NONFINANCIAL ECONOMICS

NONFINANCIAL ECONOMICS

The Case for
Shorter Hours of Work

Eugene McCarthy
and
William McGaughey

PRAEGER

New York
Westport, Connecticut
London

Copyright Acknowledgments

Extracts quoted from the following sources are reprinted by permission of the publishers: Jacques Ellul, "From the Bible to a History of Non-Work," *Cross Currents Quarterly*, Spring 1985; Philip S. Foner, *History of the Labor Movement in the United States*, Vol. II (New York: International Publishers, 1955); Karl Marx and Friedrich Engels, *Ten Classics of Marxism* (New York: International Publishers, 1948); Thorstein Veblen, *The Theory of the Leisure Class* (New York: New American Library, 1953); Max Weber, *The Protestant Ethic and the Spirit of Capitalism* (New York and London: Charles Scribner's Sons and Unwin Hyman, 1958).

Library of Congress Cataloging-in-Publication Data

McCarthy, Eugene J., 1916–
    Nonfinancial economics : the case for shorter hours of work /
Eugene McCarthy and William McGaughey.
      p. cm.
    Bibliography: p.
    ISBN 0–275–92514–5 (alk. paper)
    1. Hours of labor—United States.   I. McGaughey, William.
  II. Title.
HD4975.M38   1989
331.25′72′0973—dc19   88–28833

First published in 1989

Praeger Publishers, One Madison Avenue, New York, NY   10010
A division of Greenwood Press, Inc.

Printed in the United States of America

The paper used in this book complies with the
Permanent Paper Standard issued by the National
Information Standards Organization (Z39.48–1984).

10 9 8 7 6 5 4 3 2 1

For Richardson and Susan Okie

CONTENTS

INTRODUCTION

This book is written in support of proposals to reduce work time in order to improve employment opportunities. It is written in defense of leisure, both as a component of living standards and as a stimulus to real and meaningful use of consumer products. Shorter work hours promise a better life to the contemporary American family, where increasingly both husband and wife must work to make ends meet or where a single adult householder bears the entire burden of such responsibilities alone. They are a means to full employment, improved income distribution, and a stronger consumer market. The pursuit of shorter hours is embodied in the best traditions of organized labor. Why, then, is there entrenched resistance among U.S. policymakers to this legitimate aspiration of working men and women?

Some contend that the shorter workweek cause is a matter of its advocates trying to impose their personal values on others who may value leisure less highly. Working people, it is said, do not want more free time—they want higher incomes. The assumption of a tradeoff between leisure and material living standards seems reasonable enough, but, in fact, the connection between the two is weak. In a post-industrial society such as ours, waste becomes a principal driving force behind economic growth. Of course, the idea of waste reflects a standard of personal value, but so does wealth. The discipline of economics, neatly quantified though it appears to be, is inseparable from judgments of value. An economic undertaking may have value in terms of dollars, but in human terms be worthless.

We contend that the study of economics also properly includes consideration of the extent to which the Jeffersonian formulation of value, "life, liberty, and the pursuit of happiness," has been achieved by society. If leisure were considered from this or even a conventional economic standpoint, it would receive more sympathetic treatment in public policy. Instead, the cultural implications of leisure have overshadowed the economic. The "work ethic," in a prevalent contemporary interpretation, suggests it is good for a person to work long hours for an employer, but not for the same person to do work around the house, visit a sick friend, or organize a church picnic. We Americans seem to have lost faith in ourselves to use our time—i.e., our lives—wisely.

This book generally supports the position that organized labor has taken on this question. A reduction in work schedules can indeed be an effective remedy for the type of unemployment brought about through the installation of "labor-saving" machines. Of course there is a danger in oversimplifying. It is difficult to predict the number of jobs that would be gained or saved if work hours were reduced. The nature of the job changes with changes in technology. Pay scales and consumer markets also change. Even so, the job creation claims of the shorter workweek proposal are basically correct. Shorter work hours reduce labor supply, while more leisure stimulates a greater amount of consumption and market demand. Both changes will furnish jobs for more people than if average hours remained the same. The jobs created or saved in this way would be real and permanent jobs, not make-work or employment training. Therefore, the shorter workweek proposal is an option that should be taken seriously to the extent that the problem of unemployment itself is taken seriously.

The shorter workweek issue suffers from a lack of credibility because of its future orientation. Shorter work hours have been predicted for such a long time and with so few results that people are understandably skeptical about discussions of this kind. If we had to make a prediction, it might be that work schedules in the United States will not change unless the federal government intervenes. In that case, the matter of predicting future work schedules and the resulting shape of society would depend on predicting the future disposition of members of Congress and the president with respect to shorter workweek legislation. Our crystal ball tells us that, at the present time, their disposition runs along other lines.

But really it should be asked what business we or anyone have with crystal balls or attempts to predict the future. No one has reliable information about the future. If a book is filled mainly with predictions of coming events, one can be sure it contains speculation rather than fact. Therefore, this book takes a different approach. Instead of standing in the present and observing the future, let us for a moment stand in the past and observe the present. In such a manner we can convert past speculations into present observations of fact.

In 1959, one of the authors was chairman of the Senate Special Committee on Unemployment, a body charged with developing policy recommendations to treat the problems of employment caused by automation and technological change. Although this committee considered the proposal to reduce work hours, it was not recommended because the committee members felt that other remedies ought to be tried first. As the years went by, it became apparent that those more limited remedies were not in themselves sufficient to cure the type of long-term unemployment experienced in the nation's goods-producing industries. The shorter workweek idea ought to have been revived, but it was not. In retrospect, it is clear that the failure to reduce work schedules as unemployment rose was a significant policy mistake.

From our vantage point of the period 1958–1963, we can see what predictions were made. Critics of the shorter workweek proposal argued that if work schedules were cut, workers' living standards would necessarily suffer. Americans, they said, could not have both improved leisure and more material possessions; they had to choose between one or the other. Therefore, we as a nation made that choice. We chose higher living standards instead of more leisure. Now, today, we stand on another vantage point in time, representing the years of the late 1980s, and we see the consequences of the decision made years ago. A quarter of a century ago, Americans were promised, in effect, that if they gave up shorter work hours, they would gain a higher living standard. The plain fact is that such a promise, whether expressed or implied, has not been kept. Average real incomes have not advanced since the early 1970s. Denying increased leisure for the sake of higher living standards, U.S. workers have instead received neither.

The curious fact, though, is that GNP and total employment have continued to rise impressively during this period of dismal progress for workers. This would suggest that something might be wrong with our traditional standards for measuring economic performance. The new situation calls for a new analysis, which should acknowledge the growing amount and proportion of waste in the U.S. economy. As important as the economics of this question are however, the critical factor is political. Unfortunately, the structures of partisan politics today do not appear to be equipped to do what needs to be done economically. Our debt-driven society recoils from the thought of leisure, perhaps fearing a new age.

In any highly developed discipline, there is a tendency for thought processes to become so specialized and refined that its respected practitioners appear to lose common sense. If medieval philosophers counted the number of angels that could dance on the head of a pin, some contemporary economists deal in equally strange and fictitious concepts. To many of them, it would seem, money is reality, while leisure is an empty spot in time devoid of wealth-producing activities. Although U.S. economists in the postwar period have paid much attention to the techniques of financial manipulation by which government might keep the economy on a prosperous course, they have paid far too little attention to the way people actually work and live. That approach has produced its own set of problems, more than a few of which appear now to be coming home to roost.

If our nation is to surmount those difficulties, its policymakers will have to open their economic minds just a bit to the things outside their customary realm of discussion. Even more boldly, they might, perhaps, reconsider concepts and policy options that they once knew with great certainty to be fallacious. This book seeks to reintroduce free time into the economic formulation of the "good life" and to suggest that happiness might be counted as, in fact, a kind of prosperity.

I
AN ECONOMIC AND POLITICAL VIEW: UNEMPLOYMENT AND THE ECONOMICS OF WASTE

1
THE BANKRUPTCY OF U.S. EMPLOYMENT POLICY

Since the rise of modern industry, human beings have been competing against machines to keep their place in the production process. While the economics of production have favored the machine, people had the advantage when it came to political organization. Historically, the proposal to reduce the hours of work congruently with technological progress has been an important means by which working people sought to translate their political power into job security. It is, in our country, no longer so. Although the introduction of labor-saving equipment continues to displace human labor at a fast pace, the call for work time to be reduced has largely disappeared from discussions of economic policy. More so than in other industrialized nations, U.S. policymakers have taken a hardnosed approach to employment problems, an approach that seeks production efficiency above all else, ignoring social pain.

With more than seven million persons currently listed as unemployed, liberal and Democratic economics and politicians are rerunning their old lines, some left behind by George Meany: "The government is the employer of last resort." "The housing industry must be stimulated." "Retrain more people." "Restore the Civilian Conservation Corps." "Pass another Full Employment Act." "Restrict imports." These cries, among others, fill the air above liberal outposts, creating a pillar of fire by night. The conservatives, speaking often through the Reagan administration, recite *their* litany: "More capital investment." "Fewer government controls." "Let every employer hire one unemployed person." "Supply-side economics." "More unemployment." These calls, among others, float above the conservative camp, forming a blanket of fog by day.

The policies, both liberal and conservative, that have been pursued over the last 40 years have not accomplished their objectives. Instead they have given the nation economic instability and a stubborn unemployment rate. The Bureau of Labor Statistics has observed that unemployment's conventionally proposed remedy—i.e., economic growth—has succeeded only twice in 40 years in driving unemployment below its pre-recession levels. During the 1980s, the nation's industrial base has shrunk considerably. America's domestic manufacturing jobs have sustained a double attack from automation and foreign imports. Despite official claims, jobs—and especially good jobs—have become hard to find. The theme of full employment no longer seems to interest political leaders. Economically, a number of tough choices will have to be made. Policies in effect for decades to treat employment problems may have to be rethought and changed.

In the years immediately following World War II, economists, politicians, labor leaders, and some businessmen and manufacturers began to worry about postwar employment. Unemployment had reached a peak of 12–14 million persons, or one-fourth of the total U.S. labor force, in 1933. After some fluctuation in the intervening years, the number of unemployed in 1940, immediately before the beginning of our involvement in World War II, stood at 6.9 million persons. A year later, because of the war and war production, the figure had dropped to 3.6 million.

In 1946, with the unemployment rate hovering around 4 percent, Congress passed the Employment Act of that year. The act declared that it was the continuing policy and responsibility of the federal government to use all practicable means consistent with its needs and obligations and other essential considerations of national policy, and with the assistance and cooperation of industry, agriculture, labor, and state and local governments, to coordinate and utilize all its plans, functions, and resources for the purpose of creating and maintaining, in a manner calculated to foster and promote free-competition enterprise and the general welfare, conditions under which there would be afforded useful employment opportunities, including self-employment, for those able, willing, and seeking to work, and to promote maximum employment, production, and purchasing power. Full employment, variously defined, was the goal of the act.

In the immediate postwar period unemployment fell and business expanded. The unemployment rate, which was 4.3 percent in 1947, declined slightly until the end of 1948. In 1948/49, the country experienced the first postwar recession, which was to be followed by another in 1953/54, and then by another in 1957/58. The unemployment rate was at 4.3 percent in July of 1947, and then rose to 6.8 percent in August of 1949. In June of 1950, before the start of hostilities in Korea, the economy had recovered from the recession of 1948/49, but the unemployment rate remained at more than 5 percent of the labor force.

The effect of the Korean war was to reduce unemployment to less than 3 percent. Depression and high unemployment again followed the ending of the war, preceding recovery. By May of 1955, the production index had climbed above the pre-recession level; but the unemployment rate was 4.2 percent, compared with the pre-recession rate of 2.6 percent. The same pattern of decline and recovery followed the 1957/58 recession. Although production by early 1959 had returned to the pre-recession peak, the unemployment rate stalled at 5.9 percent.

After each of the post-World War II recessions, the unemployment rate was higher than it had been before the recession. (See Figure 1.1.) The average annual unemployment level for the decade of the 1950s was about 4.5 percent of the civilian labor force. Economists and labor evaluators then said that a rate of 3 percent was acceptable. During the 1960s, unemployment rose to a rate of about 4.7 percent. Experts moved up the "acceptable" rate to 4.5 percent. In the 1970s, unemployment was about 6.25 percent while the acceptable rate was set at 5 percent. Over the first six years of the 1980s, unemployment has averaged almost 8 percent, and the expert-accepted level has become 6 percent.

In 1959 the Senate of the United States established a special committee on unemployment. In the preceding year, 1958, the unemployment rate for the country had risen to 6.8 percent, the highest it had been since the pre-World War II year of 1941. The committee report published in 1960 listed all of the accepted and traditional ways of encouraging employment. Greater capital investment, more government employment, stand-by public works, special encouragement to the private sector, protection from unfair foreign competition, and so on, were restated, together with proposals to deal with unemployment and its consequences in the short run or for transitional periods. These proposals included better unemployment compensation programs, and special compensation to workers idled because of noneconomic political concessions in international trade.

The report included a note stating that, even if all of these things were done, there still remained the possibility that unemployment might still be too high and that the country should look into the redistribution of work opportunities in the not-too-distant future. Yet despite the passage of time between them, the Humphrey–Hawkins Full Employment Act passed in the late 1970s provided substantially the same remedies as those first passed in the 1946 act.

It was clear by 1975 that conventional measures designed to reduce unemployment had failed. Unemployment in that year reached 8.5 per-

Figure 1.1
Unemployment Rate, 1948–83

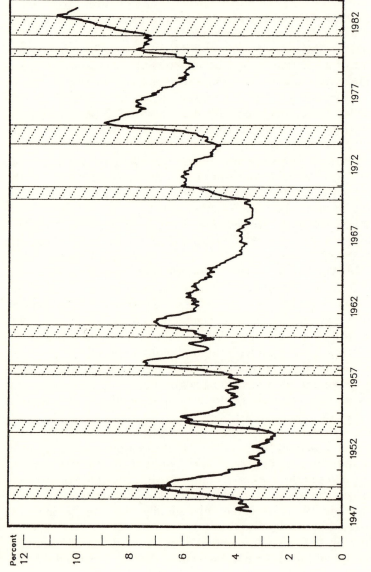

Note: Shaded areas denote recession periods.

Source: Prepared by the author.

Though unemployment rises and falls with the business cycle, the jobless rate has had an upward trend since 1970: Prior to the 1981–82 recession, the highest unemployment rate of the postwar period was 9.0 percent, reached during the 1973–75 recession. A new postwar peak of 10.8 percent was reached in December 1982.

cent. That high rate stirred scattered warnings and suggestions that a redistribution of work was in order. Dr. David Hamilton, writing in *The New Mexico Independent* of August 15, 1975, commented in an article, "You May Be Next," that "our economic policies seem designed to confirm what Marx predicted would be the course of capitalism"—namely, that "in the mature stages of capitalism, there would develop a kind of permanent reserve army of the unemployed."[1]

In that same year, Steven Kramer and Leo Friedman, writing in the August 29 issue of *Commonweal,* in an article entitled "Permanent Unemployment," made similar observations. On December 6, 1975, *The Washington Star* noted what it called "Ominous Aspects" of the job picture. The *New York Times,* in August of the same year, demonstrated modest signs of anxiety in an article entitled "The Summer of Awakening."

As unemployment began to drop in the years following 1975, largely accompanying the worst inflation in the peacetime history of the nation, the "ominous" signs seemed to have been forgotten. The "summer of awakening" was followed by an autumn of indifference. Inflation fell from a high of 13.3 percent in 1979 to 8.9 percent in 1981 and to 3.9 percent in 1982. Unemployment, however, began to rise, reaching a monthly peak of 10.8 percent in December of 1982. As inflation was wrung out of the economy, the unemployment rate subsided from an annual average of 9.5 percent in 1982 and 1983 to a level ranging between 6 and 7 percent.

In summary, if one excludes the figures during the war years, the employment charts show that chronic joblessness has been creeping up since 1969. Unemployment for 1986 hovered around 7 percent; the number of unemployed persons throughout the year averaged about 8 million on a monthly basis. (See Figure 1.2 and Table 1.1.) There has been a slow deterioration in both the fact and the norm of "full employment" over the course of the postwar years.

In view of this dismal record, why have U.S. policymakers overlooked the obvious remedy for unemployment, which is to be found in reducing the general hours of work? Most appear to have formed an impression that such a measure would somehow hurt the economy. Maybe this is because proposals for reduced work hours are associated with the Great Depression. Maybe it is because organized labor no longer supplies the political muscle to have such a proposal taken seriously. Last, but not least, professional economists have pronounced the idea to be theoretically unsound, for reasons that are best told in their own words.

YESTERDAY'S PREDICTIONS OF HOURS AND INCOME

Back in the late 1950s, the public became aware of a long-term threat to jobs from a phenomenon for which the word "automation" had

Figure 1.2
Unemployment Measures Based on Alternative Definitions of Unemployment and the Labor Force
1970–83

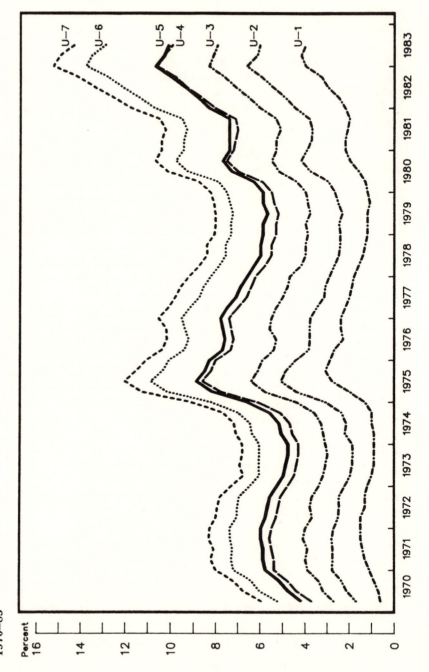

Source: Prepared by the author.

Alternative measures of unemployment differ in terms of level, but their trends are remarkably consistent.

Alternative measures of unemployment:

U–1: Persons unemployed 15 weeks and over as a percent of the civilian labor force.

U–2: Job losers as a percent of the civilian labor force.

U–3: Unemployed persons 25 years and over as a percent of the labor force 25 years and over.

U–4: Unemployed full-time jobseekers as a percent of the full-time labor force.

U–5: Total unemployed as a percent of the civilian labor force.

U–6: Total full-time jobseekers plus half part-time jobseekers plus half total on part time for economic reasons as a percent of the civilian labor force less half of the part-time labor force.

U–7: Total full-time jobseekers plus half part-time jobseekers plus half total on part time for economic reasons plus discouraged workers as a percent of the civilian labor force plus discouraged workers less half the part-time labor force.

Table 1.1

Civilian Employment and Unemployment by Sex and Age, 1947–1986 (thousands of persons 16 years of age and over; monthly data seasonally adjusted)

Year or month	Civilian employment							Unemployment						
	Total	Males			Females			Total	Males			Females		
		Total	16–19 years	20 years and over	Total	16–19 years	20 years and over		Total	16–19 years	20 years and over	Total	16–19 years	20 years and over
1947	57,038	40,995	2,218	38,776	16,045	1,691	14,354	2,311	1,692	270	1,422	619	144	475
1948	58,343	41,725	2,344	39,382	16,617	1,682	14,936	2,276	1,559	256	1,305	717	153	564
1949	57,651	40,925	2,124	38,803	16,723	1,588	15,137	3,637	2,572	353	2,219	1,065	223	841
1950	58,918	41,578	2,186	39,394	17,340	1,517	15,824	3,288	2,239	318	1,922	1,049	195	854
1951	59,961	41,780	2,156	39,626	18,181	1,611	16,570	2,055	1,221	191	1,029	834	145	689
1952	60,250	41,682	2,107	39,578	18,568	1,612	16,958	1,883	1,185	205	980	698	140	559
1953	61,179	42,430	2,136	40,296	18,749	1,584	17,164	1,834	1,202	184	1,019	632	123	510
1954	60,109	41,619	1,985	39,634	18,490	1,490	17,000	3,532	2,344	310	2,035	1,188	191	997
1955	62,170	42,621	2,095	40,526	19,551	1,547	18,002	2,852	1,854	274	1,580	998	176	823
1956	63,799	43,379	2,164	41,216	20,419	1,654	18,767	2,750	1,711	269	1,442	1,039	209	832
1957	64,071	43,357	2,115	41,239	20,714	1,663	19,052	2,859	1,841	300	1,541	1,018	197	821
1958	63,036	42,423	2,012	40,411	20,613	1,570	19,043	4,602	3,098	416	2,681	1,504	262	1,242
1959	64,630	43,466	2,198	41,267	21,164	1,640	19,524	3,740	2,420	398	2,022	1,320	256	1,063
1960	65,778	43,904	2,361	41,543	21,874	1,768	20,105	3,852	2,486	426	2,060	1,366	286	1,080
1961	65,746	43,656	2,315	41,342	22,090	1,793	20,296	4,714	2,997	479	2,518	1,717	349	1,368
1962	66,702	44,177	2,362	41,815	22,525	1,833	20,693	3,911	2,423	408	2,016	1,488	313	1,175
1963	67,762	44,657	2,406	42,251	23,105	1,849	21,257	4,070	2,472	501	1,971	1,598	383	1,216
1964	69,305	45,474	2,587	42,886	23,831	1,929	21,903	3,786	2,205	487	1,718	1,581	385	1,195
1965	71,088	46,340	2,918	43,422	24,748	2,118	22,630	3,366	1,914	479	1,435	1,452	395	1,056
1966	72,895	46,919	3,253	43,668	25,976	2,468	23,510	2,875	1,551	432	1,120	1,324	405	921
1967	74,372	47,479	3,186	44,294	26,893	2,496	24,397	2,975	1,508	448	1,060	1,468	391	1,078
1968	75,920	48,114	3,255	44,859	27,807	2,526	25,281	2,817	1,419	426	993	1,397	412	985
1969	77,902	48,818	3,430	45,388	29,084	2,687	26,397	2,832	1,403	440	963	1,429	413	1,015
1970	78,678	48,990	3,409	45,581	29,688	2,735	26,952	4,093	2,238	599	1,638	1,855	506	1,349
1971	79,367	49,390	3,478	45,912	29,976	2,730	27,246	5,016	2,789	693	2,097	2,227	568	1,658
1972	82,153	50,896	3,765	47,130	31,257	2,980	28,276	4,882	2,659	711	1,948	2,222	598	1,625
1973	85,064	52,349	4,039	48,310	32,715	3,231	29,484	4,365	2,275	653	1,624	2,089	583	1,507
1974	86,794	53,024	4,103	48,922	33,769	3,345	30,424	5,156	2,714	757	1,957	2,441	665	1,777
1975	85,846	51,857	3,839	48,018	33,989	3,263	30,726	7,929	4,442	966	3,476	3,486	802	2,684
1976	88,752	53,138	3,947	49,190	35,615	3,389	32,226	7,406	4,036	939	3,098	3,369	780	2,588
1977	92,017	54,728	4,174	50,555	37,289	3,514	33,775	6,991	3,667	874	2,794	3,324	789	2,535
1978	96,048	56,479	4,336	52,143	39,569	3,734	35,836	6,202	3,142	813	2,328	3,061	769	2,292
1979	98,824	57,607	4,300	53,308	41,217	3,783	37,434	6,137	3,120	811	2,308	3,018	743	2,276
1980	99,303	57,186	4,085	53,101	42,117	3,625	38,492	7,637	4,267	913	3,353	3,370	755	2,615
1981	100,397	57,397	3,815	53,582	43,000	3,411	39,590	8,273	4,577	962	3,615	3,696	800	2,895
1982	99,526	56,271	3,379	52,891	43,256	3,170	40,086	10,678	6,179	1,090	5,089	4,499	886	3,613
1983	100,834	56,787	3,300	53,487	44,047	3,043	41,004	10,717	6,260	1,003	5,257	4,457	825	3,632
1984	105,005	59,091	3,322	55,769	45,915	3,122	42,793	8,539	4,744	812	3,932	3,794	687	3,107
1985	107,150	59,891	3,328	56,562	47,259	3,105	44,154	8,312	4,521	806	3,715	3,791	661	3,129
1986	109,597	60,892	3,323	57,569	48,706	3,149	45,556	8,237	4,530	779	3,751	3,707	675	3,032

Source: Department of Labor, Bureau of Labor Statistics.

recently been coined. The idea of shortening the workweek through amendment of the Fair Labor Standards Act was among the suggestions offered then to deal with this problem. Generally that was the recommendation of organized labor. Some of the unions were advocating a 35-hour workweek, others a 32- or 30-hour week, but all were making essentially the same point: that the new labor-saving technologies were destroying jobs held by their members on the basis of 40 or more hours a week. At a lower level of hours, however, those jobs might be saved. This point of view did not prevail. The business community was opposed to the shorter-workweek idea. When academic and government economists joined in the opposition, the proposal was doomed.

The call for shorter working hours was not heeded a quarter of a century ago because of predictions that the economy's growth and development would be retarded by such a move. Then, as now, the object of public policy was to encourage economic growth. The U.S. economy needed to grow rapidly, it was argued, so that the nation could honor its global commitment to fight communism, build hospitals and schools, and provide a continually rising standard of living for American workers. Many believed that cutting work hours would put the economy in a straight jacket, so to speak. It would freeze industry at a particular level of development.

Economists at that time suggested that the idea that shorter hours might create jobs was based on a fallacy that they called the "lump of labor" theory. Paul Samuelson wrote in his best-selling economics textbook: "The lump-of-labor argument implies that there is only so much useful remunerative work to be done in any economic system, and that is indeed a fallacy. . . . There is no doubt that drastic shortening of hours would imply lower real earnings than a full-employment economy is capable of providing at a longer workweek."[2]

John Diebold told the Joint Economic Committee of Congress in 1960: "Unlimited demand for goods and services will prevent unemployment from automation. Since human wants are unlimited, increased productivity and production will find a market in satisfying these wants. Through greater productivity earnings will increase to such an extent that there will be a tremendous rise in our standard of living."[3]

That was more than a quarter century ago. The choice was clear: Either we could take the pessimistic expedient of shortening work time and so abort part of our economic future, or we could continue upon the upward glide-path to new heights of prosperity. Of course we chose the latter. We chose more goods and services over more leisure, firmly convinced that the two were related in a tradeoff. But were they? While it is not possible to assess the impact of shorter hours on the nation's standard of living because work hours in this country have failed to decline, it is possible to track the progress in living standards, or lack

Table 1.2
Average Hours Worked per Week in U.S. Civilian Economy, 1860–1987

Year	Average Workweek
1860	68.0
1870	65.4
1880	64.0
1890	61.9
1900	60.2
1910	55.1
1920	49.7
1930	45.9
1940	44.0
1950	42.5
1955	41.6
1960	40.8
1965	40.5
1970	39.1
1975	38.7
1980	38.5
1985	39.0
1987	39.0

Source: Prepared by the author.

thereof, given the decision to renounce shorter hours for the sake of more production.

A simple check of the facts should be enough to refute the idea of a simple tradeoff between leisure and living standards. On the hours side, Table 1.2 reveals that the average workweek in the U.S. civilian economy declined more rapidly in the earlier part of this century than in the years after World War II. In the period between 1900 and 1940, the average workweek dropped from 60 to 44 hours, which represents a decline of 4 hours per week per decade during this time. In the period between 1940 and 1980 the average workweek further declined from 44 to 38.5 hours, which represents a decline of 1.4 hours per week per decade. The period between 1940 and 1960 accounted for 3.5 hours of the 5.5

Table 1.3
Median Money Income of U.S. Households in Constant 1986 Dollars

Year	Annual Income
1960	20,807
1965	24,176
1970	27,862
1973	29,734
1975	27,949
1978	29,647
1980	27,974
1983	27,155
1985	28,269

Source: Prepared by the author.

hours decline since 1940, and the period after 1960 for 2.0 hours. Since 1980 there has been, in fact, a slight gain in average hours.

What then of living standards? The average real hourly wage in the United States more than doubled in the quarter century between the two world wars. It rose by an additional 50 percent from the end of World War II until 1970. The gain in real earnings has subsequently come to a halt and started to decline. Table 1.3 shows the median money income of U.S. families in constant dollars in the period between 1960 and 1985. There was an increase of $7,991 in annual earnings during the first thirteen years, followed by a decrease of $1,829 during the last twelve. Another indicator of real incomes has been the Bureau of Labor Statistics (BLS) series entitled "average spendable real weekly earnings of workers with three dependents." This statistical series attempted to show the constant-dollar earnings of a worker with an average-sized family after federal income and payroll taxes were deducted. As Table 1.4 indicates, average take-home pay rose from $131.08 in 1950 to $166.28 in 1965, but then fell to $151.65 in 1980—roughly its level twenty years earlier. In 1981, the BLS discontinued the series, suggesting that it had perhaps "outlived its usefulness."

The present 5-day, 40-hour schedule of weekly hours was first introduced in the United States during the 1920s. It received a boost in 1926 when Henry Ford decided to convert his automobile plants from a 6-day to 5-day week. The 8-hour day, which Ford employees received a decade earlier along with the $5/day minimum wage, remained in effect.

Table 1.4
Average Real Spendable Weekly Earnings of Workers with Three Dependents, 1950–1980 (in 1977 dollars)

Year	Weekly Income
1950	131.08
1955	143.46
1960	149.20
1965	166.28
1970	163.65
1975	164.02
1980	151.65

Source: Prepared by the author.

It says something of our declining national expectations that the present workweek standard dates back more than sixty years to the days of the Model T. One might say that we are trying to operate a space-age economy with Model T labor standards. The productivity of American labor has increased by four times since the 1920s, but average work hours have declined by less than 20 percent. The result is employment imbalance.

The present policies, which had been pursued as an alternative to reducing work hours, have not accomplished their objective of spurring economic growth. Instead, the nation has experienced prolonged economic sluggishness and a high unemployment rate. Those policies, failing to bear good fruit, need to be reconsidered.

2
THE PRODUCTIVITY
FACTOR

It has often been said that U.S. workers need to become more productive to compete effectively in world markets. The goal of achieving higher "productivity" has become a panacea. Some who use this term have a confused idea of its meaning. Increased productivity means a higher ratio between units of economic output and units of input, such as labor. In its most common definition, productivity represents "output per worker-hour."

An important feature of a modern industrial economy is, of course, its ability to produce a progressively greater volume of goods and services for each hour worked, as more advanced equipment is installed or more efficient production methods are developed. Mass-production techniques, power tools, computer-controlled equipment, more adaptable materials, and other technological innovations have increased the volume of product that a given worker can produce in a given period of time. In agriculture, too, there has been a great improvement in the productive efficiency of labor through the use of irrigation, fertilizers and pesticides, better genetic strains, bigger equipment, and larger farms. While such developments are economically necessary and healthy over the long run, they are not, as it is sometimes suggested, directly productive of jobs. The factory worker realizes instinctively that the harder and faster he works, the sooner he works himself out of a job. That assessment is not incorrect. If industry can produce the same amount of product with less labor, it will not be long in today's highly competitive business environment before the surplus labor is, in fact, eliminated.

The Luddites, British workers of the early 19th century, smashed textile-producing machines because of fears that they would become unemployed. Today, nearly everyone agrees that such a response to technological innovation would be shortsighted. When properly handled, the new technologies of production that raise productive efficiency can become a real benefit to humanity. Regrettably, however, those new technologies have not always been handled properly. They have indeed often been used to throw people out of work in order to increase employer profits.

A later generation of workers, responding to this threat, developed the idea that the harmful employment effects of machines might be avoided if employers were required to cut working hours as the machines were installed. That way, even if machines took over some of the work once performed by human beings, some work might remain, continuing to require a full crew of workers. With that purpose in mind, the trade union movements in Europe and North America carried on a struggle throughout the 19th and early 20th centuries to bring down the number of daily or weekly hours scheduled at the work place.

Intuitively we can see the logic of this argument. The more hours people work, the fewer people will be needed to complete a given piece of work. The shorter the hours, the more workers it will take to do the work. In the short run there is, in other words, a tradeoff between employment and average work hours in the production process. In the long run, of course, the situation is complicated by changes in other factors—for instance, how efficiently the people are working. Also, the amounts of work needing to be done can vary. More people, longer work hours, greater efficiency of production, or a combination of the three, would be required to complete a larger amount of work.

THE PRODUCTIVITY EQUATION

Labor economists have developed the following equation to describe the relationship among those four variables:

$$\text{Output} = \text{productivity} \times \text{employment} \times \text{average hours of work}$$

To understand how changes in productivity might affect the other economic variables, let us consider operations at the proverbial widget factory. For example, if one worker could produce 5 widgets in an hour, and there were 8 workers in the plant, and each worker worked 40 hours each week, the plant's weekly output would be 1600 widgets. Now assume that productivity doubled, so that each worker could produce 10 widgets in an hour. If all else stayed the same, the weekly output of the factory would be 3200 widgets: $10 \times 8 \times 40$. If we assume that the consumer market could not support 3200 widgets/week, but only 2400, the widget manufacturer could meet the marketplace demand for his product by

Table 2.1
Output, Productivity, Employment, and Average Hours in U.S. Agriculture, 1947–1986

Year	Output	=	Productivity	x	Employment	x	Average Hours
1947	1.000		1.000		1.000		1.000
1950	1.152		1.297		.918		.966
1955	1.204		1.646		.769		.950
1960	1.187		2.069		.634		.904
1965	1.162		2.500		.511		.909
1970	1.183		3.321		.395		.900
1975	1.317		3.980		.374		.884
1977	1.274		4.065		.353		.886
1980	1.345		4.419		.343		.888
1983	1.296		4.512		.336		.853
1986	1.890		7.329		.296		.872

Note: Change in each variable expressed as an index based upon levels in 1947.

Source: Prepared by the author.

employing only 6 workers (2400 = 10 × 6 × 40). The two unneeded employees might be discharged. Alternatively, the employer could decide to retain all 8 workers but cut their workweek from 40 to 30 hours. The equation would stay balanced: 2400 = 10 × 8 × 30. Thus there is a basic tradeoff between employment and average hours, when the levels of output and productivity are fixed.

From the above equation, it follows mathematically that, where productivity increases more rapidly than output and average hours remain constant (or nearly so), employment necessarily drops. Such an event has come to pass in the case of American agriculture. The four variables are shown in Table 2.1 Each variable is indexed to the levels in 1947. The table shows that farm productivity increased by more than seven times between 1947 and 1986, but output rose by only 90 percent. Average working hours on the farm fell by 13 percent. Employment, therefore, fell by 70 percent. In actual numbers, farm employment declined from 7,890,000 workers in 1947 to 3,163,000 in 1986. In 1920, more than 11 million Americans were employed on the farm.

SPREADING LABOR DISPLACEMENT

Historically we know that most persons who left the farm went to the city in search of a better job. The process has continued in the present decade. Fortunately, the nation's nonagricultural industries were able to provide jobs for most of the farmers displaced in past migrations. But now the same type of labor displacement that took place in agriculture is beginning to show up in other industries. Roughly 400,000 jobs were lost in the U.S. automobile industry between March 1979 and November 1982. Employment in manufacturing industries as a whole declined from an average of 21,040,000 workers in 1979 to 19,426,000 workers in 1985.[1] Government, once considered the "employer of the last resort," has ceased to be a growth industry, albeit for different reasons.

Perhaps the most dramatic example of labor displacement can be found in the use of industrial robots. Robots have always had a "humanoid" image; factory workers can relate to them as the ultimate in cheap labor. If a robot costs $6 an hour to operate and depreciate, and an automobile worker costs $20 an hour in total compensation, then the automobile companies will find a way to install those robots, despite interest expense.[2] In fact, General Motors, which employed 3500 robots in 1984, planned to quadruple that number by 1990. They were to be part of an integrated computer-based production system, whose goal was to build high-quality cars with a sharply reduced content of human labor. "Unable to lower its wages to Japanese levels, GM is making an all-out effort to slash the man-hours it takes to build a car and to reduce further its U.S. workforce of 130,000 salaried and 380,000 hourly employees," the *Wall Street Journal* reported."[3]

At facilities such as "Buick City" in Flint, Michigan, and the Saturn plant in Tennessee, General Motors planned to develop an electronic communications network linking its own plants with those of dealers and suppliers. While inventory reduction and prompt service were important benefits of the new system, an industry analyst at a New York brokerage firm pointed out that "the [main] goal of all the technology push has been to get rid of hourly workers."[4] A study at MIT has predicted that automobile employment in the seven largest auto-producing countries would drop to 2.27 million workers by the year 2000, compared with 3.64 million in 1979.[5]

Less dramatic perhaps than robots but no less menacing from an employment standpoint would be other kinds of automated devices, intended for installation in offices and other commercial places as well as plants. Among them are numerically-controlled machine tools, optical scanners used in banks and at the supermarket checkouts, electronic switching devices, and fiber optic cables used in telecommunications, word processors, and microfilm readers.

When we think that we have reached the ultimate in automated techniques, we sometimes learn that another kind of process, even more advanced, is being planned or even implemented to cut costs further. In the production of garments, for instance, the governments of the United States, Japan, and several European Common Market nations are financing a research program to develop new technologies that will enable their domestic garment industries to beat out the competition from Third World countries. "In Japan, government planners foresee bolts of fabric entering one end of a robot assembly line and emerging at the other end as finished men's business suits—all done with a minimum of human assistance," a *Wall Street Journal* article disclosed. "And in Europe, companies are developing spaceage contraptions for handling and assembling garments, including lasers and ultra-high-pressure water jets to cut fabric to computer-controlled patterns." If the technology is successfully developed, robots, using laser vision, would be able to cut fabric to precise specifications, sew pieces of cloth together, attach buttons and liners, inspect the finished product, and ship it off to a customer.[6]

Estimates of the employment impact of such innovations have ranged from negligible to catastrophic. Those who minimize their impact, often industry spokesmen, have suggested that the same or a greater number of employees would be needed to tend or service the machines—an incredible assertion, given the cost/benefit analyses that presumably supported their purchase—or they have argued that the need to stay cost-competitive has greater significance for future employment than the immediate loss of a few jobs.

EVIDENCE OF JOB LOSS

No one can argue against the evidence that blue-collar employment in particular industries or firms has been seriously hurt because of the new equipment. There is more uncertainty about the long-range employment of white-collar managerial, professional, and technical workers. Studies at Carnegie-Mellon University and Booz, Allen & Hamilton have concluded that as many as 7 million blue-collar factory workers and 38 million white-collar office workers might be directly affected by automation.[7] Already the effects of automating the office are beginning to dampen employment growth among clerical workers. A study by "9 to 5," a clerical workers' group, found that the number of clerical workers in four midwestern states declined by 100,000 persons between 1980 and 1984, even while total employment in those states was growing.[8]

In years past, workers displaced from the farm could find jobs in the city; those displaced from manufacturing became employed in services, and so forth. What happens, however, when labor displacement hits the occupational sectors that have been receiving people from other areas? White-collar employment as a whole has grown to the point that it now represents half of all U.S. jobs. Yet the Congressional Office of Technology Assessment (OTA) reported that its period of growth may be over, as office jobs show the effect of automation. In a recent report, the agency warned Congress: "It is likely that growth in office employment, as a result [of automation], will slow over the next few years; it is possible that sometime in the 1990s, the level of office employment will begin to decline."[9]

The early 1980s were a period of "takeoff" for automated production systems in the United States. "After a false start," declared a 1981 *Business Week* cover story, "America's manufacturers are finally in position to make a stunning leap into total automation. The final pieces to the puzzle of how to automate short production runs, which account for 75% of all U.S. manufacturing, are falling quietly into place." By "total automation," the article was referring to the new CAD/CAM technology—computer-aided design/computer-aided manufacturing—which allows a much smaller number of workers to create new designs on video screens, then manufacture tools, order materials, and schedule production runs in a computer-controlled environment. Expenditures for such equipment were expected to climb 35% or more annually.[10] More recently it has been estimated that 100,000 CAD work stations were in place around the world in 1985, with the total market potential put at 4 million.[11]

A study published by the International Labor Organization has taken a sanguine view of employment prospects after the installation of CAD/CAM equipment. Even though computer-aided design has increased office output by 200–1600 percent, the study reported that, so far, major layoffs have been avoided among the design engineers and draftsmen. Mainly, it said, such equipment had "enhanced the variety of tasks executed by designers and encouraged the production of a greater range and quality of drawings, plans, and project documents as well as the consideration of more alternative technical solutions."[12] To the extent that improved product design also improved sales or cut production costs, its potential labor-saving impact might be avoided or postponed. On the other hand, the increasing use of video-display terminals has introduced a new health risk for employees working with computer-based systems, which suggests a need to limit periods of exposure to the screen.

CAD/CAM systems represent an intermediate step toward what has been called CIM, or "computer-integrated manufacturing," which allows paperless processing of information from the design stage through production. Such a system, to the extent that it can be made to work, might be less sparing of jobs. At General Motors, which has sunk more than $40 billion into computer systems, the results have not lived up to expectations. For example, the computer control system at GM's Hamtramck plant has been plagued by software problems that have caused malfunctioning in the spray-paint booth and brought frequent stops to the assembly line. The Ford plant in St. Louis has experienced similar problems.[13] Where the companies install too much technology too fast and neglect training of employees, costly mistakes are more likely to happen. On the other hand, there can be little doubt that enormous cost savings are possible when the transition to an automated system is done properly. Faced with bankruptcy, Chrysler lowered its break-even point by more than one half—mainly by terminating 20,000 white-collar employees—with one of the industry's better-run computer systems. A consultant with Arthur Young, an accounting firm, claims that a properly developed CIM plant can break even at 25–30 percent of capacity, compared with 60–65 percent of capacity for conventional plants.[14]

Ironically, the chief advantage of automated production systems is no longer the cost savings to be found in eliminating blue-collar production workers. Their ranks have been thinned to such an extent in previous employment purges that the direct labor cost component of products made in the United States now runs only about 10–15 percent of total costs. Instead, manufacturers increasingly are taking aim at indirect labor and other overhead costs, which account for 45 percent of total costs. The possibility of substantial cuts in the white-collar, middle-management ranks, as well as reductions in required inventory levels, shorter lead times, and improved product quality, have become the principal justification for installing an automated system.[15]

The new structure of product costs has brought a demand for new cost-accounting methods, which depart from the traditional method of assigning overhead costs to products on the basis of direct labor. Labor becomes a controllable cost to the extent that its use can be avoided. In that regard, the focus of attention has shifted from the factory floor to the office. Company strategists are now weighing the need for supervisory and support staff against payroll costs. They are developing early retirement and other incentive packages that allow a firm to trim its administrative overhead without driving out the more valuable employees or upsetting morale.

Because of the mistakes made in automating too much too fast, many companies are now moving away from the idea of total automation and accepting instead the view that a reasonable partnership between man and machine will prevail in the immediate future. The target of cost-cutting efforts has shifted from the production employee, now a less significant item of expense, to types of expense determined to be more

Table 2.2

Cause of Employment Changes in Three Japanese Companies

Company/ Observation Period	Percentage Employment Changes	of which due to		
		Increased Output	Increased Capital/Labor Ratio	Technical Pro- gress
Japan Steel				
1967-72	1.9%	12.4%	-5.4%	-5.1%
1972-81	-1.8%	10.9%	-2.2%	-10.5%
Hitachi				
1968-71	6.6%	23.8%	-9.0%	-8.2%
1971-78	-3.5%	5.6%	1.3%	-10.4%
1978-81	1.2%	10.7%	-3.6%	-5.9%
Toyota				
1965-73	8.0%	20.2%	-5.3%	-6.9%
1973-80	1.4%	6.4%	0	-5.0%

Source: Highlights in Japanese Industrial Relations. Tokyo: Japan Institute of Labor, 1983. Reprinted with permission.

costly. Quality control, inventory control, and improved delivery times to customers have been receiving increased attention from corporate managers. That does not mean, however, that manufacturing jobs again are plentiful, or that layoffs are a thing of the past. The new systems to maintain quality or inventory control are themselves highly automated and dependent on electronic information-processing systems. It is just that employment has already been squeezed so hard that there is little juice left to be extracted.[16]

Does automation, in fact, bring employment loss? The most objective and reliable evidence suggests that it does. Some of the best studies come from foreign sources. For example, an attempt was made in Japan to determine the employment impact of the microelectronic technologies at three large firms in the period between 1967 and 1981: Japan Steel, Hitachi, and Toyota. The results are shown in Table 2.2. Even though net employment at those firms rose during most periods, analysis revealed that the "increased capital/labor ratio" and "technical progress" tended to depress the number of jobs. Employment was saved only by the factor of "increased output," which, in turn, depends on the existence of consumer markets adequate to absorb the product. These and other Japanese manufacturers had, of course, the advantage of access to the wide-open U.S. market, which allowed them to overcome the output restrictions otherwise found in a closed economic system. Another study, conducted by Japan's Ministry of Labor, confirmed these results. Employment rose at 5 percent of the surveyed firms that had introduced microelectronic technology, but fell at 30 percent of them.[17]

In 1987, the International Labor Organization published another study, *Micro-electronics and Employment Revisited: A Review*, which confirmed that general conclusion. Studies in the Japanese automobile industry, it reported, found that each robot installed in a factory replaced an average of 0.6–0.7 workers per shift. In the United States, a robot replaced one worker per shift; and, in the United Kingdom, 1.4 workers per shift. In Japan and West Germany, each microelectronics machine tool displaced two to three production workers. A similar effect was observed in Brazil. The study's author, Dr. Raphael Kaplinsky from the University of Sussex in England, declared that such technology "holds both enormous threat and great potential." That potential would not be realized, he believed, by relying on market forces alone. It would be incumbent upon government bodies to "ensure that suitable policies are proposed and implemented."

Specifically, Dr. Kaplinsky found a problem with employment: "Craft skills are being displaced and only partially replaced by a demand for higher level human resources." He also made this general observation: "Although there is evidence to support diverse views on the new technology's impact on work, levels of employment are likely to decline in the long term, either in numbers fully employed or through part-time employment or shorter working hours."[18]

3
THE EMPLOYMENT FACTOR

A common modern idea holds that the production of more material goods constitutes our duty; it also shapes our destiny. To produce more gives rise to a corresponding and complementary responsibility to consume more and, hence, to find more types of consumer products. Employment will follow from properly stimulated activity.

To stimulate the economy, it is argued that the United States ought to follow the Japanese example, not in cutting work hours or offering job guarantees to displaced workers, but simply by installing more labor-saving technology. American industry, the line is, needs to become more competitive with other nations' industries, so that we can increase our exports, or at least reduce imports, and so push our unemployment onto foreign economies. If U.S. wages cannot be reduced sufficiently to allow U.S. made goods to be priced competitively, then we must develop new types of products that are unique on world markets, or offer more advanced features on our present products. To create those new or better products, U.S. firms must devote more of their resources to research and development. More money, too, it is said, should be spent for education, which is considered a form of capital investment to support the "knowledge" industries.

Some theorists carry the argument a step further, suggesting that knowledge itself, or "information," is replacing manufactured goods as the economy's basic kind of product. Futurists speak of the transformation from an industrial to a post-industrial or services-based economy. They suggest that the U.S. economy today is unlike any other in the past, that the old economic concepts no longer apply, that we must totally change our thinking.

While such ideas may be appealing to some people, it is difficult to imagine "information" as a primary economic product. Realistically, what more information can the American consumer want or usefully consume, especially when time is limited? Do we not have at our fingertips already an almost unlimited quantity and variety of books, periodicals, recordings, and films, which may be borrowed without charge from the public library? Can we not, for a small sum of money each month, subscribe to cable television and have a choice of more than forty programs on the different channels? This brave new "information-based" economy simply is not credible in terms of people's everyday wants and needs. In reality, much of this new information is produced for the use of organizations rather than people. It takes the form of legal and accounting records, interdepartmental memos, and computer printouts, which are of momentary interest to bureaucracies and later forgotten.

Yet an undeniable shift has taken place in the economy away from manufactured products and toward services. One can either fight it or join it, a school of opinion says. Rather than cling to old ideas about the economy, one should go with the flow of progress, become "computer literate," and generally adapt to change. This way of thinking becomes a defense to concerns about the real loss of jobs in America's basic industries. The "future" becomes a generalized source of comfort and faith: if some jobs disappear, others will be created. As at the turn of the century one could not have imagined that the new-fangled automobile would some day replace the horse and buggy; so today we are largely unaware of the direction that the U.S. economy will take into the 21st century. We can, however, be confident that some new products and industries will arise to take the place of old ones, and with them will come new jobs. To believe otherwise is to lack vision—so runs the argument.

If the economy's inevitable growth and development will take care of the employment problem, there is no need for government to intervene with work-hours legislation. Despite evidence of job liquidations, we can rely on dynamic forces at work in the economy to generate enough replacement jobs without government intervention. The issue was presented as long ago as 1964 in a booklet issued by the National Association of Manufacturers; it stated:

People's wants are unlimited; it is only our capacity to satisfy wants that is limited by our ability to produce. If productivity advances put people out of work, we should be able to compute how many people were idled by each technological advance. For example, since 1910 the nation's overall productivity has increased over three times. As a result of this productivity increase it takes only one-third as much labor, on the average, to do a given job as it did in 1910. If it were true that increases in productivity or technological advances threw men out of work,

Table 3.1
Unemployment Rate and Productivity Index in Selected Years, 1910–1985

Year	Unemployment Rate	Productivity
1910	5.9%	1.000
1920	4.0%	1.193
1930	8.7%	1.459
1935	20.1%	1.596
1940	14.6%	1.792
1945	1.9%	2.043
1950	5.3%	2.216
1955	4.4%	2.577
1960	5.5%	2.898
1965	4.5%	3.473
1970	4.9%	3.790
1975	8.5%	4.103
1980	7.0%	4.257
1985	7.2%	4.609

Note: Productivity index based upon 1910.

Source: Prepared by the author.

we could conclude that two-thirds of our work force should be unemployed.... Unemployment is not the cumulative effect of improvements in productive efficiency—if it were, most of us would be out of work by now.[1]

On the face of it, this argument is compelling. Table 3.1 compares the rates of productivity and unemployment in the years 1910 to 1985. The productivity index has risen cumulatively to a level 4.5 times higher in 1985 than in 1910. In contrast, the unemployment rate has remained fairly stable except for the time during the 1930s when it ballooned to double digits. Mainly the level of unemployment fluctuates according to the business cycle. In response, one might argue that, despite appearances, unemployment has not been stable. Its reported rate has been moving upward, ratchet-like, by approximately one percentage point per decade. Furthermore, a part of the stability in the reported level of unemployment is due to tendentious changes in definition, which have depressed the official rate. These would include the increase in the lower age limit of the civilian noninstitutional population from 14 to 16, the reclassification of persons enrolled in government jobs programs from unemployed to employed, and, recently, the inclusion of military personnel in the employed work force.[2]

EXAMINING THE RECORD OF EMPLOYMENT GAINS

Even so, it is pointed out that the U.S. economy has recorded substantial gains in employment during the past decade. The magnitude of the employment gains overshadows the increase in unemployment, and is a particular source of pride for U.S. policymakers. Such statistics are used to relieve fears concerning the loss of jobs through automation or imported foreign products. There is even a tendency for policymakers on this side of the Atlantic to gloat over the achievement of the U.S. economy in generating new jobs in comparison with the dismal record of Western European economies in that regard. Employment in the United States increased by 19.2 million workers between 1975 and 1984. During the same period, the combined employment in France, West Germany, Italy, the United Kingdom, the Netherlands, and Sweden, as adjusted to U.S. concepts, remained at approximately the same level.[3]

Some cite this record as evidence of the United States' greater entrepreneurial spirit or its more "flexible" labor policies. The argument has been elevated to an almost jingoistic level of pride in the U.S. economic system, including our willingness to work long hours. During the 1984 strike in the West German automobile industry, for example, an editorial in the *Wall Street Journal* commented with ill-concealed glee: "If Germans and other Europeans are really worried about unemployment, they should look to the U.S. Back in the economic dark ages of the early 1970s, some Americans were calling for a reduced workweek. They didn't get it, of course, and during the last decade 18 million jobs have been added in the U.S. while Europe has lost 2.5 million. One result in the U.S. has been a boom in the new technology-based industries, where hardly anyone works a mere 40 hours anyway. Flexible economies produce more jobs, and more jobs with the kinds of flexible hours that hardworking people want."[4]

However what these statistics do not show is what kind of jobs have been created in the United States lately. Most of them have not been "high tech" positions in Silicon Valley, but jobs less glamorous and productive—and lower paying. The average starting salary of full-time workers in the fast-food industry, for instance, is $3.59 per hour, or $.24 per hour more than the minimum wage.[5] The Bureau of Labor Statistics (BLS) reports that, as manufacturing jobs have been eliminated, most of the new jobs added to the economy between 1967 and 1979 were in wholesale and retail trade, services, and finance, insurance, or real estate.

The average weekly or hourly earnings in each of these areas is lower than the average for private nonagricultural industries as a whole, while the average for manufacturing is higher.[6]

With respect to occupation, the areas of fastest employment growth also happen to be those that rank below average in weekly pay. The average weekly earnings of all full-time wage and salary workers in the United States in 1983 was $309. The BLS has predicted that the following occupations (shown together with their 1983 average full-time weekly wage) would add the most new positions during the 1980s: secretaries ($250), retail sales clerks ($198), janitors ($220), cashiers ($168), book-keepers ($252), nurses aides ($191), and cooks ($172).[7]

A simple head count does not always give an accurate picture of employment. When journalists attempt to describe in human terms a statistically reported trend, they usually pick familiar images or stereotypes to represent the underlying events. Consider the following facts: (1) most new jobs in the United States are created in small businesses; (2) self-employed workers have increased more rapidly than employed workers, but earn slightly less. How might a journalist imagine the type of worker behind those statistical facts: As a struggling but hopeful businesswoman who has recently opened her own boutique? As a creator of computer software? Or possibly as a distributor in a multi-level or pyramid marketing organization such as Herbalife, Shaklee, or Amway?

Although the BLS does not specifically track this type of employment, a few facts obtained from Amway promotional brochures suggest that its impact could be considerable. In 1984, Amway disclosed that it had one million distributorships worldwide, most in the United States, and that total retail sales were $1.2 billion. Typically a distributorship consists of a husband-and-wife team. In 1975, its reported retail sales were $300 million; the number of distributorships was not disclosed. If the ratio of sales dollars to people remained the same during this period—admittedly an improbable assumption—Amway gained 750,000 distributorships between 1975 and 1984.

Potentially, then, with some exaggeration, between 750,000 and 1.5 million additional persons became Amway distributors. Each would be counted as "employed" in the Census Bureau household survey by virtue of their Amway activities, even though the average income per distributorship—$1,200 per year in gross retail sales, from the above information—would not be enough to support even a minimal standard of living. How many Amway distributors might otherwise have been classified as employed or "not in the labor force," and therefore not reducing the unemployment rate, we do not know. The point here is not to disparage Amway or its way of life, but to question the interpretation of statistics when this type of worker is included in the employment figures.[8]

INTERPRETATION OF RECENT
EMPLOYMENT CHANGES

Barry Bluestone and Bennett Harrison offer some other perspectives in a report prepared for the Joint Economic Committee of Congress. They found that what jobs have been created during the years of Reagan administration have been concentrated at the bottom of the earnings scale, with most earning less than $7,000 per year (in 1984 dollars). We are moving into a two- and even three-tier wage structure in some industries or corporations. Bluestone and Harrison observed that

the slowdown in the annual rate of new job development has contributed to the much higher average unemployment of the 1980s.... [T]he record reveals a continuation into the 1980s of a strong trend toward employment growth in the service sector, with literally *no* expansion whatsoever in employment in goods production....

The redesign of full-time into part-time jobs, the disproportionate growth of part-time or part-year work, and the spread of wage freezes and concessions from one industry to another all suggest a real decline in annual earnings. In addition, demographic factors—including the continued rise in female labor-force participation and the entry of the baby-boom generation into the work-force—could also be affecting the wage distribution.... [U]nderneath the appearance of substantial overall job creation since 1973, is America proliferating low-wage jobs and perhaps even shifting toward an increasingly polarized labor-market structure?...

[D]uring the 1970s about one out of every five net additional wage-earners found a job (or jobs) paying as little as $7,000. Since 1979, that fraction has risen to nearly six in ten. While there have been some high-wage jobs created during this period, on a net basis, all of the employment increase experienced since 1979 has been generated by the creation of jobs which paid less than the median wage in 1979.

Since 1979...nearly 97 percent of net employment gains among white men have been in the low-wage stratum. During the same period, white men have experienced a net loss of one million jobs paying $28,000 or more in 1984 dollars. ...[T]he shift toward low-wage employment cannot be dismissed as simply a consequence of baby-boomers entering the workforce in the 1970s.

By 1984 total employment had increased to more than 113 million or 8 million more than in 1979. But of these 8 million net new employees, 58 percent earned no more than $7,012—the nominal dollar value that kept them in the low-wage stratum. Hence, *nearly three fifths of the net new employment generated between 1979 and 1984 was low wage, compared with less than one fifth during the preceding period.*[9]

While a rising tide may lift all boats, an ebbing one exposes and aggravates social disparities. In contemporary U.S. society, employment gains as well as gains in income have gone to particular groups, while others have been shut out. This fact may be demonstrated by the simultaneous growth in both employment and labor-force participation, on one hand, and in unemployment and retirement, on the other. The U.S. labor force has gone from around 70 million in 1960 to almost 120 million by 1986, a 71 percent increase, over the same time period that labor force participation among males 20 years and older has declined from 85 percent to around 78 percent. Meanwhile the number of persons unemployed has gone from 4 million in 1960 to reach 12 million at the height of the Reagan/Volcker recession of 1982; as of 1986, unemployment stood at 7 million, which is slightly below the average for Reagan's two terms.[10]

In 1947 there were jobs for 57 million people in the United States, while 2.3 million were unemployed. By 1960, 65.8 million had jobs, while 3.9 million were unemployed. In 1987, 110.6 million had jobs while 7.9 million did not. The unemployment rate has climbed steadily from 3.9 percent in 1947 to 5.5 percent in 1960 to 7.0 percent in 1986, while the labor-force participation rate went from 58.3 percent in 1947 to 59.4 percent in 1960 to 65.3 percent in 1986. Thus, while more and more people are working, so that the work force forms a greater and greater percentage of the population, we have unemployment simultaneously on the rise, both absolutely and as a percentage.[11]

Even though more people are touched by unemployment than it appears, the burden falls unevenly on the population. The problem is concentrated among those economically least able to withstand its ravages. Moreover, unemployment is a growing problem affecting larger and larger numbers, and proportions, of the U.S. population. Almost 25 percent of the work force faces unemployment in the course of a given year.

The following quotations from a 1983 report issued by the BLS will give demographic coloration to employment problems in the United States:

- The unemployed are more likely to be young, of a minority group, and blue collar than the labor force as a whole.
- Minority groups have substantially higher jobless rates than whites.
- Black teenagers have the highest jobless rates.
- Blue-collar workers typically bear the highest incidence of unemployment.
- Families maintained by a woman are most affected by unemployment.
- Because of the high degree of turnover, the total number of persons experiencing unemployment during a year is considerably greater than the average monthly level.
- Though unemployment rises and falls with the business cycle, the jobless rate has had an upward trend since 1970.
- Unemployment rates for adult women are usually higher than for adult men.

- Most workers become unemployed through layoff or other job loss.
- Fewer than half of the unemployed received unemployment insurance benefits in 1982.[12]

The analysis of employment trends by Barry Bluestone and Bennett Harrison shows that, besides a general deterioration in the income potential of jobs, the less even distribution of income has worked against the formation and maintenance of what has historically been considered the middle class. Not only have the traditional demographic constituents of middle-class America been threatened with loss of tenure, but would-be aspirants to such status, on the brink of success, have in recent years been pulled back before tasting the fruits of their economic ambition. According to Bluestone and Harrison:

In the 1973–79 period nearly 77 percent of the net new employment fell in the middle and upper strata. But in the subsequent period, there was an astonishing collapse of high wage employment and virtually *all* of the net job growth occurred in the low-wage sector. Only 3 percent of the two million net additional white male earners were found in employment outside the low stratum—in employment that paid more than $7,000 in 1984. . . .

[F]or both whites and non-whites, for women as well as men, the most recent period of employment expansion has failed to produce anywhere near as much real wage improvement as in the past. . . .

The continuing decline in high wage manufacturing, combined with the expansion in the low-wage retail trade and service sectors, have led to the popular perception that America may be on the verge of losing its middle class. Writers often equate "middle class" with "recipients of middle-level incomes." In those terms, our results confirm an unmistakable trend in this direction for individual working people.

Of all the demographic groups in the U.S., younger white men have been the biggest losers in the sense that *all* of the net new jobs held by this group after 1979 paid very low wages. In contrast, the share of all new jobs held by white women which pay high wages grew between 1973–79 and 1979–84, while the incidence of very low-paying work increased only slightly. The earnings of workers of color of both genders have not continued to improve as in the earlier period. Notable in this regard is the apparent halt in the previous trend toward a growing high wage share for non-white men. In the period 1973–79, 42 percent of the net employment growth among minority men was in the high wage end of the distribution. In the years since 1979, that proportion has dropped to 6.4 percent.[13]

The degree of equality in the distribution of income has been a traditional measure of social equity. By such a criterion, U.S. society has lately been retreating from its self-recognized standard of performance. Table 3.2 shows the percentage of the nation's total income going to families in each fifth of income in the period between 1950 and 1985.

Table 3.2
Distribution of Family Income in Percentages of Total Received by Each Fifth, 1950–1986

All U.S. families	1950	1960	1970	1977	1986
lowest fifth	4.5	4.8	5.4	5.2	4.6
second fifth	12.0	12.2	12.2	11.6	10.8
middle fifth	17.4	17.8	17.6	17.5	16.8
fourth fifth	23.4	24.0	23.8	24.2	24.0
highest fifth	42.7	41.3	40.9	41.5	43.7
highest 5%	17.3	15.9	15.6	15.7	17.0

Source: Prepared by the author.

In 1950, the 20 percent of families with the lowest incomes received 4.5 percent of the total income, while the 20 percent with the highest incomes received 42.7 percent of the total. The poorest fifth improved its share of total income during the 1960s, but that percentage has since declined to about what it was in 1950. The richest fifth has had the opposite experience. Its share declined during the 1960s, but then rose to its highest level for the period. The current trend, in other words, is for the income gap between rich and poor families to widen.

Part of the explanation for this development lies in changes of public policy toward poor people since the 1960s. In place of anti-poverty programs and a war-swollen economy have come periods of recession and government budget-cutting concentrated in areas that benefit poor Americans the most. The failure to reduce work hours has also contributed to the less even distribution of incomes in the following manner: The progressive annual increases in productivity have brought generally shrinking job opportunities. Those workers fortunate enough to have good jobs already continued to prosper. Others, however, were frozen out. The work force thus became polarized between "haves" and "have nots" on the basis of incumbency. The people with continuing access to income formed one, relatively affluent group. Another group, financially deprived, consisted of those who could find no place in the mainstream economy. If instead working hours had been reduced along with the technological progress, then the employment squeeze might not have occurred. Fewer people would have been reduced to scraping by on the margins of the economy.

4
THE HOURS FACTOR

In the early days of industry, manufacturing firms worked their employees 12 to 14 hours a day, six days a week, and sometimes longer, to extract a maximum work contribution for the wages paid. Banding together into unions, the workers brought pressure to bear against such practices. In time, employers were made to accept the 10-hour day as a standard day's work. The 9- and 8-hour days came later. In the 20th century, the 6-day week has given way to the 5-day week. A 5-day, 40-hour week is now the cornerstone of our work system. Statistically, the average hours worked in the U.S. economy declined from 68 hours in 1860 to 39 hours in 1986.

Some would take from those facts a complacent attitude regarding efforts to reduce the workweek further. They would say to America's workers: Be patient. Shorter work hours are inevitable. The unions are pushing for it. The work force is increasingly composed of persons, notably married women and young people, who are leisure-oriented and will make their preferences felt in the labor market. However, these things take time. You cannot force economic change prematurely or the economy might be hurt.

Such an approach is unrealistic. It were as if the shorter workweek could be gained without human intervention. Of course, someone must actively be supporting proposals for change or change will not happen. The unions may be officially on record as supporting a shorter workweek, but to say they are "pushing" for it would be an exaggeration. Married women and the young may want and need shorter hours to meet their family obligations or personal requirements, but there is a gap between their individual wishes and the institutional arrangements to accomodate them. "Flex-time" notwithstanding, the average worker has only a limited ability to influence his or her schedule of working hours.

One has to be pessimistic about the current trend of hours unless government intervenes. Work hours are not naturally becoming shorter. The reverse is true. The Bureau of Labor Statistics (BLS) has persisted in the view that workers themselves are largely responsible for such events by publishing opinion surveys showing that, given a choice between shorter hours and higher wages, workers prefer the latter. A problem with this approach is that it assumes an economic tradeoff between leisure and income that cannot be substantiated. Historically, workers with higher-than-average weekly incomes have also tended to receive shorter-than-average workweeks, and vice versa. (See Paul Douglas' *The Theory of Wages*, and more recent analysis by T. Aldrich Finegan and Peter Henle.[1]) Such a view also ignores the strong financial, cultural, and political pressures forcing people to "choose" money over leisure. Analyses based solely on the behavior of the so-called "rational economic man" are unbalanced and incomplete.

Now let us look at the record. Table 4.1 gives the annual workweek averages in the United States for the 40-year period 1947–1987. The two columns show the results from two different statistical surveys. In the first column are the averages derived from the Current Population Survey. Also known as the "household" series, these statistics are furnished by the Bureau of the Census from a monthly survey of about 60,000 families, representing a cross-section of the U.S. population of persons 16 years and older. The second column contains the averages from the "payroll" or "establishment" series. Each month more than 290,000 employers submit wage-and-hours information to state employment agencies, based on their payroll records. The information is compiled nationally by the BLS.

The two series use different definitions for the reported hours. The establishment series reports hours "paid for" by employers, and covers only production or nonsupervisory employees. The household series, a comprehensive survey of the population, reports hours actually worked. These different definitions may create differences in the reported averages. For example, if a worker took a day of vacation from a regular 40-hour job during the survey week, the household survey would show that this person had a 32-hour workweek. The establishment series, on the other hand, would report a 40-hour workweek, because the day of vacation had been paid. The two surveys also produce different figures in the case of multiple job-holding. The household series includes the hours of self-employed, agricultural, and supervisory workers; the establishment series does not.[2]

An "average" workweek suggests the schedule of an average or typical

Table 4.1
Average Workweek in the U.S. Economy "Household" and "Payroll" Series, 1947–1987

Year	Household series	Payroll series
1987	39.0	34.8
1986	39.1	34.8
1985	39.0	34.9
1984	38.8	35.2
1983	38.3	35.0
1982	38.0	34.8
1981	38.1	35.2
1980	38.5	35.3
1979	38.9	35.7
1978	39.0	35.8
1977	38.8	36.0
1976	38.7	36.1
1975	38.7	36.1
1974	39.0	36.5
1973	39.3	36.9
1972	39.4	37.0
1971	39.3	36.9
1970	39.1	37.1
1969	39.9	37.7
1968	40.1	37.8
1967	40.4	38.0
1966	40.4	38.6
1965	40.5	38.8
1964	40.0	38.7
1963	40.4	38.8
1962	40.5	38.7
1961	40.5	38.6
1960	40.5	38.6
1959	40.5	39.0
1958	40.6	38.5
1957	41.0	38.8
1956	41.5	39.3
1955	41.6	39.6
1954	40.9	39.1
1953	41.9	39.6
1952	42.4	39.9
1951	42.2	39.9
1950	41.7	39.8
1949	42.1	39.4
1948	42.8	40.0
1947	43.5	40.3

Source: Prepared by the author.

worker. When the average drops, one would therefore suppose that some or most workers must be working fewer hours per week than before. However, an average is a statistical concept, which is determined mathematically from a multitude of data. Changes in the composition of a population may affect the average as well as changes taking place

Table 4.2
Employment and Average Hours in Agriculture and Nonagricultural
Industries, 1920–1987

Year	Average Workweek		Employment	
	agricultural industries	nonagri= cultural industries	agricultural industries (000)	nonagri= cultural industries (000)
1920	60.0	45.5	11,449	30,985
1930	55.0	43.2	10,340	35,140
1940	54.6	41.1	9,540	37,980
1950	50.1	41.3	7,160	51,758
1960	48.0	40.1	5,458	60,318
1970	39.1	38.7	3,463	75,215
1980	45.1	38.3	3,364	95,938
1987	43.7	38.8	3,208	109,232

Source: Prepared by the author.

in the population itself. If the work force grows more rapidly in industries that schedule shorter-than-average hours than in industries that
schedule longer-than-average hours, the employment shift will bring
down the general workweek average even if the average hours remained
the same in each industry. In fact, this has been the case. The older
goods-producing industries, with stable or declining employment, have
tended to schedule longer hours than the newer services-providing industries, where employment had grown. As a result, the overall average
has dropped statistically more than the individual experiences of workers
would warrant.

For example, the average workweek of the U.S. civilian economy has
been affected by the employment shift between agriculture and nonagricultural industries. Work hours are normally longer in agriculture.
Table 4.2 shows the number of Americans employed in agriculture and
in nonagricultural industries, and their average workweeks, in years
1920–1987. It can be calculated that if agricultural employment had
comprised the same percentage of total employment in 1987 as in 1920,
the average workweek in the entire economy would have been 40.12
hours in 1987 instead of 39.0 hours, as reported. Therefore, the employment shift between agriculture and nonagricultural industries ac-

Table 4.3
Calculation of Average Workweek in 1987 if Employment Mix by Industry had been the same as in 1964

	historical			calculated		
Industry	1964 employ= ment (000)	1964 per= cent	1987 employ= ment (000)	employ= ment if 1964 percent (000)	1987 ave. hours	man-hours (000)
mining	497	1.2	530	843	42.3	35,647
construction	2,637	6.5	3,924	4,471	37.8	169,017
durables mfg	7,213	17.8	7,458	12,230	41.6	508,789
non-dur. mfg	5,569	13.7	5,564	9,443	40.2	379,605
whole. trade	2,823	7.0	4,637	4,787	38.2	182,853
retail trade	8,046	19.8	16,228	13,643	29.3	399,738
transp. & pub. util.	3,490	8.6	4,456	5,918	39.1	231,382
fin., insur. & real est.	2,347	5.8	4,844	3,980	36.3	144,460
services	7,939	19.6	21,135	13,462	32.5	437,499
total	40,561	100.0	68,776	68,776	36.19	2,488,990

1987 workweek as reported   34.8

difference   1.39   hours

Source: Prepared by the author.

counted for 10.5 percent of the 10.7 hours by which the average workweek in all industries declined between 1920 and 1987.

Within the nonagricultural sector, industries that schedule relatively short hours have added employees at a faster rate than industries where hours are longer. Table 4.3 shows the number of production or non-supervisory workers employed in private nonagricultural industries in 1964 and 1987, together with their 1987 average workweek. The non-supervisory workers in retail trade averaged 29.3 hours of work each week in 1987. Their share of the total employment rose from 19.8 to 23.6 percent between 1964 and 1987. Workers in "other services," whose workweek averaged 32.5 hours in 1987, showed an even more rapid employment gain. On the other hand, workers in durable-goods and nondurable-goods manufacturing, who together averaged 41.0 hours of work per week in 1987, declined from 31.5 to 18.9 percent in their share of total employment between 1964 and 1987. If the various industrial groups had each employed the same share of the total in 1987 that they had in 1964, the average workweek in all industries would have been 36.19 hours in 1987 instead of the reported 34.8 hours. The extra 1.39 hours per week caused by the change in the employment mix represents 35 percent of the 3.9 hours by which the average workweek declined during this period.

Both the "establishment" and "household" series have reported an average workweek less than 40 hours in recent years. In fact, only a minority of American workers work fewer than 40 hours a week. That discrepancy is due to the fact that part-time workers, averaging less than 20 hours of work in a week, are reflected in both sets of figures. Average scheduled weekly hours, derived from a third survey, give a more accurate picture of work for the typical full-time worker. Between 1959/1960 and 1979–1981 the average scheduled workweek of office workers in metropolitan areas declined from 39.0 hours to 38.8 hours. The average for plant workers declined from 40.5 hours per week to 39.7 hours per week during this period. Office workers in finance, insurance, and real estate, and to a lesser extent in services, generally have scheduled workweeks shorter than 40 hours. Less than 10 percent of factory workers in manufacturing do. About 80 percent of plant workers, but slightly less than 60 percent of office workers, are scheduled to work exactly 40 hours a week. Overtime hours are, of course, not reflected in these figures.[3]

IMPACT OF THE FAIR LABOR STANDARDS ACT

Since the end of World War II, the trend among full-time workers in the United States has been to concentrate work schedules at the 40-hour level rather than to reduce them further. The BLS defines a full-time worker as someone who works 35 or more hours a week. Between 1955 and 1970, the percentage of full-time workers who worked 35–39 hours increased from 7 to 9 percent; those who worked 41–48 hours dropped from 21 to 15 percent; those who worked 49 or more hours increased from 49 to 53 percent.[4] Earlier studies found that, curiously, the percentage of workers in the longest hours category was increasing. The nonagricultural wage-and-salary workers who worked 49 or more hours a week rose from 12.9 percent of all full-time nonagricultural and wage-and-salary workers in 1948 to 18.2 percent in 1965, and to 21.7 percent in 1987.[5]

An explanation of this pattern might lie in the application of the Fair

Labor Standards Act (FLSA) to particular groups of workers. Because employers have to pay a premium wage to employees covered by the act for work performed beyond 40 hours in a week, there would be a financial incentive for employers to switch them from work schedules above 40 hours a week to schedules at or below 40 hours. Further drops to levels below 40 hours would not be due to the FLSA but to other influences. Actually, employers have an incentive to schedule exactly 40 hours of work: The rising cost of fringe benefits, hiring, and training makes hiring employees for fewer work hours a week less attractive, while hours beyond 40 in a week would incur the "half time" overtime premium. On the other hand, certain employees, such as those in managerial or professional positions, are exempt from the overtime-pay provisions of the FLSA, or they have job skills in short supply. Their work hours might therefore rise without restraint. Such employees, plus those at the lower end of the pay scale, account for most of the people who work 49 or more hours a week.[6]

The Fair Labor Standards Act, passed in 1938, brought a 40-hour standard workweek to blue-collar manufacturing workers, starting in October 1940. At first, only about one third of the nation's 33 million nonsupervisory wage-and-salary workers were covered by the law. The lower-paid workers in agriculture, services, and retail trade were generally not covered. Over the years an increasing number of workers have come under the law's jurisdiction through amendments, until by September 1980 it applied to 81 percent of all employees in the goods-producing sector and to 51 percent of employees in the services-providing sector. The 1961 amendments extended coverage to 3.6 million workers, concentrated in retail trade, services, and construction. The 1966 amendments added 10.4 million people, including certain types of farm workers. The 1974 amendments brought government employees, including postal workers, under FLSA jurisdiction. Finally, the amendments passed in 1977, affecting 2.4 million persons, repealed the overtime exemptions for hotel, motel, and restaurant workers.[7]

Until the 1960s, the FLSA applied mainly to blue-collar employees in manufacturing, construction, transportation, and public utilities. Agricultural, retail, service, and financial workers were not covered. A larger percentage of full-time wage-and-salary employees worked more than 40 hours a week in industries that were not covered than in industries that were covered. There was, however, a tendency in all industries for the percentage of people working the longer hours to decline between 1948 and 1960, while the percentage working 40 hours a week or less increased. In manufacturing industries as a whole, the percentage of full-time wage-and-salary workers working 41 or more hours per week declined from 29.2 to 24.9 percent during this period. In agriculture and in wholesale and retail trade, where workers were not eligible for overtime pay, the percentage of such workers dropped, respectively, from 85.7 to 75.6 percent and from 62.0 to 49.8 percent.[8] The FLSA appears to have been an influence to reduce hours, but in a general way. Regarding retail trade employees affected by the 1961 amendments to this law, Peter Henle observed: "The fact that reductions in worktime have been industry wide suggests that either the rapid transfer of new practices induced by an hours standard or the presence of other factors such as the shift to the suburbs or the availability of part-time workers may be affecting the hours pattern for the industry as a whole."[9]

PART-TIME AND FULL-TIME EMPLOYMENT

In fact, the growth and development of part-time employment may have been one of the most important results of the Fair Labor Standards Act. Part-time employment is defined as employment for 1–34 hours a week. The BLS has developed two categories of part-time workers: those who voluntarily work part time and those who work part time "for economic reasons." "Economic reasons" include slack work, materials shortages, or repairs to plant and equipment, jobs begun or ended during the survey week, and a person's inability to find other than part-time work. There is also another group of people who actually worked less than 35 hours a week, but are included in the full-time workforce. They are persons who worked part time "for other reasons," which include employment for less than 35 hours a week because of vacations, holidays, illness, bad weather, and other noneconomic reasons. The BLS definitions assign someone to the full-time workforce if that person usually works full time—35 or more hours a week—even though the person in the survey week may actually be working less than 35 hours or be unemployed. Someone who usually works part time, regardless of actual status, would be in the part-time workforce.

Table 4.4 shows the relationship between these various categories and their respective employment records in 1987. A total of 119,865,000 Americans were included in the civilian labor force that year, of whom 20,929,000 (17 percent) were in the part-time workforce and the remainder in the full-time workforce. Only 79 percent of the people in the full-time workforce actually worked 35 or more hours per week, however.

The distribution of part-time employees varies considerably by industry. The two industrial groups that have added the most new employees—wholesale and retail trade and services—also utilize part-time workers the most extensively. On the other hand, the group that has lost the greatest share of employment, manufacturing, employs full-time workers almost exclusively. Together, these trends have had a significant impact on the workweek average. Besides showing a significant variation

Table 4.4
Full-time and Part-time Workforce in 1987

	number of persons (000)	average workweek	man-hours worked (000)
Full time			
Full-time schedules, worked 35 or more hours	78,522	44.91	3,526,421
Part-time for other reasons, usually work full time	8,209	27.9	229,031
Workers on full-time schedules, total at work	86,731	43.3	3,755,452
Workers on full-time schedules, not at work	4,517	0	0
Total employed full time	91,248	41.16	3,755,452
Part time for economic reasons, usually work full time	1,706	24.2	41,285
Unemployed - full time	5,976	0	0
FULL-TIME WORK FORCE	98,930	38.38	3,796,737
Part time			
Part time for economic reasons, usually work part time	3,695	21.0	77,595
Part time for other reasons, usually work part time	14,395	19.2	276,384
Part time - not at work	1,393	0	0
Total - employed part time	19,483	18.17	353,979
Unemployed - part time	1,446	0	0
PART-TIME WORK FORCE	20,929	16.91	353,979
U.S. Civilian Labor Force	119,865	34.63	4,150,716
Total at work	106,530	39.0	4,150,716

Source: Prepared by the author.

by industry, part-time employment has important demographic characteristics. American women 20 and over are more than three times as likely as their male counterparts to be working part time. Teenagers of both sexes are twice as likely as the women 20 and over to work part time. The increased percentage of female workers in the workforce has accompanied the rise in part-time employment.[10]

Each year the BLS reports the average workweek of full-time workers in addition to that of all workers. In 1987, full-time workers averaged 43.3 hours per week. All workers averaged 39.0 hours per week that year. Full-time workers in 1968 averaged 43.9 hours per week, while all workers averaged 40.1 hours per week. The decline in the average full-time workweek between 1968 and 1987 was 0.6 hours per week. The decline in the average workweek of all workers during this time was 1.1 hours per week. Therefore, 55 percent of the one hour decline in the general average was due to declining workweeks among the predominant group, the full-time workers. The remaining 45 percent of the decline was due to shortening hours worked by the part-time workers or else to the compositional shift in the workforce between full-time and part-time workers, as the latter gained a larger share.[11]

In summary, the statistical decline in the average workweek to a level below 40 hours does not indicate that an "average" worker in the United States now works less than 40 hours a week or that weekly work schedules of 40 hours are being abandoned in favor of shorter schedules. The "average" or predominant type of worker is still a full-time worker, and this person averages more than 43 hours of work each week. Instead, what progress has been made in reducing the statistical average for the workweek since World War II is due largely to three developments:

1. The employment mix has changed. Jobs have shifted from industries where longer hours are worked to industries where shorter hours are worked.

2. Part-time employment has increased relative to full-time employment.

3. In some industries, application of the Fair Labor Standards Act has prompted a reduction in weekly hours from higher levels down to 40.[12]

A RETREAT FROM SHORTER HOURS

The trend is clearly away from shorter hours. In the early 1960s, International Brotherhood & Electrical Workers local #3 in New York City negotiated a "breakthrough" contract, giving electricians a 25-hour workweek. Subsequently, its members went quietly back to a 35-hour week because of competitive pressures from non-union contractors. In 1976, the United Automobile Workers waged a month-long strike against Ford to add "paid personal holidays" to its members' annual paid leave. At the time, some commentators considered this to be a back-door approach to a 4-day workweek. In 1982, such benefits were among the "give backs" that the union granted to U.S. automobile manufacturers. In the same year, the air-traffic controllers' union, PATCO, was busted while striking for a 4-day week.[13]

In the meantime, attempts to achieve shorter hours through legislation have stalled. Bills submitted in Congress to reduce the statutory workweek have failed to attract more than a handful of co-sponsors. A study of Philip Morris Inc. found that the average American had 31 percent less leisure time in 1984 than in 1973. The median number of hours worked increased from 40.6 to 47.3, according to this study, while personal free time fell from 26.2 to 18.1 hours per week.[14]

LEISURE IN OTHER FORMS

What about paid vacations and holidays? Even if progress toward a shorter workweek has stalled, it could be that workers are continuing to receive greater amounts of paid leisure on an annual basis. In the immediate postwar period, there seemed to be a definite trend toward such benefits. Prior to World War II, it was customary for blue-collar workers to take time off without pay to observe major holidays such as Christmas; employers were somewhat more generous with their white-collar employees. The practice of paying for holiday leave received a boost from several decisions of the National War Labor Board, which allowed as many as six paid holidays to be granted within wage stabilization guidelines. Employers took advantage of this method of competing for scarce wartime labor. With respect to paid vacations, only about one fourth of the nation's union workers in 1940 were covered by contracts providing this type of benefit. The contracts typically called for one week of paid vacation per year, or two weeks at the most. By 1957, 91 percent of workers covered by major collective bargaining agreements received paid vacations, and in a majority of these contracts senior workers received annual vacations of at least three weeks.[15]

Economists at BLS have estimated that U.S. workers received an average of 0.3 weeks of paid vacation in 1940, 1.3 weeks in 1960, and 1.9 weeks in 1968. Since then, the average paid vacation is estimated to have risen by another one tenth of a week. Not only have the benefit increases been less generous than in earlier periods, the average length of vacations has been adversely affected by a decline in the percentage of high-seniority employees. The percentage of workers taking full-week vacations without pay has increased, indicating that workers' interest in receiving more leisure in this form has not slackened. With respect to paid holidays, BLS economists have estimated that in 1940 office workers in the United States received an average of 5 days per year, while plant workers averaged 1 day per year. By 1968, this had increased to 8.0

Table 4.5
Estimates of Annual Hours of Paid Leisure Gained by U.S. Full-time Workers, 1940–1979

Source	Period	Additional Hours of Paid Leisure per Year			
		Shorter Workweek	Longer Vacation	More Holidays	Total
Hedges & Taylor	1968-1979	25	4	10	39
Moore & Hedges	1960-1969	30	15	4	49
Henle	1940-1960	75	48	32	155
total	1940-1979	130	67	46	243

Source: Prepared by the author.

paid holidays per year for office workers, and 7.5 holidays per year for plant workers. Today, both groups average slightly less than 10 holidays per year.[16]

Table 4.5 summarizes the average gains that U.S. workers have received in the form of shortened workweeks, paid vacations, and paid holidays for three different periods of time. Peter Henle did the computation for the period 1940–1960; Geoffrey H. Moore and Janice N. Hedges for the period 1960–1969; and Janice N. Hedges and Daniel E. Taylor for the period 1968–1979. The table shows that the total gains in paid leisure were substantially larger in the first 20-year period than in the comparable combined period between 1960 and 1979. The slowdown is most noticeable in the area of paid vacations and holidays.

Those who contend that U.S. labor standards are among the most advanced in the world will be sorry to learn, from Table 4.6, that the U.S. average of two weeks of annual paid vacation is comparable with the legal provisions in Czechoslovakia, Italy, and Greece, but falls well below the legal standards in most other European nations. It also fails to meet the standard set by the International Labor Organization in its 1970 Holidays with Pay convention, calling for workers with one or more years of seniority to receive a minimum of three weeks of paid vacation. The U.S. provision of ten paid holidays per year is comparable to European practice. In the United States, of course, paid vacations and holidays are a matter for employers or collective bargaining to decide rather than being set by law.[17]

This is not to say that we in the United States have failed to achieve any advances in leisure. The preferred method of distributing leisure in recent decades has been to increase the number of people who do no

Table 4.6
Statutory Provision for Paid Vacations and Public Holidays in Several European Countries

Country	Minimum Days Annual Paid Vacation	Number of Holidays
Austria	20	13
Belgium	20	10
Bulgaria	14	7
Czechoslovakia	10	7
Denmark	25	10
Finland	20	5
France	25	10
Germany (East)	18	9
Germany (West)	15	11-13
Greece	10	6-12
Hungary	15	8
Ireland	15	8
Italy	10	10
Luxembourg	25	10
Netherlands	15	8
Norway	21	10
Poland	14	8
Portugal	15	12-14
Rumania	15	8
Spain	23 *	14
Sweden	25	11
Switzerland	15	4-5
Turkey	12	15
United Kingdom	none	8
USSR	15	8
Yugoslavia	18	7

*calendar days

Source: Prepared by the author.

remunerative work at all but, in some cases, nevertheless receive financial support. Unemployment itself could be considered such a form of leisure. Lives spent on welfare, employee absenteeism, disability, and involuntary part-time employment also bear a resemblance to paid leisure. In a more recognizable form of employee benefit, one finds such practices as prolonged vacations or sabbaticals, sick leave, and, above all, retirement. All make paid employment a precondition of receiving the benefit and are awarded, by and large, on the basis of seniority. In such cases, the period of leisure is more sharply separated from the period of work to the point that a separate class of nonworkers, or nonworking former workers, is created.

Table 4.7
Persons not in the Labor Force, by Reason for not Working, 1967–1987

Category	1967	1970	1975	1980	1985	1987
Not in labor force	52,484	54,280	58,655	59,425	62,744	62,888
Percent of civilian noninstitutional population	40.4%	39.6%	38.3%	35.4%	35.2%	34.4%
Not participating because of -						
School attendance	6,745	7,126	7,730	7,621	7,743	7,798
Poor health, disability	4,509	4,358	5,461	5,115	4,717	5,156
Household respon= sibilities	32,564	33,068	32,443	29,880	28,453	26,990
men		201	217	297	372	457
women		32,867	32,224	29,583	28,081	26,533
Retirement	5,313	5,918	7,851	10,738	14,857	16,237
men		5,216	6,428	7,919	9,985	10,353
women		703	1,423	2,819	4,872	5,884
Think can't get job	732	638	1,082	970	1,204	1,026
Other	2,622	3,165	4,081	5,100	5,771	5,679

Source: Prepared by the author.

The BLS puts many of these people into a category called "not in the labor force." The major subcategories include nonemployment because of (a) education, (b) poor health or disability, (c) household responsibilities, (d) retirement, (e) discouragement about finding a job, and (f) other. Table 4.7 shows the numbers counted in each subcategory in selected years between 1967 and 1987. As the table indicates, the total number of Americans classified as being "not in the labor force" increased numerically but declined as a percentage of the civilian noninstitutional population in this period. The two remaining categories, employment and unemployment, increased in both respects. Within the "not in the labor force" category, the greatest change involved persons who were absorbed in "household responsibilities" and "retirement." Those not participating in the work force for the first reason, predominantly women, declined by 5.5 million persons between 1967 and 1987. Those not participating for the second reason, largely men, increased by 10.9 million persons. One might say that younger and middle-aged women were pouring into the work force as older men in even larger numbers were leaving.

When leisure is put on an all-or-none basis, it raises questions of social equity comparable to those cited earlier in regard to the distribution of income. The problem is perhaps most acute in the case of a single-parent wage-earner, more often female than male, who must find enough time in the day to combine paid employment and childcare responsibilities with personal requirements. At the same time that a 25-year-old woman, for instance, may be struggling against physical stress and fatigue to do all that, her 60-year-old father may be settling into a life of leisure through early retirement; or another woman, her own age, may have chosen to go on welfare. Like financial poverty, an inadequate provision of leisure time can become a source of misery and a type of social injustice.

5
OUTPUT: USEFUL OR WASTE

Now we come to the fourth variable in the equation describing the production of goods and services: output. Output is the factor which is balanced against the three input factors. The equation, again, reads:

Output = productivity × employment × average hours of work

In an earlier chapter we applied this equation to the farm economy. Between 1947 and 1986 agricultural output rose by 90 percent, while productivity rose by 633 percent and average work hours declined by 13 percent. That combination of changes brought about a decline in farm employment of 70 percent, or 4.5 million persons. Evidently the situation in agriculture was different from that in the U.S. economy as a whole. Employment has not declined in the U.S. private economy, but instead has risen to a level 70 percent higher than it was in 1947. In numbers of persons employed, it rose from 58.1 million persons in 1947 to 92.9 million persons in 1986. The remaining three factors have also been different from their equivalents in the farm economy. Between 1947 and 1986 the average productivity of U.S. workers rose by 14 percent, average working hours declined by 15 percent, and output rose by 254 percent. The productivity gains in the private economy generally were not as great as those in agriculture, the hours decline was somewhat larger, and the gains in output were substantially larger.

Table 5.1 summarizes the changes that have taken place in output, productivity, employment, and average hours in the private business sector in years since 1947, according to BLS data. The changes are expressed in terms of an index based on levels prevailing in 1947. In

Table 5.1
Output, Productivity, Employment and Average Hours in the U.S. Private Business Sector, 1947–1986

Year	Output	=	Productivity	x	Employment	x	Average Hours
1947	1.000		1.000		1.000		1.000
1950	1.133		1.151		1.002		.984
1955	1.373		1.339		1.058		.970
1960	1.530		1.506		1.076		.946
1965	1.934		1.804		1.136		.944
1970	2.218		1.969		1.246		.906
1975	2.470		2.131		1.320		.878
1977	2.762		2.227		1.416		.878
1980	2.948		2.212		1.550		.862
1983	3.036		2.294		1.555		.853
1986	3.536		2.439		1.707		.850

Source: Prepared by the author.

each year, the product of the indexes representing productivity, employment, and average hours equalled the index representing output. Output is clearly the key to the differences we have found between agriculture and the private economy in general. Output in the general economy was 3.5 times higher in 1986 than in 1947 while farm output rose by a comparatively anemic 90 percent. It would appear, then, that the greater increase in output is the principal explanation for the fact that employment was able to rise in the U.S. private economy despite the failure of working hours to decline as productivity gains took place.

HOW SOLID IS OUTPUT?

Output implies a certain volume of goods and services, which are the basis of a community's material living standards. The higher per capita output, the more prosperous the community would seem to be. The reported statistics show that output in the U.S. private economy tripled between 1950 and 1984 while the U.S. population rose by 55 percent. Per capita output therefore almost doubled. Would that not be a fair representation of average living standards? The average citizen, the supposed beneficiary of gains in U.S. per capita output, may be skeptical of such claims. How can the statistical evidence of higher living standards be reconciled with the conflicting evidence of one's own eyes? An American of today might ask: If people are becoming so much more prosperous, why can so few families starting out nowadays afford to buy a house of their own? Why are so many Americans in their early 20s moving back into their parents' home in order to save money? Why, in contrast to their grandparents' generation, do both husband and wife today have to work to make ends meet? In terms of statistics, how do we reconcile the substantial gains in per capita output with figures, cited earlier, showing that the real income of U.S. wage-earners has been declining since the early 1970s?

We need to take a closer look at output. Farm output is something that we readily comprehend and that we can appreciate for its contribution to our material well-being. Farmers grow wheat for the bread we eat, raise corn and soybeans to feed livestock, maintain cows to milk for dairy products, and so on. We can see a personal need for these various farm products. At the same time we can understand why farm output might have risen by a comparatively small percentage amount since 1950. Once people have reached a certain level of per capita physical consumption, they become satiated. Well-fed people do not want larger quantities of food forced down their throats just because the farm economy can produce those larger quantities. Economists say that the demand for farm produce is relatively "inelastic."

It is quite another matter with economic output in general. Only a small part of the output from the U.S. private economy has to do with food production or the production of physical goods. The rest is more nebulous. The particular kinds of products being furnished in the economy are continually changing. They are so various in kind that we can hardly characterize them in a few images or descriptive categories. Output, like employment, changes as the economy itself develops new wants and needs and new products to meet the changing demand. The volume of output in the general economy is more elastic than in the farm economy because of our capitalistic ingenuity in developing new kinds of products and working them into the economy and into our daily lives. At the same time, we must begin to question how necessary or useful some of these products really are.

How solid is U.S. economic growth? As the economy develops new forms of enterprise, there is both growth and decay. We do know, at one end, what kind of job is being eliminated. Generally this is a job to do or produce something of obvious use. It is a job to grow food, build cars, dig ditches, pump gas. At the other end, we do not clearly see the nature of the emerging job. If past experience is any indication, this job will likely involve some form of "services." The services sector of the gross national product (GNP) now accounts for half of the total, compared with less than one third in 1950. Beyond that, it is unclear what a typical job of the future might be. One would assume that the job would include activities that are to some degree useful to people, but that cannot be known for certain. The nature of the job tends to follow the nature of the product with which it is involved. Employment takes shape around those activities of production and distribution that furnish the various goods and services for the market. As various as jobs are, so is the nature of economic output.

Output for the private business sector would be a composite of all goods and services produced in the private economy—a forced mixture of "apples and oranges", so to speak. It should be noted, however, that the U.S. government's data-gathering techniques have not kept pace with changes in the nature of economic activity. A particular problem has been the failure to give the burgeoning services sector even a fraction of the scrutiny given manufacturing activities. Only one third of the Standard Industrial Classification (SIC) codes pertain to services, for instance, while two thirds of GNP occurs in this sector. Services are a softer kind of output than goods; they are less easily defined in physical terms. The present chairman of the Federal Reserve Board, Alan Greenspan, who once headed an economic consulting firm, cited his own occupation as an example of generating ill-defined output: "I defy anyone to set an indicator of physical volume for this business," he said.[1]

Just as not all jobs are alike in their provision of income or degree of usefulness, so not all output is alike. The possibility that we will now explore is that much of the apparent gain in living standards, as represented by the statistical increase in per capita output, does not consist of goods and services that are useful to people or even desired by them, but of one or another form of economic waste. A more spurious kind of growth therefore has taken place in the U.S. economy in recent decades than what people sometimes are led to believe. The word "waste" is, of course, a pejorative term. The BLS does not have a statistical category representing wasteful economic activities, and if it did, the series would soon be discontinued. "Waste" implies that certain economic acativities are superfluous, and could be eliminated without regrets. It suggests, as well, that what certain people do for a living has little value or use to society. That in itself guarantees an immediate constituency to demand that its function be differently characterized.

HOW TO DEFINE WASTE?

Our attack on waste will not be an attack on particular persons or groups, but a more general kind of criticism. In that respect, it is unlike the type of campaign against waste in government that political "conservatives" have pursued. The Grace Commission, for instance, has compiled a list of wasteful expenditures made by the federal government. Among other things, the commission report revealed that Social Security checks continue to be sent to 8,000 persons who have died, that most domestic military bases are strategically worthless, that federal specifications for a mousetrap run 700 pages, and that much of the government's data-processing equipment is obsolete.[2] Those are all valuable pieces of information, deserving corrective action. Nevertheless, the thrust of such criticism is a partisan attack on the public sector, implying that the private sector is comparatively unwasteful or efficient. That particular angle may be interesting to some, but it is not our theme.

The discussion of waste in this book will focus on a different kind of waste, not a kind that suggests that particular persons are corrupt or foolish, but a kind that suggests that the system itself is corrupt or foolish. Is it possible to be objective about such matters? One person's waste is another's opportunity. To some people it might seem, for instance, that the "Pet Rock" was a good example of waste—an amusing kind of product but basically unnecessary. A "Cabbage Patch" doll is individually registered with the manufacturer, and receives its own birthday cards. This too seems extravagant, but, as wasteful things go, the Cabbage Patch doll is one of the better products on the market. Anything that can bring a smile to a small child's face is, to adoring parents, well worth the purchase price. It has been reported that the average American family owns 2.3 television sets. Is that a tell-tale sign of our national proclivities toward waste? Not necessarily. Lyndon Johnson used to watch three sets at a time, and some in today's audience may have equally diverse television-viewing interests. We are not Puritans here, intending to kill someone's sport; we are simply seeking to expose waste in its grimmer and more useless forms.

Perhaps the subject can be approached in this fashion. Let us suppose that in primitive society the economy starts out like a sapling, developing to supply materials essential for human life. More and more of these materials are supplied, until a condition of abundance is achieved. Further growth spills over then into kinds of production not so useful or necessary. The economy develops in crooked patterns of useless, meaningless enterprise. Farther out on the economic spectrum, the activities make even less sense. They become frivolous, extravagant, bizarre, and, eventually, self-destructive. Meanwhile, the interior parts start to decay, so that, despite its superabundance, the economy neglects basic functions. The growth areas begin to feed on themselves. Healthy parts of the economy are drained to nourish the unhealthy. Sane, reasonable, and productive enterprises are mercilessly squeezed to extract resources to feed predators. Thus in successive stages of growth, saturation and ruinous decay, the economy moves from the production of necessities to waste.

The root of the problem would seem to be not economic scarcity but abundance. Scarcity would breed sensible solutions, but abundance breeds waste. Too much production and sale of products leads to a saturation of markets. With the saturation of domestic markets, new ones abroad must be found. Eventually, world markets, too, become saturated. When there is no further opportunity for constructive growth, it is time for ruin and decay. Under the circumstances, then, it might be helpful to find a more benign form of waste to relieve the pressures leading to overproduction. If someone could sell this idea, government might solve the problem of economic overcapacity by a ditch-digging program of the following sort: In the morning a crew of workers would arrive with picks and shovels to dig ditches. In the afternoon, another crew would shovel the dirt back into the ditches and pack it down hard. Each crew would be told that "enemies" had undone their work from the previous day. By the current reporting procedures, both sets of activities would be included in the official statistics of GNP. The more dirt shoveled in and out of the ditches, the higher the community's living standards would be objectively found to be.

The phenomenon of economic waste is not new to Americans. We have had at least a century of experience in dealing with the kinds of behavior inspired by waste and the social problems it creates. In the late 1920s, a report of President Hoover's Committee on Recent Economic Changes identified the shift away from production of necessities, saying that "as a people we have become steadily less concerned about the primary needs—food, clothing and shelter...and we now demand a broad list of goods and services which come under the category of 'optional purchases'—optional in the sense that this portion of income may be saved or spent, and if spent the manner of this spending may be determined by the tastes of the consumer or the nature of the appeals made to him by the industries competing for his patronage." The report, issued in 1929, incorrectly concluded, however, that "economically we have a boundless field before us.... [T]here are new wants which will make way for newer wants...by advertising and other promotional devices, by scientific fact finding [and] by carefully predeveloped consumption...As long as the appetites for goods and services are practically insatiable, as it appears to be...it would seem that we can go on with increasing activity...."[3]

ECONOMISTS ON WASTE

If the economics of waste has its own special economist, he would be the Minnesota-educated college professor, Thorstein Veblen, who published *The Theory of the Leisure Class* at the turn of the century. Veblen introduced the idea of status-seeking waste into modern economic theory. Of its essential nature, he wrote that "the expenditure in question is no more and no less legitimate than any other expenditure. It is here called 'waste' because this expenditure does not serve human life or human well-being on the whole, not because it is waste or misdirection of effort or expenditure as viewed from the standpoint of the individual consumer who chooses it. If he chooses it, that disposes of the question of its relative utility to him.... In strict accuracy nothing should be included under the head of conspicuous waste but such expenditure as is incurred on the ground of an invidious pecuniary comparison."

Veblen's entire theory is summarized in those last three words. They mean that the expenditure was made primarily for the purpose of showing that the person who made it has more money than other people do. The expenditure gives evidence of financial prowess, which, in turn, is the basis of social standing in our society. Veblen wrote:

The basis on which good repute in any highly organized community ultimately rests is pecuniary strength; and the means of showing pecuniary strength, and so of gaining or retaining a good name, are leisure and a conspicuous consumption of goods.... Accordingly, both of these methods are in vogue as far down the scale as it remains possible.... No class of society, not even the most abjectly poor, forgoes all customary conspicuous consumption.... Very much of squalor and discomfort will be endured before the last trinket or the last pretense of pecuniary decency is put away.

Veblen believed that the economy had an almost unlimited capacity to accommodate this form of waste. He wrote:

[T]he end sought by accumulation is to rank high in comparison with the rest of the community in point of pecuniary strength. So long as the comparison is distinctly unfavorable to himself, the normal, average individual will live in chronic dissatisfaction with his present lot; and when he has reached what may be called the normal pecuniary standard of the community, or of his class in the community, this chronic dissatisfaction will give place to a restless straining to place a wider and ever-widening pecuniary interval between himself and this average standard.... If, as is sometimes assumed, the incentive to accumulation were the want of subsistence or of physical comfort, then the aggregate economic wants of a community might conceivably be satisfied at some point in the advance of industrial efficiency; but since this struggle is substantially a race for reputability on the basis of invidious comparison, no approach to a definitive attainment is possible.[4]

Veblen's theory, developed almost a century ago, is surprisingly contemporary, as indeed it has been in previous periods of affluence such as the 1920s. We have our designer clothing and specialty foods, which make a social statement as much as they satisfy a functional need. The idea that conspicuous consumption of services and goods may have real economic significance clearly applies to our current situation. Veblen's opinion, stated above, was that economic growth might continue indefinitely along those lines; there was theoretically no limit to the volume of goods and services that upscale consumers might demand in the process of improving their living standards.

Besides conspicuous consumption, Veblen took "conspicuous leisure" to be a kind of financial exhibition. He wrote that "a life of leisure is the readiest and most conclusive evidence of pecuniary strength." In this respect, the times may have left Veblen's theory behind. Veblen was writing at a time when the vast majority of Americans worked in agriculture or other laboring jobs. In an economy dominated by productive jobs, a nonproductive or leisure condition would have been unusual; and only the unusual can become a mark of social distinction. In today's economy, on the other hand, many or most occupations have become nonproductive. Leisure comes perilously close to them in economic appearance. What we have today, therefore, in our scheme of social values, is not conspicuous leisure, but instead, conspicuous labor.

Nowadays the fashionable posture is to be seen doing work, even base blue-collar work, while the leisured person has become an object of scorn. This attitude is prevalent, for instance, among New York investment bankers and others who do work widely considered less useful, but who do it at such handsome rates of compensation. In every city or town, one sees prosperous-looking young men or women driving pick-up trucks or utility vans for everyday transportation. In bureaucracies, the term "shop" has come into vogue to indicate a department where someone works. An academic degree leading to a predictably lucrative occupation is sometimes called a "plumbing license." By such colorful expressions, contemporary Americans are displaying a certain "labor chic," which can be understood as a consequence of the economy's increasing scarcity of "real" work despite the growing number of jobs.

A purpose of this book is to identify in some detail the kinds of economic activities that have developed as an alternative to more leisure. If Americans want more goods and services, or what economists call a "higher standard of living," what is it exactly that they have received? What have they gained from giving up opportunities for more free time, and was the price worth the purchase? These are questions that economic policymakers ought to have asked, but did not investigate sufficiently. The real value of leisure must be weighed against the real value of additional goods and services to be had from additional hours of work, if we are to make an intelligent judgment in this regard.

Such questions are not new. The issue we are raising here is much the same as that which Benjamin Franklin posed in a letter written in 1784. Writing to an American friend from France, Franklin asked:

What occasions then so much want and misery? It is the employment of men and women in works that produce neither the necessaries nor conveniences of life, who, with those who do nothing, consume the necessaries raised by the laborious.... Look round the world and see the millions employed in doing nothing or in something that amounts to nothing.... Could all these people, now employed in raising, making, or carrying superfluities, be subsisted in raising necessaries? I think they might.... It has been computed by some political arithmetician that if every man and woman would work for four hours each day on something useful, that labor would procure all the necessaries and comforts of life, want and misery would be banished out of the world, and the rest of the 24 hours might be leisure and pleasure.[5]

Adam Smith held a similar point of view. He wrote in *Wealth of Nations*:

Whatever be the actual state of the skill, dexterity, and judgment with which labor is applied in any nation, the abundance or scantiness of its annual supply must depend, during the continuance of that state, upon the proportion between the number of those who are annually employed in useful labor, and that of those who are not so employed.... The labour of some of the most respectable orders in the society is, like that of menial servants, unproductive of any value, and does not fix or realize itself in any permanent subject, or vendible commodity, which endures after that labour is past, and for which an equal quantity could afterwards be procured. The sovereign, for example, with all the officers both of justice and war who serve under him, the whole army and navy, are unproductive laborers.... In the same class must be ranked, some both of the gravest and most important, and some of the most frivolous professions: churchment, lawyers, physicians, men of letters of all kinds, players, buffoons, musicians, opera-singers, opera-dancers, etc.... Both productive and unproductive laborers, and those who do not labour at all, are all equally maintained by the annual produce of the land and labour of the country. This produce, how great soever, can never be infinite, but must have certain limits. Accordingly, therefore, as a smaller or greater proportion of it is in any one year employed in maintaining unproductive hands, the more in the one case and the less in the other will remain for the productive, and the next year's produce will be greater or smaller accordingly.[6]

A WAY TO APPROACH THE SUBJECT

The economic task at hand is therefore to make a distinction between productive and nonproductive kinds of work, and between useful and wasteful kinds of products. While attempting an objective treatment of the subject, we are also forced into making value judgments with which some may disagree. It would be convenient for our purposes if the Bureau of Labor Statistics kept records of the number of jobs and dollars that were related to wasteful production. In the absence of such statistics, this book will make its case on the basis of examples and illustrations within several categories representing economic waste. The reader is invited to consider from personal experience the wasteful nature of these activities and the extent they are found in the U.S. economy.

Perhaps the best way to begin this discussion would be to identify undertakings which, in our view, do not represent economic waste. The closer the economy sticks to the furnishing of necessities, the more useful its products tend to be. That does not mean, however, that one must accept as an ideal an economy stripped down to the level of bare subsistence. Other kinds of goods and services are also useful, even if they are not strictly necessary. For starters, there are products such as food, clothing, shelter, and, perhaps, basic transportation and medical care. No one would quarrel with the need to work to obtain these kinds of economic products. People naturally want and demand them. Each human being has a natural level of need for such products, first to stay. alive, and then to feel comfortable and happy. In their case, consumer demand would exist, without further encouragement, because of conditions that life has imposed upon humanity.

In conditions of affluence, the level of material provision that seems natural and appropriate can be raised. A person can require new kinds of food to satisfy the physical appetite for food and derive pleasure from the process of satisfaction. Likewise, a larger quantity and variety of clothing, a better-built house, faster and more convenient transportation, and so forth, can supply life's needs more abundantly. Consumer demand is created from people's self-discovered needs and wants. A greater per capita amount of products, and a higher quality and greater variety of them, are said to raise the material standard of living. The products are useful because people want to use them in various ways. Therefore, they are not waste even if their consumption goes beyond satisfying minimal needs.

A national economy can raise the level of consumer demand in still another way. After the individual needs are met at higher levels of satisfaction, the economy as a whole can expand the volume of consumer demand by extending its provision of benefits to more people. Population growth would be an obvious way to raise the system-wide demand for various products. Another way, less obvious, would be to encourage a more even distribution of incomes and leisure. A given amount of produce will be consumed more usefully, or will be appreciated to a greater degree, if it is shared with more people. If people who have previously been excluded from the system are given a full share of prosperity, their entry will expand its capacity for consumption more than if the same goods or services were distributed to persons who had enough already. For a person with three cars in the garage, the purchase of a fourth car might be personally less satisfying than the same purchase by someone who was buying such a product for the first time. In summary, economic growth that is not waste can occur in supplying products that raise the per capita living standards and in extending the benefit of this prosperity to more people, either through the growth of population or a broader distribution within the existing population.

In order to rise above economic subsistence, people need two things. First, they must have enough money to purchase the consumer products that they desire. Second, they must have enough leisure to carry on useful or personally satisfying consumption. If those two conditions are met, then economic growth can take place in ways that contribute to human effort and happiness. If not, the surplus is likely to be taken in the form of waste.

As it has previously been revealed, the U.S. economy has not lately done well in either respect. Per capita real incomes have been declining since the early 1970s, and the distribution of incomes has become less equal. Likewise, workers have failed to achieve across-the-board reductions in worktime. Also, the distribution of leisure has become less equal as benefits such as shorter workdays and workweeks have been forsaken while workers have retired or otherwise withdrawn from the workforce entirely. As a result, people have less money to buy consumer products and less time to find a use for them. For the money and time that is made available, a shrinking portion of the population is able to participate in the distribution of benefits. One might suspect, therefore, that the statistical gains in GNP, suggesting a generally rising standard of living, do not reflect useful production and consumption but, to an increasing degree, what we would call "economic waste." Something may have been produced in greater abundance, but not the kinds of products that people truly need or want. Conversely, the conditions permitting an expansion of useful production and consumption have been undercut.

FOOD AND DRINK AND SOME OTHER PRODUCTS

If this argument is correct, one ought to find confirmation in statistics relating to products such as foods. The evidence does not suggest significant production gains in this area. Table 5.2 shows the per capita consumption of several major food items in years between 1960 and 1983. Eggs, milk, citrus fruit, fresh vegetables, and coffee have all experienced stable or declining levels of consumption. Soft drinks, which are heavily advertised and promoted, were a big gainer. In fact, those products have become America's most consumed beverage. Diet soft

Table 5.2
Per Capita Consumption of Major Food Commodities, 1960–1983 (in pounds unless otherwise indicated)

Commodity	1960	1965	1970	1975	1980	1983
Meats (carcass weight)	173.7	175.6	192.2	180.3	180.2	176.2
Eggs	334	313	309	276	272	261
Milk	302	292	277	267	250	238
Citrus fruit	33.7	29.2	29.3	29.4	28.9	28.8
Vegetables:						
fresh	105.7	98.3	99.1	98.0	107.5	77.2
canned	44.4	47.6	51.1	51.9	49.8	47.1
Potatoes	109	107	117	120	118	121
Wheat flour	118	113	111	114	117	116
Coffee	15.8	14.8	13.7	12.2	10.3	10.2
Soft drinks (gallons)	13.6	19.2	23.7	27.3	37.8	40.0

Source: Prepared by the author.

drinks, some of whose ingredients have been linked to health hazards, represent the fastest-growing segment of this market. Their per capita consumption in 1985 was almost double what it was in 1980.[7]

With respect to the quality and variety of food products, the U.S. economy is certainly capable of making an improvement here. Food-processing firms have aggressively developed and marketed new products for persons who want to upgrade their eating habits. For awhile it seemed that there was a trend, for instance, toward upscale frozen foods that could be cooked in microwave ovens. That trend has been reversed. Between 1985 and 1987, the market share of frozen entree and dinner items priced at $2.50 or above has dropped from 51 to 33 percent, with a corresponding increase in items priced under $2.50, according to the Campbell Soup Company. Analysts explained that consumers found that the higher-priced gourmet foods were often foods of ordinary quality sold in packages with attractive pictures. "Photography inflation" is what Campbell Soup's market-research director called this. Another problem, as revealed in a *Wall Street Journal* article, was that today's time-squeezed "yuppie" consumers were finding it more convenient to order food from a take-out service rather than to buy frozen foods: "For some who want to eat in nanoseconds, shopping for even microwavable items is too time consuming."[8]

In general, one might say that the trend in U.S. food consumption is away from the basic food products or even food delicacies and toward highly processed foods that suit people's special problems. The first problem is a shortage of time. That accounts for the popularity of foods or food services that will deliver the prepared product quickly and conveniently. The second problem is the tendency, through excessive consumption of food and lack of physical exercise, for people to put on weight. Diet foods and drinks, catering to this need, have captured a growing share of the market. Pick-me-up soft drinks and other such beverages, which suit the frenetic pace of contemporary life, have become more popular than water.

Besides food, an economy can expand into other areas of useful production such as the production of transportation equipment. For decades the personal automobile has been a symbol of American affluence, with many models and colors from which to choose. Americans have demanded oversized, overpowered, overfueled vehicles as an extension of their personalties. But now some experts are saying that the automobile industry may have reached a point of saturation and become increasingly a repair business. Automobile ownership per U.S. family declined from 1.22 vehicles in 1978 to 1.17 in 1983.[9]

Even so, the parade of new products available to the American consumer has continued. Video rental shops have appeared in every neighborhood (sometimes in abandoned service stations) next to the bars, fast-food restaurants, laundromats and convenience stores. The electronics industry has become the new symbol of a dynamic consumer economy. In 1984, the most important home electronic products in terms of annual sales revenue were color television sets, video cassette recorders (VCRs), home computers, and telephone equipment. VCRs were a hot item that year, as video games were two years earlier; and before them, such products as CB radios, pocket calculators, and stereos. "Camcorders" are the latest electronic gadget to win the hearts and dollars of the buying public.

There is reason, however, to doubt the consumer value of a product such as the personal computer. How much of its popularity is due to the joy and excitement of using the product and how much to a fear-driven sense of need to improve one's technological skills in an era of declining job opportunities? A man who had bought several personal computers said this of his consumer motivation: "I think the single most important reason to have a computer at home today is the future.... Your child's future job will depend on it. I don't think there are many parents who would like to see their kids without jobs." In that context, "computer literacy" has become a symbol of future employability rather than an authentic consumer pleasure.[10]

6

SOME COMMON
VARIETIES OF WASTE

Economic waste can best be described as a condition of production seeking consumption. The normal process is for consumption to seek production. There is, in other words, first a human need, which brings a
desire for consumption, and then production to satisfy that consumer
need. In an economy of waste, on the other hand, production comes
first, and consumption is forced to conform to its requirements. The
priority of production is of course, one of the basic tenets of "supply-
side economics," an unfortunate ideological hypothesis adopted by economists in the Reagan administration. Adam Smith, progenitor of conservative economists, knew better. He wrote in *Wealth of Nations:*

Consumption is the sole end and purpose of all production; and the interest of
the producer ought to be attended to, only insofar as it may be necessary for
promoting that of the consumer. The maxim is so perfectly self-evident that it
would be absurd to attempt to prove it. But in the mercantile system, the interest
of the consumer is almost constantly sacrificed to that of the producer; and it
seems to consider production, and not consumption, as the ultimate end and
object of all industry and commerce.[1]

In an economy of waste, the basic economic problem is not need but
lack of consumption. Production is readily available in sufficient supply,
but where to find the markets? Markets, of course, should be formed
around a need. Therefore, if the need does not exist, the challenge is
to make one exist by artificial means. Wasteful economies, in other words,
push goods and services off on sometimes unwilling customers. Their
purpose is to find an outlet for production with or without people's

consent and cooperation. In such an economy one would find the high-pressure salesman brow-beating people into buying products that they do not want. If the product is unwanted, then it is economic waste.

Is the U.S. economy, however, a system built on peddling unwanted merchandise? Certainly this is one of our economy's mainstays, but the situation is more complicated than that. An economy of waste peddles its waste in ways more subtle. It has many "sacred cows," considered requirements of decency in such a "civilized" society. The highest achievement, however, is to be able, by ingenious means, to sell or place an economic product for which no real need exists. Such ingenuity, if it had been applied to space technology, might have taken us to the ends of the solar system. Instead, we are left with an accumulation of waste, in many different varieties.

In this chapter, we will discuss some of the types of waste to be found in the U.S. economy. The discussion will include numerous illustrations and examples. The major categories of waste would include the following. Economic waste can occur when:

1. Goods and services for which there is an insufficient demand are aggressively marketed.
2. Products that cannot be sold in the domestic market are exported to foreign countries.
3. National rivalries lead to war.
4. Products are used to exhibit status or social rank rather than to satisfy other, more substantial, human needs.
5. Government legally mandates unnecessary activities.
6. People are socially compelled to spend money in observance of commercial holidays.
7. The seller of a product decides what or how much of it the purchaser will buy.
8. Personal consumption is required to gain income.
9. The system of career development breeds incompetent personnel.
10. Goods and services that used to be free come to be sold commercially.
11. Considerable economic resources are thrown into self-defeating routines of ruin and repair.

Starting at the top of the list, we will discuss each category of waste with reference to specific forms and examples. Although it may not always be possible to measure each category statistically, the reader may recognize from personal experience the extent to which such activities claim the community's economic resources.

Table 6.1
Estimated Advertising Expenditures by Medium, 1965–1986 (in millions of dollars)

Year	Newspapers	Television	Direct Mail	Other	Total	Total as % of GNP
1965	4,426	2,515	2,324	5,985	15,250	2.21%
1970	5,704	3,596	2,766	7,484	19,550	1.97%
1975	8,234	5,263	4,124	10,279	27,900	1.80%
1978	12,214	8,955	5,987	16,174	43,330	2.00%
1980	14,794	11,474	7,596	19,686	53,550	2.03%
1983	20,582	16,789	11,795	26,684	75,850	2.30%
1986	26,990	22,585	17,145	35,420	102,140	2.41%

Source: Prepared by the author.

MORE AGGRESSIVE SELLING

The production of goods adds obvious value to a product. Its subsequent marketing or selling, while a necessary function, does not. The consumer admittedly gains something by way of information about a product, but mostly the information is intended to encourage purchase of one seller's brand rather than another's. From a macroeconomic standpoint, the competing efforts to push rival products largely cancel each other out. Yet they must all be tallied in the cost of products and be included in GNP.

The question is how prevalent the marketing function has become. If this function claims an abnormally large or growing share of the total economy, it could be considered a significant form of economic waste. The news media play a large role in selling commercial products, especially low-ticket items such as food, beverages, drugs, and grooming aids. Table 6.1 shows the dollars spent for advertising in the principal media in the years 1965–1986. Although advertising expenditures fell as a percentage of GNP during the first ten years of this period, they have subsequently recovered. Direct mail and television commercials account for a growing share of the advertising dollar, while newspaper advertising has declined somewhat in relative importance. To cope with the growing segmentation of the consumer market and media fragmentation, companies are turning to a variety of specialized sales-promotion techniques, including sponsorship of sporting events or contests, sweepstakes, rebates, and dealer incentives.

According to an article in the *Wall Street Journal*, the merchandisers of products for new or expectant mothers prefer direct mail. Such a woman will typically be contacted at least a dozen times about products ranging from diapers to stretch-mark removers to baby shoes. Although the cost of direct mail runs about $1 per mailed piece, marketing managers feel this is the best way to corral a rapidly changing group of customers. "Every day there's 10,000 new [babies] born, but, unfortunately, 10,000 kids who are toilet trained, too. The sooner we get to their parents, the better," the vice president of Kimberly-Clark's paper-diaper division observed. A woman in her eight or ninth month of pregnancy is considered most receptive to the promotion of baby products. Therefore, many advertisers use mailing lists of such women compiled from frontline sources including maternity shops, childbirth-training classes, and even obstetricians and gynecologists.

Once a new mother is hooked on a product introduced in this way, the trick is to reinforce her brand loyalty by offering discount coupons. The coupon redemption rate for this group is nearly twice the general average. Gerber Products, on the other hand, uses direct mail to sell not only babyfood products and life insurance but also $2.50 recipe books showing how to turn babyfood into low-calorie meals for adults. Ross Laboratories distributes free packets of its infant formula at hospitals. Although such an approach is less obtrusive than advertising, some mothers who are attempting to breastfeed their babies feel that the marketers of infant formula, in the words of a New Jersey woman, "hit you at a very vulnerable time."[2]

Besides media advertising, the marketing function includes other kinds of activities that increase the convenience of buying a product or exert immediate selling pressure. There is nothing like a live human being to induce a decision to buy. In the area of financial services, the commissioned sales agent, relying heavily on the telephone, does much of the marketing. One-quarter million men and women are employed in the business of selling life insurance. When marketplace demand for their product falters, insurance sales agents have approached prospective clients with tie-ins to other services, including the arrangement of student loans and homeowner's mortgages. Telemarketing techniques have been extensively used to sell a variety of products. Merrill Lynch has trained 1000 of its brokers to go after the owners of small businesses who might need help with credit, insurance, and personal investment decisions. "When you have them by the credit," a Merrill Lynch executive explained, "their hearts and minds will follow."[3]

The U.S. economy has long depended on consumer credit to persuade people to purchase products that they cannot immediately afford. With high rates of inflation, Americans were persuaded that a "buy now, pay later" policy made good financial sense. Yet the surge of personal borrowing has continued into the 1980s, after inflation appeared to be brought under control. While the GNP has grown at an average annual rate of 8.6 percent since 1980, personal debt has grown by 9.4 percent. Household interest expense in 1985 rose to 10 percent of disposable personal income, compared with 5 percent in 1970. Mortgage debt and consumer credit stood at a record 19 percent of disposable personal income, compared with 8 percent in 1952.[4]

Aggressive marketing used to feature such gimmicks as gift stamps and newspaper coupons that would help the shopper to save money. Although this form of merchandising is not dead, the emphasis in retailing has shifted to "convenience" buying. Stores offering fast checkout counters and extended hours have captured a growing volume of sales. According to a survey conducted by the Food Marketing Institute, today's shopper is more interested in saving time than money.[5] More than half the food stores opened in 1984 were "superstores," having more than 30,000 square feet of space. Cub Foods, a pacesetter in this area, grosses $800,000–1 million per store per week—about four times the weekly volume of conventional supermarkets. Its customers typically spend $40–50 during each visit. The superstores stock a complete line of grocery products, displayed in-bulk in a warehouse-like environment. "It suggests there's massive buying going on that translates in a shopper's mind that there's tremendous savings going on as well," explained an executive of Cub's parent company.[6]

Retailers have hired high-priced design consultants to create a shopping environment that will pull customers into a store and persuade them to buy all kinds of merchandise. A news report disclosed that "a good design's influence should be subliminal. Layout, lighting, color and signs should work together to make it easy for you to find what you want and [be] tempted by merchandise you didn't know you wanted." One trick of the trade is to place a sparse selection of products at the entrance and an attractively illuminated display toward the rear, so that customers are enticed to walk through the entire store. Other arrangements are meant to encourage impulse buying: "Display 'vignettes'—in which several garments are arranged together just as you might wear them—often persuade customers to buy more. Small, easy-to-buy items such as earrings and chewing gum are displayed at most cash registers." Store lighting is used with good effect to create a buying mood: "Lighting can enhance the color of the merchandise and draw you to items the retailer especially wants you to see—'the moth effect,' says Dee Ginther, an associate professor of design at the University of Minnesota."[7]

Manufacturers of consumer products spend enormous sums of money in seeking to differentiate their product from others on the market through heavily advertised brand names. Although part of this expenditure represents a legitimate effort to communicate product differences, much is simply commercial propaganda. The companies advertise that they have a better brand of bottled water, petroleum, or fresh vegetables than what Mother Nature gave competitors. "Several companies are planning to put their brand names on fresh food," it was revealed in the *Wall Street Journal.* "Aided by advances in biotechnology, which companies claim will make produce taste better and last longer, the quest to develop fresh, branded food is one of the highest priorities in the industry."[8]

In the drug industry, product differentiation has gone beyond the stage of research, advertising, and marketing promotion. The truth-in-advertising requirements of the Federal Communications Commission have created a new kind of marketing warfare in which lawyers man the frontlines of battle. A strategically placed lawsuit, which challenges rivals' claims in a television commercial, can effectively tie up or delay the introduction of competing products or, perhaps, uncover competitors' trade secrets. "I call it the fifth 'P' of marketing—for plaintiff," a college marketing professor observed. Tylenol, until its reputation was besmirched by an unknown poisoner, was one of the more adept players at this game.[9]

Americans are thoroughly used to the hard- or soft-sell of commercial products. Our moral indignation is not aroused when such tactics are used upon ourselves, but, curiously, we may have a soft spot in our hearts for other, more innocent victims of the practice. The Nestlé boycott, which ended in January 1984, began a decade earlier as a protest against Nestlé's effort to sell infant formula to often impoverished mothers in underdeveloped countries in preference to breastfeeding their babies. Nestlé characterized the campaign as an "attack on the world's free economic system." The World Health Organization eventually adopted a code limiting aggressive sales tactics to promote infant formula on a 118-to-1 vote, the United States casting the lone negative vote. Nestlé consented to the code, and the boycott ended.[10]

EXPANDING EXPORT MARKETS

When domestic markets have been developed to the limit, businesses cast a hungry eye upon virgin territories abroad in search of new sales opportunities. The export trade allows production surplus to be profitably sold and domestic jobs to be saved. The United States enjoyed healthy trade surpluses in the decades immediately following World War II, but no more. The U.S. merchandise trade balance has shifted from modest surpluses in the 1960s and early 1970s to deep red ink. In 1986, the deficit (excluding military grants) reached $144 billion. The United States has lost its comparative advantage in most manufactured products. Agricultural products still show a surplus, but not on the scale enjoyed in earlier years. Once blessed with ample domestic gas and oil reserves, we now import billions of dollars' worth of petroleum products each month.[11]

As a nation advanced in merchandising techniques, the United States still enjoys an advantage in products such as soft drinks and toiletries, which are sold by cultivation of a personal image. The peoples of developing nations associate these products with Western sophistication, and will spend sorely needed currency to have them. The Gillette Company, for example, sends portable theaters to remote Third World villages to show films teaching men how to shave. In Mexico, where the great majority of shavers use plain or at most soapy water, it has introduced a product called "Prestobarba" ("quick shave") to encourage them to trade up to shaving cream. With a stagnant market for razor blades in the United States and other developed countries, Gillette's executive vice president for international operations states: "The opportunities on the blade side really lie in new geography. In the Third World, there's a very high proportion of people under 15 years old. All those young men are going to be in the shaving population in a very short time." Since 1969, the share of total company sales from Latin America, Africa, Asia, and the Middle East has risen from 10 percent to 20 percent, while the dollar volume of sales to these areas has increased sevenfold.[12]

While cigarette consumption has declined in Europe and the United States during the past five years, it has increased sharply in Africa and Asia, despite food shortages. A study published five years ago in a British medical journal claimed that the people of Bangladesh were spending about 20 percent of their incomes on tobacco products. The article suggested that "smoking only five cigarettes a day in a poor household in Bangladesh might lead to a monthly dietary deficit." One reason that the tobacco companies are pushing sales in Third World nations is that these nations permit unrestricted advertising on radio and television and do not require health warnings on cigarette packages. Cigarettes sold in the developing nations often have higher tar and nicotine levels that those sold in the United States. Foreign governments often profit from cigarette sales, either through collection of excise taxes or from domestic cigarette production. Third World peoples account for one third of the world's annual consumption of tobacco products, worth $200 billion, and their share is rising. This segment of the export market is "where the growth is," according to an industry analyst.[13]

WAR

Only a Hitler would be cynical enough to choose war deliberately as a means of marketing a nation's surplus production and putting people back to work. There have been government leaders, however, who have

Table 6.2
Expenditures for National Defense, 1950–1986 (in billions of dollars)

Year	Current Dollars	Percent of GNP
1950	12.4	4.7%
1955	42.7	11.0%
1960	48.1	9.5%
1965	50.6	7.5%
1970	81.7	8.2%
1975	86.5	5.7%
1980	134.0	5.0%
1985	252.7	6.4%
1986	273.4	6.6%

Source: Prepared by the author.

been "forced" into adopting this disagreeable solution. War does have a number of immediate economic advantages. Its products, while destructive, are generally agreed to be necessary. Although governments must often resort to deficit financing to pay for wars, few citizens at the time complain. World War II lifted the United States out of the Great Depression. The Vietnam war gave us prosperity in the 1960s.

Since the dropping of atomic bombs on Hiroshima and Nagasaki, war involving the two superpowers has become too brutal and destructive a prospect to be chosen for economic reasons. While rejecting war itself, however, we have discovered a new mode of military enterprise, called the "cold war," which is a state of continuous military preparedness. Such an arrangement allows production without the need of subsequent consumption. Its economic rationale remains impeccable: We must continue spending for this kind of waste so long as our Soviet adversaries hold up their end of the arms race.

Table 6.2 presents expenditures for national defense in years between 1950 and 1986. Defense expenditures declined as a share of GNP in the decades following the Korean War, but the Reagan administration has lately reversed that trend. Today military production is one of the few dependable sources of growth in the U.S. economy. Sales of arms and military aircraft remain a bright spot in the nation's sagging balance of trade. In rural Minnesota and the Dakotas, for instance, a representative of the Defense Logistics Agency's St. Paul office made the rounds of small farm-supply manufacturers hurt by the slumping farm economy, urging them to bid on defense contracts. His mission has been tagged "beating plowshares into swords."[14]

The military seems also to have taken over much of the U.S. space program, replacing the atmosphere of open scientific adventure with secrecy inspired by concerns of national security. More than one third of the space shuttle payloads through 1994 will have a military purpose. While NASA lacked the relatively minuscule funding to send a space probe to greet Halley's comet, the U.S. Air Force conducted tests of its anti-satellite technology in space. An observer with the Federation of American Scientists summed up the new program: "We are spending more and more money to put things in space, and at the same time we are spending more and more time shooting them down."[15]

Certain aspects of the nation's military expenditure seem to make little sense even by the grim logic of war. One is the enormous overhang of personnel costs, especially outlays for military retirement. There is a town in Florida called "Niceville," near Eglin Air Force Base, which has more military retirees than the combined forces serving under George Washington during the Revolutionary War. Former budget director David Stockman irritated residents of this and similar communities when he charged that "institutional forces in the military are more concerned about protecting their retirement benefits than they are about protecting the security of the American people. When push comes to shove, they'll give up on security before they'll give up on retirement."[16]

Another senseless pursuit is the "doomsday" planning that underlies U.S. strategic policy. Preparations are now being made at the Pentagon to fight World War IV. In that scenario, World War III has already been fought. However, a Poseidon submarine carrying nuclear missiles has managed to escape thermonuclear destruction by concealing itself beneath the Arctic icecap. This will be the spearhead of victory for the United States in the next round of battle with the Soviet Union. The important thing is to maintain contact with the nation's underground commandpost. Therefore, the Reagan administration is proposing to spend $18 billion for a new "hardened" communications system that can withstand nuclear attack. The project reportedly enjoys "top priority" in the Pentagon's budget.[17]

STATUS-SEEKING CONSUMPTION

Waste is in the eye of the beholder. We all know what is meant by "conspicuous consumption" or consumer spending that is intent on "keeping up with the Joneses," but to identify a particular kind of expenditure with such waste is often difficult. An expensive sportscar might be bought for the sheer pleasure of driving it fast down the highway. A silk scarf might provide an exotic creature comfort. As followers of an objective science, economists ought not to point their fingers moralistically at people and suggest that this or that product is necessarily a waste of money.

Yet there is in the contemporary economy a strong component of spending for products that are conspicuously extravagant and unnecessary. The social need to buy the more expensive goods for the sake of their expensiveness creates a category of waste that might be objectively identified. In the 1980s, one would associate this kind of economic behavior with the so-called "yuppie" phenomenon. The media identify them by their type of consumer expenditure. They drive Porsches or BMWs, or drink Perrier. The key word to describe them is "upscale." This is where the consumer market in this decade appears to be headed. The era of consumer mass merchandising is fading. "Within the last 5 to 10 years, price has graduated to 'value'," the president of Dayton-Hudson department stores has observed.[18] Actually, retailers are going where the money is. Because of the polarization of incomes in American society, it makes less sense to aim for the general consumer, because that approach would hit the shrinking middle. Aim rather for the bulge of purchasing power on the upscale side.

Some of the big mass merchandisers, including Sears and J.C. Penney, have been actively courting the "yuppie" dollar. Penney spent $1.5 billion to remodel its stores to their liking, and Sears spent $1.7 billion. Whereas Penney put on a "Salute to Italy" promotion show and lured Prince Charles and Princess "Di" into a Washington, D.C. area store, Sears relied more heavily on big-name promotions featuring Hollywood celebrities such as Johnny Carson and Cheryl Tiegs.[19] During the 1984 Christmas season, "retailers that stocked high-priced merchandise such as 'upscale fashions' and videocassette recorders reported the highest sales gains," a New York trade official told the *Wall Street Journal*.[20] Automobiles such as the Oldsmobile Cutlass, a rung above Chevrolet, have become top sellers. "In 1984 the upscale cars showed the greatest increase at Ford," a company analyst declared. He attributed this trend to "a dichotomy in the wage structure. There aren't many $7-an-hour starting jobs in the steel mills anymore, so buying power has been taken away from younger people."[21]

Since the October 1987 stockmarket crash, merchants have tended to shun the yuppie image, which had become too much an advertising cliché. The idea of "having it all" materially had drawn much criticism. Worse yet, some of the yuppies had lost their jobs—and their ability to respond productively to the ad campaigns. In the new environment of financial fearfulness, a new type of advertisement was beamed toward the young urban professionals, stressing value and durability. Buying the new Porsche was declared to be a sound "investment," considering its high resale value. Advertising executives were aware of a contradiction in the new approach. The *Wall Street Journal* reported:

When pressed, some advertisers admit they are trying to reach the same group, just using different labels. They still must unload their microwave ovens, their Rocksports and Reeboks. "We will still be going after people in that same age and economic group," says Richard Shriner, Jr.... And agents say that casting calls for commercials still come in just as frequently for young, 30-ish actors who look as though they work hard, play hard, and spend big—yuppies by another name. "In some parts of the world, yuppie has become a bad name. It isn't around here," says Hollywood agent Sandra Joseph.... "All of us [in advertising] are pushing consumption. If you don't buy, we're all in trouble."[22]

A generation ago, writers such as Vance Packard catalogued the conspicuous consumption associated with Americans' love of the automobile and their mass migration to the suburbs. Such phenomena, now thoroughly familiar, have continuing economic consequences. The suburban lifestyle, centering on single passenger use of the automobile, increases the nation's demand for petroleum products, mostly imported. It has been estimated that the use of intra-city public transportation is three times as efficient in use of fuel per passenger mile as transportation in a private automobile with an average passenger load.[23] Yet patronage of public transportation has declined significantly over the years, both in relative and absolute numbers.

In Minneapolis–St. Paul, for example, the mass-transit system handled a total of 238 million linked passenger trips in 1920. By 1950 it was down to 140 million passenger trips; and to 72 million trips by 1980. Not coincidentally, the percentage of Twin Cities residents living in the two core cities as opposed to the rest of the seven-county metropolitan area declined from 81.0 to 32.5 percent between 1920 and 1980.[24] Suburban living reduces population density, which makes it less economical for the public-transportation agency to provide service to areas where the bulk of the population lives. People do not ride the bus because service to their area is not convenient or not available—and the service is not available because there are insufficient customers. Although people buy automobiles and suburban homes for reasons of use or personal pleasure, it is understood that the motive of exhibiting social advancement also plays a part in their decision.

Sometimes a number of the wasteful categories overlap, as when large advertising budgets create a social image for more expensive products, which may then be damaging to one's health. A small Minnesota brewer complained that his company could not compete against the Millers, Budweisers, and Strohs of the industry. "Everybody drinks labels, they don't drink beer. They drink advertising," he said.[25] Drinking beer or its ads may be good clean fun, but some of the other mind-altering substances are not. Snorting cocaine has become associated with the fast-track lifestyle of the rich and famous. The drug's illegality adds something to its air of forbidden excitement, besides driving up the price.

To complete the economic circle, drug addicts need treatment, and the treatment providers need to bring their service to the addicts' attention in a cost-effective manner. So there is a boom in "substance abuse advertising," directed either at the addict himself or at family members. Because cocaine appeals primarily to status- or power-hungry individuals, an executive with Ogilvy & Mathers's health advertising unit explained that "what you do is make them understand that they can lose their job, everything they're trying to build." Advertisements for the treatment of alcoholics, on the other hand, are often pitched at housewives. "We'll show them their life. We'll have a woman laying in bed at night, not knowing where her husband is," another marketing manager revealed. The Ogilvy & Mather executive was bullish on substance-abuse advertising. "The basic concept is now being extended beyond substance abuse to depression and suicide and so on," he said. "These are still younger products, so there's a greater response. There's still cream to be skimmed."[26]

GOVERNMENT-MANDATED WASTE

In the fall of 1964, Ronald Reagan catapulted onto the national political stage with a nationally televised speech on behalf of Senator Barry Goldwater's presidential campaign. "Already the hour is late," Reagan said. "Government has laid its hand on health, housing, farming, industry, commerce, education, and, to an ever-increasing degree, interferes with the people's right to know. Government tends to grow; government programs take on weight and momentum, as public servants say, always with the best of intentions. 'What greater service we could render if only we had a little more money and a little more power.'... Today in our country the tax collector's share is 37 cents of every dollar earned. Freedom has never been so fragile, so close to slipping from our grasp."[27]

Government expenditures represent a collective decision to commit economic resources in a certain way. The individual taxpayer is confronted with a legal requirement to divert funds to purposes that may offer little personal benefit. "Nothing is easier than the expenditure of public money. It does not appear to belong to anybody. It is easy to bestow on somebody," a sign in a Congressional office declared.[28]

In addition to the waste that it directly creates, through taxation and spending, government has burdened the economy with unnecessary and sometimes unhelpful regulation. In 1978 it was estimated that compliance with government regulations cost American industry $135 billion annually.[29] Government tax policies, offering hidden subsidies to particular industries, divert investment dollars to the favored industries from other areas that may have greater economic merit. The railroads and public utilities bear a proportionately lighter tax load than the computer industry, for instance. Federal tax provisions that allow accelerated depreciation of commercial buildings over unnaturally short lives, and subsequent capital-gains treatment on their sale, are said to have contributed to the glut of office space in many cities.[30]

The U.S. economy is also financially worked by special entrepreneurs of waste, otherwise known as private attorneys. Their business is expropriating a percentage of whatever waste they can discover and run through the courts. The arrangement allowing attorneys to receive payment on a contingent-fee basis creates an open incentive for people to initiate expensive lawsuits. There is no cost to the plaintiff, unless victorious; but, for the plaintiff's attorney, a potential "pot of gold" may lie at the end of the litigious rainbow. A major disaster such as the MGM hotel fire in Las Vegas can yield as much as $90 million in attorney's fees.[31] Pennzoil's attorneys in the lawsuit against Texaco took several times that. Indirectly, attorneys cost the economy billions more than their own fees each year by forcing other sectors to take excessive precautions to protect themselves from lawsuits. The fear of medical malpractice suits motivates doctors to prescribe unnecessary tests and procedures that can pose additional risks to the patient. It has been estimated that "defensive medicine," inspired by fear of lawyers, accounts for almost one third of all tests performed by doctors. The annual price tag for Medicare patients alone runs $20 billion.[32]

One of the ways that waste from the legal system is transmitted to the rest of the economy is through liability insurance. It is estimated that more than $70 billion was spent in 1985 to settle liability claims in and out of court. Liability costs increased by 61 percent between 1981 and 1985. The *Wall Street Journal* reported that "the soaring cost and worsening shortage of liability insurance are taking their toll on businesses, professionals and local governments across the country. The crisis is forcing companies to raise prices or accept smaller profits, change their operations and eliminate products and services." Cessna Aircraft, for instance, stopped building several types of small planes when liability insurance, which had reached 30 percent of the products' total cost, put prices out of customers' range. A ski resort in Pennsylvania was forced to raise the price of lift tickets 25 percent because of a six-fold increase in the cost of liability insurance.[33] Potential lawsuits against corporate board members have brought a boom in directors' and officers' liability insurance, while persuading many eligible persons not to serve. "I just can't afford to expose my personal assets to the risk," said a former director of a Houston-based oil and gas drilling business. "The legal profession is striking out at every place it can find a pocket. And I just happen to have a pocket."[34]

One can argue that the enormous economic costs associated with the legal system are purchasing a higher quality of law enforcement, civil liberties, and product safety for American society than is to be found elsewhere. Certainly, most attorneys are not "ambulance chasers," forever trying to drum up business. People come to them with legitimate complaints, and they render valuable assistance in those matters. On the other hand, one must look at the legal system as a whole to judge the value of the service rendered to society by this type of enterprise. Justice is dispensed on a "win/lose" basis, so that the economic result is zero.

What exactly is the "service" that the private attorney gives? Is it not to ensure that a client's case is adequately presented in court, or otherwise advantageously handled, so that the client receives "fair and equal treatment under the law"? One wonders why the courts are incompetent to provide such treatment without attorneys? It is not "fair and equal treatment" that clients want from expensive legal services, but *better than* fair and equal treatment; or else they want protection against an adversary seeking such an advantage in the courts. This is a system that allows parties with money to purchase "better justice" for themselves than those who cannot afford a high-priced attorney. Access to the public courts, ideally, ought to be free. Instead, government-sanctioned technicians of legal interpretation skim off material amounts of wealth in the guise of serving "justice." It is hard to escape the conclusion that the private legal system flourishes to the extent that the laws are interpreted or administered unequally and, therefore, unfairly.

COMMERCIAL HOLIDAYS

Besides the waste mandated by government and the legal system, there is what might be called "socially mandated" waste. A notable feature of the American way of life has been the conversion of religious or national holidays into commercial events that socially coerce people into buying things they do not need or want. Christmas is by far the most important "commercial holiday"; it has been estimated that, on average, Christmas sales contribute more than one third of retailers' annual sales and half to three fourths of their profits.[35] Of the 7 billion greeting cards that Americans buy annually, 2.2 billion are bought at Christmas.[36] Christmas also provides an occasion to lubricate the wheels of commerce with suppliers' gifts to purchasing agents, office parties, and the like.

The new commercial holiday of Christmas focuses on the persona of Santa Claus, while the old religious one featured Jesus. Santa's tenure, never secure, has thus become subject to the test of commercial appeal. During recessions, for instance, he can become a victim of economically inspired layoffs. Sears, Roebuck & Co. employed only 35 Santas nation-wide in the Christmas of 1983 compared with 400 in 1978. The jolly elf character apparently took up valuable floor space in the stores that could be more advantageously used to display merchandise. A Sears spokes-man remarked: "Santa Claus isn't part of economic reality today. He doesn't reflect directly on the sales and profit sheet. He's part of the overall reduction in personnel."[37]

Seeing what Christmas could do for their business, merchants have cast an eye upon other holidays during the year to find a commercial application. Valentine's Day, which used to honor a saint, has become an occasion to sell roses, greeting cards, and boxes of candy. Over $500 million was spent on candy for Valentine's Day in 1985. There were 850 million greeting cards sold to demonstrate love on that day.[38] Thanks-giving Day, in a practical way, honors the food industry, especially turkey farmers. Washington's birthday, in its less patriotic version, has become a day when greedy shoppers could paw through tables of marked-down merchandise. Now it has become plain "President's Day," much as the old Armistice Day has been converted to the more generic and com-mercially adaptable Veterans Day.

Some formerly religious holidays, including Halloween and St. Pa-trick's day, now feature a different kind of spirituality, which is to be found in bars or at weird costume parties. Small children learn to beg for bags of candy. Congress has also created a new kind of nonreligious, nonpatriotic holiday, which frankly identifies the groups of people who are to receive gifts. Mother's day, Father's day, and National Secretaries' week are some of the better-known examples. Mother's day has become the main revenue producer for the retail floral industry. Grandparent's day is a new entry, acknowledging an area of demographic growth, which was created after the candy industry's attempt to honor the nation's elderly with "Sweetest Day" bombed.[39]

With its gift-giving theme, a commercial holiday virtually guarantees that money will be spent wastefully, because the purchaser does not know what gift the recipient needs or wants. Such a system greatly increases the chance of redundant possessions, wrong clothing sizes and colors, and so forth. The requirement that the gift must be a "surprise" rules out the possibility of prior consultation between donor and recipient. While holiday gift-giving does not coerce spending to the degree that legally mandated consumption does, to refuse to enter wholeheartedly into its Potlatch spirit marks one as a "Scrooge" or, worse yet, someone who truly does not care about friends or family members.

SELF-DETERMINED MARKETS

The free market acts to control costs by setting up an adversarial relationship between buyer and seller. The buyer normally makes the decision whether to purchase the seller's product at the asking price. The quantity of product purchased depends on the buyer's estimation of need. The buyer has a financial incentive to purchase as little of the product as possible at the lowest possible price. In some situations, however, the decision whether or not to buy is placed in the seller's hands, because the seller is considered technically more competent than the buyer to make decisions in the seller's area of expertise. The service that the seller extends to the buyer includes a determination of its need. Thus, a conflict of interest is created between the seller's responsibility to make an honest determination of that need and his own desire for higher income. It is a virtual prescription for waste.

This type of waste often arises among professionals who stand in a fiduciary relationship with clients. For example, a stockbroker might be authorized to buy and sell shares of stock in the client's account to increase the value of the portfolio. The client entrusts this power to the broker because the broker is closer to and more knowledgeable about investment opportunities. Unfortunately, a stockbroker normally gets paid only when shares of stock are bought or sold; there is no reward for sitting on an adequately growing portfolio. Under pressure to generate revenues for the firm as well as to increase their own commissions, brokers are tempted to trade excessively in the client's accounts. This practice, known as "churning," is on the rise. A former American Stock Exchange official has charged that "the compensation system that prevails in the securities industry actually encourages brokers to churn accounts. ... He [the broker] is under powerful financial inducements to be a high-pressure salesman: to overtrade his customers' accounts, and to do it in highly speculative securities that yield the biggest commission."[40]

Every time a stockbroker churns an account and earns a dollar commission, GNP rises. No one has benefited economically from this transaction, except for the broker himself. Lawyers and accountants have also been known to profit from such arrangements. Even when they do not abuse their clients' trust, professionals may take advantage of their discretion to decide how much billable time is required to prepare a case adequately. A pair of attorneys on opposite sides of the case can effectively collaborate in running up client's billings on both sides, though adversarily intentioned. "The business of the law is to increase the business of the law," Charles Dickens once observed.[41]

Likewise, public-accounting firms that are engaged to audit the books of client firms are themselves sole judge of the extent to which it is necessary to gather evidence in order to render an unqualified opinion on the financial statements. Being by nature cautious and careful individuals who have lately become a favorite target of lawsuits brought by disgruntled investors, they will, of course, want to do a thorough job.

Table 6.3
Health Care Expenditures and Prices, 1950–1986 (1967 = 100)

Year	Health Expenditures		Consumer Prices	
	billion dollars	percent of GNP	medical care	all items
1950	12.0	4.5%	53.7	72.1
1955	17.3	4.5%	64.8	80.2
1960	26.9	5.3%	79.1	88.7
1965	41.9	6.1%	89.5	94.5
1970	75.0	7.4%	120.6	116.3
1975	132.7	8.3%	168.6	161.2
1980	248.1	9.1%	265.9	246.8
1985	425.0	10.7%	403.1	322.2
1986	458.2	10.9%	433.5	328.4

Source: Prepared by the author.

Although the client's top managers nominally control the purchase of accounting services, they are apt to be more interested in obtaining a favorable report, which reflects favorably upon their own performance as managers, than in limiting audit procedures to hold down costs for the firm.

Perhaps the largest area of waste relating to self-determined markets would be that in the healthcare field. Table 6.3 shows the growth of health expenditures, both in current dollars and percentage of GNP, in years between 1950 and 1985. The table also shows the rising level of prices charged for medical services compared with the general price level. Healthcare services today account for more than twice the percentage of GNP that they claimed in 1960. Their costs have inflated far more rapidly than the average for all goods and services. Admittedly, part of the growth in healthcare expenditures may be attributed to the delivery of more and better services. Americans are living longer, are generally healthier, and are placing heavier demands on the healthcare industry than ever before. On the other hand, this is also an industry largely immune from the normal cost-control mechanisms found in other areas of the economy. If a doctor says that certain tests or procedures are necessary to diagnose or treat an ailment, who is the patient to disagree?

The problem is compounded by the fact that it is often a third party, an insurance company or the government, who pays for the recommended treatment, and not the patient. Because the more exotic and expensive types of treatment advance a doctor's or a hospital's reputation more than the routine practice of sound public health, some critics charge that an inordinate share of the healthcare dollar is devoted to a relatively small number of patients in advanced stages of illness, which could be better used elsewhere. Government health programs reflect the vagaries of legislative whim. For example, while the federal government spends billions of dollars each year on kidney dialysis treatment, it is reported that an elderly Medicare recipient living in Washington, D.C. who loses a pair of eyeglasses has to wait a year for a replacement pair.[42]

In this category, too, should be put bureaucracies generally. A bureaucracy represents a self-determined market because its very size insulates decision making from immediate pressures of the marketplace. Instead, the decisions tend to reflect considerations of internal politics. There is every incentive for a manager to play up the importance of his particular function by requesting additional staff. The more employees who report to a manager, the higher up the manager is apt to rank in the bureaucratic hierarchy, and the more richly he deserves to be compensated. Bureaucracies obstruct the flow of information that would be needed to make an intelligent market decision about buying or selling their service. Only the bureaucrats themselves know for sure what kind of work it is they do; consequently, their expertise in deciding how much of the service an organization might require is relied upon heavily.

Government bureaucracies can generate waste by incestuous relationships with their constituencies. It has been reported, for instance, that a quasi-public regulatory agency, which is actually controlled by the Sunkist Corporation, has kept the U.S. Department of Agriculture from approving a new shrink-wrap process that would keep lemons fresh for months and thus allow prices to drop dramatically.[43] A decade ago, the General Accounting Office (GAO) charged that persons in the Bureau of Labor Statistics who were conducting the surveys of private-sector wages upon which federal salaries are based had tilted the occupational comparisons toward the higher-paying jobs in private industry. This practice was estimated to inflate civil servants' wages by an extra one billion dollars annually.[44]

Although public-sector bureaucracies have a reputation for being unusually bloated and resistant to pressures for change, those in the private sector are also beginning to receive recognition as producers of waste. Table 6.4 shows the number of nonproduction employees in U.S. manufacturing industries in years between 1950 and 1987, as well as their percentage of total manufacturing employment. There has been an increase in both over the years. The chairman of Acme-Cleveland Corporation, which cut its corporate staff from over 100 employees to under

Table 6.4
Nonproduction Employees in Manufacturing as Percent of Total Employment, 1950–1987

Year	Number of Nonproduction Employees (000)	Percent of Total Employment
1950	2,718	17.8%
1955	3,594	21.3%
1960	4,210	25.1%
1965	4,628	25.6%
1970	5,323	27.5%
1975	5,280	28.8%
1980	6,071	29.9%
1985	6,212	32.0%
1987	6,100	31.9%

Source: Prepared by the author.

40, has noted that "there is [a] tendency of multidivision companies to build large corporate organizations that are bloated with redundant corporate, group and middle-management people doing many of the things responsible line managers are supposed to do.... As a general rule, I think that whenever you have more than five layers in an organization, there is probably something wrong.... In addition to being much too costly, I doubt any senior manager can really know what is going on when he is that far removed from the action."[45]

The rash of corporate takeovers and mergers in the 1980s increased the size of many organizations. They also brought extravagant fees for the investment banking firms that provided "escort services" to the contending parties. Morgan Stanley, for instance, received $14 million for advising Conoco with respect to its takeover by Dupont. Dupont, in turn, paid First Boston Corporation $15 million for advice from its point of view. The investment bankers argued, of course, that their services were worth the price. Their fees were based on how much "guile, shrewdness and instincts" they brought to the job according to one participant. When asked whether the bigger mergers required more work, the chairman of First Boston, George L. Shinn, replied testily: "You bet your neck it does. You have to have crews of people—lawyers, accountants, bankers—and they work round the clock. There have to be people who make out the strategies, people who massage the figures and do the layouts. Everybody from the chairman down to the associates gets involved."[46]

CONSUMPTION TO GAIN INCOME

More of our personal expenditures are made for the purpose of gaining and keeping a job. In that respect, they resemble capital investments more than consumer expenditures, and should not be considered part of anyone's "standard of living." One of the largest outlays is for education. The average cost of attending a public 4-year college was $5,300 in the 1985/86 school year; it was $9,600 for a private 4-year college.[47] Students who pursue a Ph.D. degree can expect to pour almost $100,000 into their educations.[48] Over the years the amount of educational preparation required to land a given entry-level job has escalated. In 1940 the median number of years that Americans 25 and older had spent in school was 8.6 years; in 1980 it was 12.9 years.[49]

A common opinion is that Americans are devoting more time to education in order to acquire the skills that they will need to handle the much more complicated work found in today's economy. Yet it has never been established that formal education improves a person's ability to solve complex technical or managerial problems. Thomas Edison had three months of schooling. Henry Ford went through the sixth grade. Even today, a surprising number of top business leaders and other "achievers" have limited educations. Yet employers are clearly demanding more advanced academic credentials from persons desiring to be hired by their organizations. The increased competition for jobs leads students more deeply into the process of acquiring better credentials.

The tragedy is that while Americans have gone to greater lengths to prepare themselves for a career, the career opportunities have become less promising. Peter Drucker has detected "a growing mismatch of jobs and job seekers" due to changing technological and demographic conditions. "When the baby-boomers entered the work force there was a vacuum in management positions. But the newcomers now will find that the pipelines are full. Most of the baby-boomers have gone as far as they will go in management and will stay in their present jobs another 30 years or so. There is thus a total mismatch between reality and perfectly normal expectations of the young people now entering the work force."[50]

Although employment policy puts great emphasis on job training, less attention has been paid to what employers actually want in persons applying for entry-level positions. A 1984 report of the National Council on Employment Policy suggests that specific career preparation may be relatively unimportant. It observes that "employers report in survey after survey that what they are seeking in young employees is, first, the basic skills needed to learn on the job, and, second, the dependability and world-of-work skills to show up on time and follow instructions. Vocational skills are less frequently required, although important for some jobs such as secretarial work. Employers do not usually give academic or other tests, and have little basis for judging the dependability of those with limited work experience."[51]

The excessive competitiveness in U.S. education has instead produced such dubious pursuits as attempting to improve college SAT scores. "The [SAT] tests drive the high-school curriculum because the teachers know they're going to be judged by how well their students do on tests. Do we want our kids practicing verbal analogies as one of the most important things they learn in high school?" the president of an educational foundation asked. College admissions officers feel pressure to admit students with high SAT scores, because the public tends to rank colleges by the average score of the students they have managed to attract. Inevitably these trends produce a secondary industry of coaching high-school students on how to take the tests. It is an industry that has developed mostly within the past ten years.[52]

On the fringes of the educational world, waste flourishes in some of its more outlandish forms. The Internal Revenue Service allows professionals to deduct personal expenses connected with the continuing education requirements of their profession. The courses that doctors, lawyers, and others are required to take are not necessarily night classes at educational institutions located close to home; many are given in faraway places such as Hawaii or Las Vegas. Doctors who travel to Maui in pursuit of their continuing medical education can find such electives as "Diving Medicine in Depth" and "Big League Baseball Sports Medicine" (with guest lecturer Mickey Mantle). "CME, as long as it's a quality course, can be done in plain vanilla, or it can be done in butter pecan with whipped cream and a cherry," exclaimed the chairman of the AMA's Continuing Medical Education advisory board.[53]

Over on the poor side of the tracks, a number of privately owned trade schools have learned how to milk government grant and loan programs intended to help low-income students. The current regulations allow schools to keep 25 percent of the full year's tuition if a student attends class for at least one day. A school reaps maximum profits by luring as many students into school as possible by a package of students aid subsidies and then having them drop out early. That way, several groups of students can enroll in the same course during the same school year. Some schools were found to be using telephone "boiler room" teams to recruit students from poor neighborhoods. A GAO audit of such programs, which cost the taxpayer nearly $1 billion a year, found that 83 percent of the schools studied had not consistently maintained academic standards.[54]

Besides education, proper attire ranks high on the list of expenditures required to get ahead in a career. At the Wharton School of Business the lecture hall was packed to hear a "real world" talk on the subject of executive dress. "The discussion focuses on the acceptable ratio of natural fiber to synthetics, the proper shirt collar configuration, the importance of the over-the-calf sock," an article in the *Wall Street Journal* reported. "Some of the students say they are prepared to shell out more than $1,000 for their fast-track outfits." One speaker warned students against wearing ankle-length socks. " 'I know it doesn't amount to a hill of beans in reality,' he said; 'but believe me, they [the corporate recruiters] watch for it.' " The women MBAs were advised to spend a minimum of $1,200 on their business wardrobe by Mrs. Freddy Leventhal, representing a New York store that catered mainly to businesswomen. "Shoes must be all leather, and $95 is the least you can pay for them," she admonished. A representative of the Elizabeth Arden cosmetics firm gave the Wharton students this shot of plain talk: "Those of you in marketing know that people are always looking at the packages. Packages should stand out. Don't wait until you get in the real world and your package is passed up for another one."[55]

WASTE IN CAREER DEVELOPMENT

For all the money "invested" in its "human resources," American industry has not always managed to bring forth workers' best productive performance. The root of the problem may lie in its oversupply of labor. The immense overhang of formal education in the career-development process has contributed to the mass underemployment of the nation's workers. Missed opportunities to use acquired skills and knowledge on the job take a toll of personal frustration and lost economic activities. Another type of waste has to do with an arbitrary and misguided system of personnel management, which limits people's opportunities to do useful work by steering them into tight career slots. Such a career-development system could even be described as an occupational "caste system," one designed to keep people in their place rather than to employ them more productively.

During periods of labor shortage such as the years of World War II, Americans showed what they could do. Occupational standards were relaxed, and workers responded with their best effort. After the shortage had ended, barriers to productive employment were erected. The caste system took hold. The basis of this system is a belief that working people are divided into two categories. There are managers and laborers, professionals and clerical types, self-starters and persons who need to be given directions. The career structure takes the shape of a hierarchy, in which job positions are vertically linked by their presumed requirement of a greater or lesser degree of independent thinking. In such a scheme, the occupation that supervises the work of another is deemed superior to it, because supervision involves a more complex type of skill. The reward for being superior in the occupational hierarchy is, of course, to receive a higher rate of pay. Each field has its own caste structure, which preserves and justifies its highly stratified order of rank and income distribution.

A particular feature of this system is that, while an employee might rise to positions of greater responsibility and pay within the same caste, it is difficult to be promoted anymore from one caste to another. To break occupational castes, it is normally necessary to return to school and obtain another set of credentials. In general, the American system of careers regards workers as specialized labor commodities rather than as persons with a range of talents. Workers receive their identity as a productive commodity through their educational preparation, modified by subsequent work experience. In interviewing job applicants, an employer hopes to hire someone whose exhibited qualifications match as closely as possible the requirements of the position being filled. Because personnel departments insist on hiring people by an "objective" selection process, employees are moved into narrow and increasingly inescapable career tracks. This system creates an overly rigid labor force, in which employers claim to have shortages of "qualified" workers, even as many intelligent, energetic, and willing persons who could do the work are not allowed to try.

The career system in Japan works differently. A researcher at the Japan Institute of Labor describes it in the following words:

Japanese workers are more flexible in regard to the scope of their jobs and are adjustable to changes. They are more than willing to help others, sometimes beyond their own job definition.... The flexible attitude of Japanese workers toward job definition is the result of a lifetime employment system where workers are expected to work on various kinds of jobs in succession until they reach retirement age. They are not employed for a certain job with certain skills and experience, but are instead employed fresh from school without any qualifications except for a certain level of education. Transfer from one job to another and from one work place to another is routine. What kind of job it is is not very important for Japanese as they expect this rotation of jobs in their long careers, with promotion closely connected to such rotation. Thus they are more company-oriented than job-oriented and are more concerned with the fate of the company than their Western counterparts.[56]

American-style management has been accusesd of being too autocratic. The hierarchical scheme of organization wastes manpower to inflate a manager's sense of self-importance. Peter Drucker has suggested that, ideally, an organization should be structured according to the flow of information rather than organizational rank. "With nothing more high tech than the quill pen," he wrote, "the British...in India...came out with the world's flattest organization structure, in which four levels of management staffed by fewer than a thousand Britons—most of them youngsters barely out of their teens and 'lower middle management'—efficiently ruled a subcontinent."[57] The "Peter Principle" states that in a hierarchy, individuals tend to rise to their levels of incompetence. Nonthreatening kinds of incompetence are "usually tolerated by the system," Peter observed, but "supercompetence frequently leads to dismissal because it disrupts the hierarchy. That is why it is more objectionable than incompetence within an organization. Ordinary incompetence is a bar to promotion, but is not a cause for firing."[58]

The American system of careers emphasizes the recruitment of talent, which its professional keepers presume to know, even for the most lowly and worst-paying positions. In this age of "participatory management," the *Wall Street Journal* found that employers increasingly are using psychological tests to screen applicants for entry level blue-collar or clerical jobs. At a large paper company in Wisconsin, for example, "applicants for nonunion machine-operator jobs are put through 'leadership-simulation' exercises." Some independent insurance agencies have begun to hire clerical and customer-service employees using a 109-question personality test "designed to measure such traits as motivation to please others, organization, desire for detail work and 'people orientation'." A trucking company hiring for clerical positions wanted people "good at detail work" but instead found some who "displayed traits such as assertiveness, well suited to supervisory jobs." In the last instance, a vice president of the firm predicted that those "assertive" new employees would eventually be promoted.[59]

NEWLY COMMERCIALIZED SERVICES

When the white man pushed the American Indian off his land in the early 19th century, the Shawnee chief Tecumseh tried to stem the erosion of tribal territory by preventing further deals between the whites and individual Indians. He complained to the Indiana territorial governor, General William Henry Harrison: "The only way to stop this evil is for the red man to unite in claiming a common and equal right in the land, as it was at first and should be now.... No tribe has the right to sell, even to each other, much less to strangers.... Sell a country? Why not sell the air, the great sea, as well as the earth? Did not the Great Spirit make them all for the use of his children?" [60] Something of the same sort is now happening in the services sector. The GNP statistics suggest that more services are being produced each year. Part of this growth, however, may not be real, but represent merely the assignment of dollars to activities that used to be done for free. As the Indians' tribal hunting grounds became private property through a monetary transaction, so are these services being commercialized.

When experts say that the U.S. economy is changing from a goods-producing to a knowledge-producing economy, what they may mean is not that the quantity or quality of knowledge has increased but that more knowledge is being claimed for profit. Words covered by trademarks become a private brand name. Singers copyright their songs, writers their scripts. Thoughts and ideas that used to be exchanged freely among scholars have come to acquire a commercial value. Where Plato's academy once was dedicated to the pursuit of truth, academic institutions today have become a business much like any other. The University of Minnesota maintains a patent office to market professors' discoveries and inventions and to control the distribution of proceeds from royalties. The director of this office declared: "It used to be and still is that inventors publish their research without patents because people think it is for public knowledge. But if you only publish something, potentially no one will pick it up. The main thing is to get it out to industry."[61]

The knowledge-producing professors have become go-getters not unlike those in the business world. They write books, publish papers, give lectures or participate in scholarly conferences, or do consulting work in industry or government. In essence, they are merchandizing themselves. They are seeking to become established brand names in the academic world or in what is sometimes called the "real world" of commerce, government, and the professions. A conservative think tank, the Heritage Foundation, has learned to market these people to best advantage. The *Wall Street Journal* reported that "Heritage operates something it calls its 'academic bank', a computerized list of 1,200 conservative academics whose expertise can be marshaled for newspaper pieces and congressional testimony. Last year, these academics testified at a rate of more than once a week—with their transportation costs to the hearings picked up by Heritage. After all, says Mr. Feulner [Heritage's president], 'We translate the theoretical into the practical.' "[62]

As academic life becomes more commercial, it acquires greater impact on GNP. The production of knowledge itself may not have changed, but its economic weight has increased. If not waste, this must be considered a spurious kind of economic growth. Attaching dollars to such activities does not increase the amount of the underlying production. In a like manner, the U.S. economy has appeared to grow as work once confined to family life became commercialized. This is primarily a result of the changing economic role of women. The past forty years have seen a steady increase in the proportion of married women who have sought gainful employment. The labor-force participation rate of married women over 16 in the United States living with their husbands rose from 23.8 percent in 1950 to 52.8 percent in 1984. For married women with children under 6 years of age, it rose from 11.9 percent to 51.8 percent during that time.[63]

As more women have ventured forth from the home to seek outside employment, much work that was once done for free within the household has been placed in the hands of outside businesses. American families are eating out more often at restaurants. About 32 percent of a family's average food budget is now spent on meals consumed away from home, compared with 17 percent in the early 1960s.[64] The growing use of facilities such as day-care centers, nursing homes, and commercial cleaners can also be attributed, in part, to the employment boom among women with family responsibilities. Although such services represent a growing share of GNP, the volume of the service itself may not have changed that much. It is basically the same meal, whether cooked by mother or a family-style restaurant. Economically, the difference lies in the fact that the home-cooked meal was excluded from GNP because no money was exchanged, while the one provided commercially is included. It shows up as "growth" on economists' radar screens.

New business opportunities have arisen from the loss of women's free time. In a *Good Housekeeping* survey, 68 percent of the women surveyed reported that their housekeeping standards had suffered "a great deal." An article in the *Wall Street Journal* told how:

many companies are trying to make household chores quicker, easier and more interesting—sometimes at a fat price. Take, for instance, the seven-fingered Venetian blind duster that retails for $9. These days, time-scrimping housekeepers can also find plastic collars that will keep the socks paired through laundering and decorative stove-burner covers that will hide burned-on goo indefinitely.... Many consumers are washing their hands of the dirty work altogether, and not just wealthy matrons.... Maid services are springing up. McMaid, Inc., in Chicago, offers everything from a traditional, all-day personalized housekeeper to an express service, in which a team of four swoops through an apartment in an economical 30 minutes. McMaid has already expanded to New York City and plans to franchise nationally.

The Whirlpool Corporation plans to aid the harried housekeeper with "robotic arms that could be programmed to transfer laundry from washer to drier. Whirlpool thinks such robots will eventually wash dishes and windows, take groceries out of the shopping bag, scan the bar code and put them on the proper shelf in the pantry."[65]

It is not hard nowadays to find some type of business offering to supply for profit some service that could once be had for free. The health clubs are booming, though they charge hundreds of dollars annually for providing strenuous ways to move one's body. Persons who want advice on how to cope with life in today's more complicated world can buy professional help from counselors of various kinds. In all, the "advice" industry in the United States is estimated to take in $15 billion a year. Management consultants claim $4 billion of this amount; psychologists and others involved in personal consulting claim $6 billion; those who give advice concerning personal finances account for the remaining $5 billion.[66] There is even a kind of business that advises people on how to spend their free time meaningfully. The person with a cause to promote used to be able to speak from a soap box, wear a sandwich-board sign, or tack up handbills on a wall or fence. He can still do those things, but today's public is not much impressed with poverty-stricken messages.

One of history's more memorable events took place when the Apostle Paul preached the Gospel to philosophers in the marketplace of Athens. If he tried to do that today in one of our American shopping malls, chances are he would be escorted to the door by uniformed security guards. The attorney representing a shopping-center mall that had ejected leafletting members of a religious group put the question of civil liberties into perspective: "In order to freely speak and freely publish," he said, "you have to do it with property. You have to use your own property and not be forced to use that property for someone else's speech."[67]

RUIN AND REPAIR

Earlier in the book it was suggested that the government might guarantee full employment by sponsoring a two-part program of digging ditches and filling them up again. If that possibility seems far-fetched, consider how many occupational services are concerned with undoing the consequences of a previous damaging event. For example, a person might drink alcohol to excess. Subsequently, he would receive a variety of treatment services. Money is spent in both phases: first for the alcoholic beverages, the entertainment, and related expenses; then for the medical care, counseling, and so on, associated with the cleanup. Both sets of expenditure contribute to GNP. Both, therefore, are interpreted as representing a higher standard of living. Yet common sense tells us that most of the money was wastefully spent. Looking at the whole cycle of activities, the net effect in terms of good health would be zero. The person might have been better off if he had experienced neither the phase of drunkenness nor of detoxification and cure, but simply stayed sober the entire time.

Recovering alcoholics may not be willing to dismiss their experiences so lightly, for it was deep-seated personal need that originally drove them to drink. Why is it in our society that so many young men and women from good homes seek out personal ruin, and are not content with the comfort and serenity of a middle-class life easily within their grasp? This urge to self-destruction suggests that the human spirit requires considerably more care than what we have thus far been willing to give. In a real sense, then, it would seem that the American standard of living might improve if fewer goods and services were produced but people had a greater chance to pursue understanding and personal happiness. Reduced hours of work would give them that chance. But instead of allowing more leisure time and making room for spiritual growth, U.S. society apparently has decided to push coercively for further growth of the economy. Naively it is assumed that this effort will create greater prosperity. Instead, the additional economic resources are dissipated, to a great extent, in the self-defeating cycles of ruin and repair.

This category of waste encompasses such a large part of modern economic life that our brief discussion here cannot do it justice. Still, we will attempt to identify some of the specific kinds of activity involved in the process and suggest how much they might cost. The category of "ruin" includes such problems as unemployment, sickness, poverty, crime, chemical dependency, divorce, suicide, child abuse, emotional disturbance, and domestic violence. Each contains the element of waste. We assume such things just happen, but dare not ask why they happen so frequently. The category of "repair" includes clean-up activities associated with each type of ruin. Although they cost money, the expenditure is considered necessary so long as the initial problem exists.

In a society well advanced toward waste, the repair phase has developed full-blown industries to deal with each kind of problem. These industries include organizations with budgets to meet, and people who have devoted their careers to the repair process. One may ask what would become of the repairers if nothing needs to be repaired? Is not the very mechanism that has been formed to correct a ruinous problem itself a device to seek out or promote the problem? Cannot, in other words, a solution pushed too hard become part of the problem that it was designed to handle? Economic waste does occasionally take that form as well.

Expert testimony has linked unemployment with other of society's vexing problems. Dr. Harvey Brenner of Johns Hopkins University told a Congressional committee of a study he had done, showing that the rise in unemployment that took place during the 1969/70 recession had resulted in higher suicide rates, increased admissions to mental hospitals, and more deaths due to alcoholism and heart-related diseases.[68] The former Minneapolis chief of police, Anthony Bouza, has observed that "crime is a symptom of a society disease that has its roots in poverty, in the creation of an underclass, in the exclusion, the creation of a large number of unskilled people, mostly black, mostly Hispanic, the creation of a surplus population."[69]

Crime is expensive; it is no longer a marginal kind of economic activity. On the "ruin" side, estimates of the money earned from narcotics dealing run between $50 billion and $75 billion a year, according to federal law-enforcement agencies.[70] It is estimated that American businesses lose $40–50 billion annually in embezzlements, fraud, and other white-collar

Table 6.5
Federal and State Prisoners, 1950–1986

Year	Number	Rate per 100,000 population
1950	166,123	110.3
1960	212,953	118.6
1965	210,895	109.5
1970	196,429	96.7
1975	240,593	113.3
1980	315,974	139.2
1985	481,393	200.6
1986	523,922	216.0

Source: Prepared by the author.

crimes.[71] Criminals are finding new ways to take money through the manipulation of automated teller machines in banks, credit cards, and computers. Organized crime skims billions of dollars from the U.S. economy. The President's Commission on Organized Crime issued a report in January 1986, charging that four of the nation's major unions, including its largest, the Teamsters, were controlled or influenced by organized crime. In addition, it claimed that gangsters had infiltrated many businesses, bringing "broad-based corruption to a number of industries." A study commissioned by this group estimated that organized crime takes in between $41.6 billion and $106 billion annually in gross revenues.[72]

On the "repair" side, costs are equally staggering. Richard Nixon's "law and order" campaign brought increased appropriations for the Law Enforcement Assistance Administration (LEAA), which helped local police departments buy equipment. Between 1968 and 1980 the LEAA spent more than $7 billion, yet the crime statistics grew worse during this time.[73] The prisons are bulging with convicts. Table 6.5 shows the increase in the number of federal and state prisoners between 1950 and 1985. After declining in the 1960s, their number and rate per 100,000 population have soared. Additionally, about 150,000 Americans reside in local jails.[74] The criminal justice system is truly a growth industry. During the 1970s, total expenditures for the police, the courts, corrections, and legal services rose from $8.5 billion per year to $26.0 billion. The rate per 10,000 population of full-time equivalent employment in those areas rose from 38.0 to 53.5.[75] The employment of private security guards in the United States tripled between 1969 and 1983, reaching

1.1 million workers. An article in the *Wall Street Journal* suggested that many of these people, sometimes with criminal records and usually poorly paid, were themselves security risks.[76]

There are indications, too, that the law-enforcement process has, through overly zealous or aggressive tactics, crossed over into a position of becoming part of the problem it was meant to solve. Increasingly, the police are resorting to sting and decoy operations, which precipitate crime. Crusades against drunk driving, wife beating, child abuse, and so forth have created a political climate in which police-state measures are sometimes employed against accused perpetrators of such practices. A combination of police officials, social workers, psychologists, attorneys, and judges has been empowered to take children away from their parents, ruin people's reputations, and saddle them with ruinous legal bills. The number of big-city police departments encouraging or requiring officers to make arrests in cases of minor domestic violence tripled between 1984 and 1985 according to the Crime Control Institute. Media attention to the problem of domestic violence and lawsuits against police departments were cited as principal reasons.[77]

The problem of child abuse, once neglected, has also received overkill treatment. Between 1982 and 1985, the number of lawsuits against child-protection workers for failing to protect abused children doubled. The result has been a "better safe than sorry" attitude among child-protection professionals, according to Douglas Besharov, author of a recent book on the subject. "Social workers," he explained, "fear they will be blamed if there was any reason, however minor, for thinking that the child was in danger. Hence they are under great pressure to take no chances and to take children from their parents whenever they might be criticized for not doing so. Ironically, this kind of defensive decision making is breeding further litigation—as parents have begun to sue workers for violating their civil rights."[78]

The "helping" professions have helped children in Minnesota to inappropriate kinds of treatment, according to Connie Levi, then majority leader of the Minnesota House of Representatives, who chaired a special task force on juvenile justice. Rep. Levi told a church audience of children "falling through the cracks and drifting through the system" with changes in treatment funding. "Kids slide back and forth between the mental-health system, the child-welfare system, and the juvenile [justice] system," she said.

As you know, the mental health/chemical health industry—and it is an industry in Minnesota—is very large, very complex. What has happened in the past six years is that we have slipped into what I consider to be "third-party-payment-driven" diagnosis in terms of placement of children.... Children are being labelled as chemically dependent or emotionally disturbed in many cases without adequate diagnosis. . . . because, you see, the insurance company will pick up the tab for the treatment. . . . Once you are labelled as chemically dependent or emotionally disturbed as a young person, that will stay with you for the rest of your life; it isn't like a delinquency charge which is expunged upon reaching adulthood. . . . When the subcommittee was in Brainerd, [staff members of] the Brainerd Learning Center . . . testified . . . that they had a number of kids there—court-ordered there—that were inappropriately placed were now appropriately there, but it was their fourth, fifth, or sixth program, and they were so counseling-wise and weary that it was almost impossible to reach them.[79]

For people as fortunate as we Americans appear to be, it is strange that so many of us seem to be recovering from something. Either we are recovering from alcohol or drug abuse, or we need counseling to handle death or divorce, or we are dieting or trying to give up smoking. There are support groups for exconvicts, wife beaters, childless couples, and single parents. Certain emotional types are told they have "love addiction." Others need counseling to overcome a tendency toward procrastination or chronic lateness.[80] Workaholics must be professionally advised concerning their gluttonous appetite for staying at the office. Psychologists have found ways of strengthening people's "intimacy skills," teaching them to become more assertive, helping them to cope with stress or connect intellect with the emotions. One of the more amusing interdisciplinary exercises, reported on CBS's "60 Minutes," concerned a bank in Lincoln, Nebraska, which collapsed leaving thousands of uninsured depositors. Bank officials called a meeting of the depositors. "They had a psychologist up there on the stage that told us how to learn to live without the money," recalled an elderly depositor. "I was hoping they would tell us how we could live *with* the money."[81]

Usually ruin and repair happen separately. An exception was made when pari-mutuel betting on horse races came to Minnesota. After years of discussion about the advantages and disadvantages of legalized gambling, the voters finally approved the idea, and a new race track was built. Recognizing that this enterprise might aggravate the problem of compulsive gambling, though, the Minnesota Legislature decided to spend part of the state's share of revenues from the track on a demonstration project for the treatment of gambling addiction. An expert on problem gambling was brought in from an eastern city, who announced that he would set up chapters of Gamblers Anonymous across the state. "I know you have hundreds of compulsive gamblers in Minnesota," he said at a news conference. "That means hundreds of miserable lives that could be salvaged through treatment." No fanatic, this expert disclosed that he personally supported the concept of legalized gambling and himself liked to bet on the horses once in awhile. For a portrait of the compulsive gambler, he suggested that such persons tend to be "exceptionally bright, very industrious, exceedingly energetic, athletic, highly competitive, action-oriented, and workaholic."[82]

One might say that American society allows its citizens considerable freedom to indulge themselves in the pleasures of this world, even to the point of flirtatious encouragement. But woe to the person who goes too far—he is pounced on, made to submit or apologize, and become permanently branded. We seem to have a cultural fixation on "cops and robbers." The legal profession waits for the moment of weakness—a death, divorce, personal injury, defective product—then moves in swiftly for the kill. After a slow start, the Dalkon shield birth-control device quickly generated more than 5000 personal injury suits against its manufacturer, A.H. Robins Co., thanks in part to an informative brochure prepared by a Twin Cities law firm. Robins made some money off the device; then the attorneys made some money off Robins. One attorney, evidently with a grim sense of humor, is said to have ordered a set of solid-gold cufflinks in the shape of a Dalkon shield.[83]

Cigarette smoking has been called one of the nation's principal health hazards. Department of Health and Human Services statistics indicate that this practice costs Americans $13 billion a year in medical bills, $4 billion in bills paid by Medicare and Medicaid, and $25 billion in lost productivity. Nearly 350,000 persons die annually from smoking-related illness.[84] Congress reacted to the threat by requiring the tobacco companies to put health warnings on the cigarette packages. Later it banned cigarette advertisements on radio and television. The industry has fought back with payments to legislators, usually in the form of speakers' fees and honoraria. In 1984, the Tobacco Institute topped the list of lobbying organizations paying the most to members of Congress.[85] The $60 billion-a-year alcoholic beverage industry has reacted to charges of its products' damaging effect on health by sponsoring a health study of its own. The study found that moderate drinkers had a smaller chance of being hospitalized for coronary problems than teetotalers.[86]

In the space of one generation, U.S. society has been permeated by a drug culture of major proportions. The National Organization for the Reform of Marijuana Laws, an advocacy group, claims that despite well-publicized attempts at eradication by the federal government, the value of U.S.-grown marijuana reached $18.6 billion in 1985, making it the nation's largest cash crop.[87] Besides their obvious cost in wasted lives and poor personal health, drugs used at work cost U.S. employers $70 billion a year in lost production and health-related expenses according to a Congressional report, plus an estimated $33 billion a year in pilferage of merchandise and equipment by employees. Employees with a drug or drinking problem have four times as many accidents, are absent from work sixteen times as often, and make five times as many workers compensation claims as the average employee according to this report. The problem became so bad at the General Motors plant in Mansfield, Ohio, that the company hired undercover agents to work on the assembly line and infiltrate the drug rings. General Motors estimates that one out of ten employees has used drugs or alcohol on the job.[88]

Cocaine is the drug of choice for busy executives. "What generally begins as social use of the drug can often lead to dependency, fostered by unremitting job pressures," a *Wall Street Journal* story on the subject explained.

"The ethics of the 1980s are work, work, work, and cocaine is the stimulant that supposedly allows people to put in more time in an effective manner," says Richard L. Miller, director of a drug treatment program in Emeryville, Calif. In New York, Regent Hospital has treated sales and marketing executives, bank officials and securities traders. "These people have must-succeed personalities," says Arthur Greenberg, the hospital's co-director of substance abuse treatment. "Their sense of self-esteem is largely based on their incomes." He recalls a broker the hospital treated recently. "His cocaine intake was based on the Dow Jones average," Mr. Greenberg says. "Some major movement, downward or upward, and his cocaine use would escalate." ... Around Wall Street, cocaine is traded in elevators, cafeterias and bathrooms. Dealers typically seem well-dressed and well-to-do. ... The executive drug user remains well insulated from the sleazy underworld of street dealers and drug smugglers. "The dealer he sees drives a Porsche and wears a beeper."[89]

For every breakdown, someone stands to profit. Potholes cost the average American motorist about $187 a year, mainly to replace damaged tires. The roads near Washington D.C. have an average of 121 potholes per mile, the highest rate in the nation.[90] Consequently, a Maryland man named Reginald Giles has built a thriving business from selling used hubcaps, which he has picked up along the highways, at a reasonable price.[91] U.S. firms are reported to be spending two to three times as much as they did ten years ago to combat the problem of international terrorism.[92] G. Gordon Liddy of Watergate fame has cashed in on this with a course of security techniques. The near epidemic in shoplifting has created lucrative business opportunities for Viaticus Group of Cranston, Rhode Island, which produces tapes with subliminal messages that are imbedded in the background music played in stores. For instance, the message might whisper "You are honest, don't steal," or it would feature the fleeting sound of a police-car siren or the clanging door to a jail cell. With claims to cut shoplifting losses by 25 percent, the firm's sales in this line have doubled every year for the past four years.[93]

The U.S. divorce rate has increased from 2.2 per 1000 in 1960 to 5.2 per 1000 in 1980.[94] With this unsettling social trend, an entirely new industry has blossomed to handle the problem in its various ramifications. The American Bar Association estimates that 11,000 attorneys now specialize in divorce, compared with 700 in 1980. Divorce mediation, a field that did not exist ten years ago, now has 4000 practitioners.[95] In addition, psychologists, counselors, private investigators, and other professionals are kept busy helping divorced or separated couples with their personal problems. A real estate agent claims that a single divorce can produce three separate housing transactions: sales of the divorcing couple's home and a replacement purchase for each erstwhile partner.

In spite of the repair boom, the American consumer often has difficulty in finding reasonably-priced repair services for such products as clothing, household appliances, and electronic products. An outraged columnist complained, for example, that a dealer wanted $27.00 to replace a broken plastic mixing cup on his Hamilton Beach Scovill blender, when the entire blender had originally cost him $26.95. How can it be that services of this sort are so expensive when the U.S. economy has moved so heavily into "services"? An article in *Forbes* magazine has suggested a number of reasons. The trend toward discount retailing has left inadequate profit margins for the stores to provide adequate customer service. More products are manufactured in preassembled, solid-state units, which do not allow individual components to be fixed. Product technology is changing so fast that the training of repair technicians lags behind. Basically, however, the problem with repair services has to do with the relative expensiveness of labor, as new technologies of production have reduced the per-unit cost of manufacturing labor. It therefore becomes cheaper to throw away a broken product and buy a new one than to spend money for repair.

The *Forbes* article summed up the economics of the repair business in these words: "Manufacturing today is heavily automated, done by machines rather than by human labor. Machinery is, in the long run, much cheaper than labor. That's what makes the mass consumer society possible. Repairing, however, takes human labor that is expensive by nature. Today's moderately-priced watch, for example, is built almost entirely by machinery; it can be repaired only by expensive craftsmen. Thus it is usually more economical to replace the watch than to repair it. Wasteful? Of materials maybe, but saving of human labor."[96]

The lesson to be drawn here has to do primarily with knowledge. Through knowledge, in the form of applied technology, the productivity of labor has greatly increased. But an economy built on knowledge has a dark side, which is the human inability to grasp this knowledge as required. The voluminous knowledge required, for instance, on the production side, to maintain a complex computer system or, on the consumption side, to make intelligent purchasing choices in the vast market of available goods and services, has grown beyond the scope of normal intelligence. And that, in turn, leads straight to waste. Waste occurs when people make mistakes in ignorance of the required knowledge.

The more knowledge is required in economic functions, the more waste will occur. The more waste occurs, the more labor is required additionally to cope with the situation. At some point, the process becomes self-defeating. We should not, as intelligent creatures, continue with panglossian dreams of progress onward and upward through economic growth, but take the time to sit down to consider what it is we are actually doing. Maybe then providing more leisure will begin to make more sense.

7

SHAKING THE WASTE
OUT OF THIS
ECONOMY

To be honest about this economy, waste is not the exception but the rule. Some of America's most productive workers, its farmers, have been reduced to 3 percent of the workforce, and are being shaken out further. While the freest of the free-market competitors are competing to death, state-protected monopolies thrive. A wasteful economy is spiritually debilitating. Part of the problem America had with the Vietnam war was that the operations was surfeited with equipment; it was a logistics-intensive war. People's natural inclination is not to waste, but to maintain reasonable frugality and decorum in their lives. People are proud of themselves for having done well with what they have, not for indulging in an excessive, senseless use of materials.

A new spirit of selfishness is loose in the land. Those who are personally well off like to think of themselves as being tough "survivors" in this land of waste. But can we ignore the warnings? While President Reagan in good Hollywood fashion speaks of "a shining city on the hill," the United States has lost some of its appeal to foreigners seeking to start a new life in a free and humane society. There are 45,000 Hmong living in a Thai refugee camp who are legally permitted to enter the United States but refuse to go because of stories they have heard from relatives and friends about this country via cassette tape. They have heard of social pressures to break up families, of personal indignities suffered by women in hospitals, and how healthy Hmong men have died mysteriously in their sleep.[1]

Among American males 15–24 years of age, the suicide rate tripled between 1964 and 1977.[2] Some blame this on young people's declining horizon of opportunities, or the overly competitive and over-programmed lives that today's generation of high-school students live. They are the first generation of Americans expecting to be economically less well off than their parents. Too often, they bear the brunt of decisions imposed by force on a largely defenseless population—by the police, the courts, social workers, educators, the military, and other bureaucratic instrumentalities—as the nation's democratic ideals are forgotten.

We are living in a nation hungering for new ideas, new attitudes, and a bold spirit. Even the yuppies are tired of this tireless materialism. They, too, want to make room for spiritual things. Unfortunately, a prevalent attitude in the business world and other places of power is that the road to happiness and success is paved with the willingness to work long hours for an employer. An article that appeared in the *New Republic* several years ago referred to this phenomenon as "the macho of time." Commenting on its presence among top officials within the Carter administration, the article asked: "What could they possibly be doing for all these hours? And if all these important people are working so terribly hard, why isn't there peace and prosperity throughout the land? A veteran observer of foolishness in high places explains the Washington time macho this way: 'If you can't measure output, you measure input.' Since policymakers cannot often point to anything objective they've accomplished, all they can do to assure themselves and the rest of us of their value is to put in long hours."[3]

SOCIAL PRESSURES TO WORK LONG HOURS

U.S. employers have not been generous in providing free time. The 40-hour week has been in place for more than a generation, and little progress has occurred beyond that point. Our typical 2-week annual paid vacation falls below minimum international labor standards. Although the workweek has declined statistically, part-time work is increasing relative to full-time work. The reality is that many people, especially married women, are moving from no hours of paid employment to some hours. In the stereotypical two-parent family, both husband and wife are more apt to hold jobs nowadays. Consequently, the family unit as a whole has less leisure time than in previous generations.

The increasing time pressures from work have stunted the development of family and other personal ties. Although the government has attempted by various means to coax welfare mothers into paying jobs, a Congressional report cites the shortage of childcare facilities, which "can foreclose the possibility of employment, training, education, and even the opportunity to job hunt," as a principal reason for the disappointing results.[4] Columnist Joan Beck questions, however, whether our society should "settle for putting millions of children into day care for billions of hours without trying to develop alternatives. Instead of pushing employers to provide day care, it would make more sense to pressure them to restructure some jobs to fit the new work force that includes so many young parents. Flexible hours, part-time positions . . . shared jobs, telecommuting and other strategies allow mothers and fathers to spend more time with their young children while earning money and keeping up careers."[5]

Behind the failure of U.S. working hours to adapt more readily to human needs there are definite cultural attitudes. Americans are proud of being "hard-working people," not like those lazy Europeans. John Molloy, who taught the nation's corporate climbers to dress successfully, informed readers of a subsequent book, *Live for Success*, that "winners do something else. They work. Losers talk a good job . . . They are more likely to tell you how tired they are and how much they have sacrificed for the company. The fact is, they don't work very hard. They tend to be clock-watchers. Even if they work for themselves, they will quit at 5 o'clock or a few minutes ahead of time. They simply do not put in the same number of hours as successful people."[6]

The posture of working long hours has long been a management fad. A *Wall Street Journal* article noted that among recent MBA graduates who went into consulting or investment banking, "there is a New York culture; it's almost a macho image: 'I work more hours than you do.' " Down at Salomon Brothers, were found lining up for coffee at 7:15 A.M. Henry Kaufman, the firm's research head, declared: "We are looking for people who don't look at the endeavor as a 9-to-5 business. For some of us, it's a 24-hour business."[7] Over at Gulf & Western headquarters, a spiral of lighted windows was seen late at night leading up to a row of lights on the top floor where the company's CEO, another long-hours prodigy, was presumed to be laboring at his desk.[8]

Work, work, work—that is the ticket to success in financial circles. Ivan Boesky, the famed arbitrageur convicted of insider trading, was an exemplar of the "work ethic" as practiced today on Wall Street. An article in *Time* magazine described his living habits in the these terms: "Boesky was terribly good indeed, thanks to frantic 20-hour work days, obsessive research and a natural trader's ability to talk on several telephones at once. . . . Boesky works like a machine and claims to sleep only two or three hours a night. He rises at 4:30 each morning and climbs into his chauffeured limousine. . . . At work Boesky stands behind his desk and punches buttons on a 300-line telephone console as he studies flickering stockmarket figures."[9]

The new corporate style merges the hours of leisure and work, leisure being decidedly the junior partner. A column in *Advertising Age*, entitled "The Next Trend," advised readers to use their leisure productively: "Never again will you waste two hours playing racketball when all your best contacts are in the aerobics class down the street."[10] The president of an executive recruiting firm warned corporate climbers against letting their hair down at company picnics. "The guy who strikes out the executive committee during the softball game may not be doing himself any favors," he observed. "Behavior at a company picnic is just one of countless small ways—seemingly unrelated to job performance—in which candidates for senior management are judged," a reporter for the *Stamford Advocate* revealed.[11]

In this age of technical specialization, the boss cannot be expected to know how well each employee is doing his job. Lacking a good measuring stick, he uses "effort" as a substitute measure. If an employee regularly works long hours, it is assumed that he is putting his all into the job. Such people therefore get promoted into management positions. There are several opinions as to whether working long hours actually improves work performance. On the negative side, a study conducted by two IBM researchers found that "working long hours may have little to do with a manager's effectiveness."[12] A management consultant has called the workaholic boss "an 18-hour-a-day menace." The workaholic manager, he said, was "a contradiction in terms, because if you're a workaholic, you can't be a manager. A workaholic placed in a management position ... is one of the most divisive forces roaming the corridors of the industrialized world."[13] Even so, almost 60 percent of corporate CEOs who were surveyed in 1984 admitted to working 60 or more hours per week, up from 44 percent in 1980.[14]

With such attitudes among the economic elite, it is unlikely that the U.S. economy will spontaneously progress toward shorter work hours. Whatever movement occurs in hours usually goes in the other direction. On the manufacturing front, General Electric was able to persuade union employees at its Lynn, Massachusetts, plant to accept mandatory 12-hour shifts by threatening to renege on a promise to upgrade the plant and instead to build another in New Hampshire for nonunion labor.[15] Many retailers are pushing for repeal of "blue laws," which prohibit commerce on Sundays. The issue was big in Houston, where some of the large discount department store chains formed a group, "Texans for Blue Law Repeal," with a $300,000 war chest to fight opposition from the smaller stores.[16] Dallas-based Southland Corporation, parent of the 7-Eleven convenience store chain, sets the pace in contemporary retailing with its 24-hour daily schedules. Attitudes are different in other industrialized countries. In West Germany, for instance, every store in the country is legally required to close at 6:30 p.m. on weekday evenings, and at 2 p.m. on Saturdays.[17]

Prior to being elected governor of Minnesota, Rudy Perpich served for three years as an international sales representative for Control Data Corporation in Vienna, Austria. The European attitude toward work hours evidently made an impression on him. He recalled in an interview:

I came to work one time, and these Americans had asked their Austrian secretary to come in on a Saturday morning.... I went out to the other area, and here's this lady, this Austrian.... crying. And she was *crying*. I said, what, I thought someone had died. She said, "They made me come to work today." She says, "This is my day." Yep, that's the kind of feeling she experienced having to go to work on Saturday.... She had certain things she had to do—shopping, whatever—but that's family, it's not for work. And I think that's good. We talk about juvenile delinquency in America, I think a part of it is we're all going to meetings all the time in the evening.... [In Austria] from Saturday noon until Monday morning, you can't even buy a quart of milk. That's family time.[18]

CONSUMPTION, THE FORGOTTEN ELEMENT

Family time indeed. We seem to have forgotten the end of all this business. Man the producer—if the Wall Street gambler can be called that—has become our economic model. Man the consumer, man the human being, has been taken for granted, as if such a person will automatically be found who can validate the production or make it worthwhile.

How do economists know that in requiring abnormally long hours of work the economy will necessarily produce an endlessly expanding quantity of useful products and not waste? Is it not negligent for powerful persons who are themselves insulated from economic hardship to entertain carelessly optimistic views of how others will fare under their policies? How can they assume that the millions of workers who are discharged from basic industries will unfailingly be picked up somewhere else; or that while wages are being squeezed to make American businesses more competitive, enough people will continue to have enough money in their pockets to buy all the consumer products that industry can produce; or that the pool of money and spending habits we call the U.S. market can be endlessly tapped by businesses all over the world without any thought to its financial replenishment? And free enterprise will take care of everything! Consumer markets do not grow in nature; they need to be grown. One would hope that some economists would again give thought to the process of building or "growing" a strong American market—demand-side economics, if you will—through full-scale wages paid for real, productive work.

The shorter-workweek proposal is not a give-away program to pay people for doing nothing. Rather it is a program to allow more people to become productive. It is also a way to beat back the encroaching wilderness of waste to a more tolerable perimeter. The key to the success of this approach is markets. Paul Hoffman, who administered the Marshall Plan and later headed the United Nations' early economic-development programs, told reporters upon his retirement in 1972 what he had learned from years of successful experience in this area: "One illusion is that you can industrialize a country by building factories. You don't. You industrialize it by building markets."[19]

Building a thriving market means that enough people or organizations with a desire to buy products become financially authorized or empowered to purchase what they want. Increased wages, which put more "financial authorization" into workers' pockets, strengthen the consumer market in an obvious way. So does increased leisure. It creates a greater opportunity for working people usefully to consume products. It also gives more people an opportunity to become employed and earn a wage. Instead of the nation's income becoming concentrated in the hands of a few, a larger part of the population can participate in this process of producing and consuming consumer products. The aggregate wants and needs of these more numerous people, supported by the required financial authorization, will expand the market to a point beyond what it otherwise might have been.

The new ideology called "supply-side economics" denies that insufficient markets have much to do with a sluggish economy; instead, the problem is said to be production. According to this view, the way to national prosperity is to encourage more business activity to take place in a nation by lowering the tax rate and offering various other business incentives, which, in turn, will cause more people to become employed and pay taxes. Eventually government will recover from economic growth what it lost through tax cuts—so the proponents argue.

Supply-side economists see leisure as an enemy of growth and prosperity. A prominent supply-sider, Paul Craig Roberts, then assistant secretary of the Treasury, wrote in the *Wall Street Journal*:

The administration wants to cut personal income tax rates, not in order to give people more money to spend, but in order to increase incentives to earn more taxable income. Today people are taxed at unprecedented high rates on any additional income they earn.... The inevitable results of little reward for extra effort are worsening work attitudes, high absenteeism rates, reluctance to work overtime and to assume risks, and the lowest personal savings rate in anyone's memory. For the supply-side policy to work, taxpayers don't have to respond to marginal tax rates by giving up vacations, going on a double shift and saving all their income. When you have a work force of more than 100 million people, small individual responses result in a large aggregate effect. If the average number of hours worked per week rises from 35 to 35.5, GNP rises by $24 billion.[20]

This is the financial view of economics. The main reason that leisure is in disrepute among Treasury Department officials is that they can't tax it. A proposal such as the shorter workweek, which would redistribute the burden of work and its income more evenly, would reduce the tax collector's take from a given volume of economic activity. Therefore, it cannot be. From a less parochial point of view, however, one sees that supply-side economics has things backwards. Mere production accomplishes nothing; there must be some sense of a role for consumption.

To economists who look only at the financial side of the economy, leisure represents only lost wages, lost taxes, and lower production. Achieving prosperity seems a matter of persuading people to rise from their easy chairs and start engaging in some income-producing activity. There is even a psychologist at Washington University in St. Louis who has experimented with pigeons to find ways of motivating them to work harder for their economic reward—say, peck a plastic button more times before the bird seed comes out of the feeder—in preference to leisure. Certain economists have shown an interest in his work.[21]

People, however, are not like caged pigeons. Their economic behavior is imbedded in a larger scheme of life that includes other values besides the efficient production of goods. In a real-life human economy, increased leisure increases consumer demand, which then calls forth more production. "People who have more leisure must have more clothes. They must have a greater variety of food. They must have more transportation facilities," said Henry Ford. "This increased consumption will require greater production than we now have. Instead of business being slowed up because the people are 'off work,' it will be speeded up because the people consume more in their leisure time than in their working time. This will lead to more work. And this to more profits. And this to more wages. The result of more leisure will be the exact opposite of what most people might suppose it to be."[22]

The choice, therefore, is not between a larger or smaller economic pie, but it is a decision whether or not to regain rational control of a system drifting off in the direction of waste. The makers of public policy should again look to the provision of basic wants and needs. Over the years powerful institutions have been created with a gargantuan appetite for money, requiring continual growth of GNP to stay solvent. The economy is managed to accommodate that need. Working people are required to march at a pace dictated by the metronome of compound interest rates and escalating commitments to the different constituencies of waste. It matters not whether production is useful or wasteful, just that a larger number of dollars are attached to it to meet financial targets.

MARXIST CRITICISM

The capitalist system is on trial, as it has been for at least a century and a half, over this question of waste. Karl Marx did not contend that capitalism would be overthrown because of a decline in the work ethic, or a failure to keep pace with production. The problem was insufficient markets. An early socialist thinker, Fourier, described it as a "crisis from plethora." Capitalistic economies were perceived to go through cycles of feast and famine, as the accelerating forces of production outran their capacity to absorb the output. In such circumstances, Fourier said, "abundance becomes the source of distress and want."[23]

Engels described the process at some length. He wrote:

The ever-increasing perfectability of modern machinery is, by the anarchy of social production, turned into a compulsory law that forces the individual industrial capitalist always to improve his machinery, always to increase its productive force. The bare possibility of extending the field of production is transformed for him into a similar compulsory law. . . . But the capacity for extension . . . of the markets is primarily governed by quite different laws, that work less energetically. The extension of the markets cannot keep pace with the extension of production. The collision becomes inevitable, and as this cannot produce any real solution so long as it does not break in pieces the capitalist mode of production, the collisions become periodic. Capitalist production has begotten another "vicious circle."

Thus it comes about that the economizing of the instruments of labor becomes at the same time, from the outset, the most reckless waste of labor . . . that machinery [quoting Marx] "the most powerful instrument for shortening labor time, becomes the most unfailing means of placing every moment of the laborer's time and that of his family at the disposal of the capitalist for the purpose of expanding the value of his capital." Thus it comes about that overwork of some becomes the preliminary condition for the idleness of others, and that modern industry, which hunts for new consumers all over the whole world, forces the consumption of the masses at home down to a starvation minimum and in doing this destroys its own home market.

Engels believed that this:

economic bankruptcy recurs regularly every ten years. In every crisis, society is suffocated beneath the weight of its own productive forces and products, which it cannot use, and stands helpless, face to face with the absurd contradiction that the producers have nothing to consume because consumers are wanting. The expansive force of the means of production bursts the bonds the capitalist mode of production had imposed upon them. . . . Nor is this all. The socialized appropriation of the means of production does away not only with the present artificial restrictions upon production, but also with the positive waste and devastation of productive forces and products that are at the present concomitants of production, and . . . with the senseless extravagance of the ruling classes of today, and their political representatives.[24]

Marx himself used military imagery to describe the process of labor displacement. He wrote:

Machinery supplants skilled laborers by unskilled, men by women, adults by children; where newly introduced, it throws workers upon the streets in great masses....This war has the peculiarity that the battles in it are won less by recruiting than discharging the army of workers. The [capitalist] generals vie with one another as to who can discharge the greatest number of industrial soldiers. The economists tell us, to be sure, that those laborers who have been rendered superfluous by machinery find new avenues of employment....But even if we assume that all who are directly forced out of employment by machinery...do actually find some new employment, are we to believe that this new employment will pay as high wages as did the one they have lost? If it did, it would be in contradiction to all the laws of political economy.[25]

Events of the past ten years have brought this Marxist apocalyptic scenario, for the first time in half a century, back into focus. Policies of the Reagan administration have stripped away the protective padding that since the 1930s has shielded American workers from the kind of grinding wage competition described by Engels and Marx. While fighting the spread of Marxism to the tiny Central American nation of El Salvador or Nicaragua, the U.S. government tolerates the greater risk of political destabilization in Mexico and South America, where problems of servicing foreign debt have stifled the national economies. At home, the stage is set for a more explosive political situation with the dismantling of New Deal "welfare state" programs, unmitigated labor displacement, the ravishing of agriculture, and a sharper polarization in the society between its more and less affluent members.

POLITICS ABOVE ECONOMICS: STANDING MARX ON HIS HEAD

The materialistic philosophy of Marx and Engels teaches that a society's economic relationships determine its political and social institutions. In a society that has advanced to a high degree of waste, however, a curious reversal takes place: Politics comes to control the society's economic institutions. It is not that government necessarily controls the economy, but that politics in its broader sense controls economics. The "who you know" becomes a more critical part of economic success than the "what you know," in other words.

Collectively, the economic function remains important. It is, for instance, essential that the farmer continue to produce food for people. Individually, however, this matters little. Farmers are "a dime a dozen." We are all, no matter how indispensable we think our particular occupational skill, a "dime a dozen" in an economic sense. We can each, individually, be replaced, as many learn, to their great distress during a recession when they are laid off or forced to retire just to save some dollars.

What matters, then, to individuals in an economy such as ours is not so much the ability to do productive work as having access to income—

and that is a political rather than an economic decision. There is in any organization a political nucleus that has such power by virtue of its legitimate succession to rank and authority. Political access to income requires this group's blessing. Where an organization requires particular work to be done, then the person who can do it well will likely receive the blessing. But where the organization's economic place is too comfortable and secure to be immediately threatened by poor workmanship in its ranks, then other, noneconomic factors may decide who is to be rewarded how much. In an extreme case, the decision makers will decide to reward only themselves. Though heirs to the work of their predecessors, they will pretend personally to deserve such a generous reward by "supply and demand" for their managerial service.

The official line always downplays the political side. It is said that by working hard or smart for a long period of time we will eventually receive our just economic reward. We like to think ours is a unique function; that belief gives us a sense of security. But, in fact, we all hold our incomes by the grace of someone else. We hold our jobs, our pensions, our rents, our dividends and our interest payments by the grace of someone else. · Work remains the main source of economic provision. The more the economy consists of wasteful pursuits, however, the less needed a particular piece of work becomes, and the more precarious the livelihood obtained from it.   The shorter workweek would push the balance back from the political toward the economic. With a leaner economy—where work was more necessary—production workers would have more leverage as suppliers of a laboring service. They would command more income and enjoy more real economic security.

The Reagan revolution was a revolution against waste, but only against a particular kind: waste in government. Waste is a bigger problem than that. The real wastrels are not so much the "welfare cheats" as the more prosperous types of gougers and racketeers. While punishing the people on welfare, this administration has not given them enough of a chance to better themselves through work. Therefore, the main effort against waste will have to come from another political direction. This would be a battle extending the fight against waste from the public sector—or from the poor people's corner there—to the entire economy. The waste of unemployment and of missed opportunities should also be recognized. As the Reagan revolution sought to crunch the resources available to government to waste, so might the next one crunch the resources available to economic life in general, creating space for individually chosen pursuits.

Our political institutions have the power already to seize the economy by the collar and shake the waste out of it. But, truly, waste will never completely disappear. Waste can be anything beyond what is needed to sustain life. Is there any reason, however, not to choose a better form of waste? If in a thousand years the artifacts of our civilization are unearthed and examined, we would want to have left something more than storage boxes filled with legal, medical, and accounting records. We could use our economic surplus instead to colonize space, increase historical or scientific knowledge, feed the world's hungry, provide education for the sake of its own experience, or rebuild the cities and farms. Or else, we could give people the opportunity, in the form of leisure, to create their own kind of waste. Why make people pay for someone else's waste—give them a blank page to fill with expressions of their own. That is another meaning of freedom, the ability to choose one's own form of waste.

8
AN ECONOMY BUILT
ON MONEY AND DEBT

Current public policy looks at the economy through a lens of money. All wealth is dollar-denominated. If an activity does not leave a trail of money, it is economically invisible and of little public concern. The housewife complains that her unpaid housework is not valued by the society; only when she abandons the role of full-time mother and homemaker does she become an economically significant person. The same stigma attaches to leisure. Business sees it as unproductive time. Government cannot find a way to tax it. Therefore, leisure is considered to be something negative. In economists' eyes, a decline in the average workweek signals the approach of a recession, while long workweeks with much overtime mean that the economy is booming. The goal of economic policy seems to be to have as many people as possible each working as many hours as possible, producing and earning wealth measured in dollars.

In reality, an economy is more than an excuse for exchanging money. There is a physical side to its activities as well as a financial side. Money itself is a figment of the economic imagination. Money is a yardstick, not a commodity. "Money as money is nothing. It is just something to make bookkeeping convenient."[1] These are the words of H.L. Hunt, not Lenin or Marx. If money is a yardstick, then the idea of a community's running out of money becomes quite absurd. No more can we run out of dollars financially than we can run out of inches or miles in space. If there is insufficient money for the economy to function properly, the government can always create more. The financial mechanism by which the economy is regulated exists in the form of symbolic tokens. If unconducive to economic good health, the monetary medium can be changed.

Of course, there are limits to what government can do with money. A society cannot continually be tampering with its system of money, or people lose confidence in the system altogether. Confidence in the society's money is closely related to confidence in government itself.

The U.S. economy is staggering beneath a heavy load of debt. In 1985, total public and private debt in the United States exceeded $8 trillion. This represented the highest ratio of debt to GNP since World War II. The ratio, which remained stable at 1.45 to one for most of the postwar period, took a jump to 1.63 to one in the 1980s. In November 1985, consumer installment debt reached a record 18.9 percent of after-tax income. The savings rate in 1985 was a mere 4.6 percent—lowest in 27 years. More than one fifth of the amount owed by U.S. consumers was borrowed on credit cards. U.S. business has borrowed about as much as consumers—roughly $2.1 trillion apiece—while government at all levels has borrowed $1.8 trillion. It takes 16 percent of GNP to pay interest on the debt. A growing share is owed to foreigners.[2]

Some money is borrowed for the sake of a future economic benefit, such as buying a house or financing a college education. Some, including most consumer credit, is borrowed to finance present consumption. A particularly disturbing feature about the current debt, on the other hand, is how much of the indebtedness represents the cost of past benefits. In the federal budget, for instance, the three largest categories of expenditure comprise payments for Social Security retirement and disability insurance, national defense, and interest on the national debt. All three to a large extent represent obligations from the past. When debt takes this particular form, it can no longer be claimed that the debt is a normal part of business or can be sustained from present and future productions of wealth. One must anticipate a stage at which the burden of servicing the debt will become unbearable and a cataclysmic adjustment must be made.

Some refer to this prospect as a "debt bomb." Whatever its name, there is a combination of financial pressures in the nation's economy that threaten to bring a collapse in the next period of economic weakness. The unfunded actuarial liabilities of our public and private retirement programs run into the trillions of dollars. The national debt itself exceeds $2 trillion—a remarkable increase from the $400 billion that worried some people in 1970.[3] A collapse could well come at any of several points of financial vulnerability, where the U.S. government has committed its resources. For instance, the Federal Savings and Loan Insurance Corporation guarantees deposits in the nation's saving-and-loan associations, half of which are considered to be financially unsound.[4]

The debts owed by developing nations to world banking institutions and the Western commercial banks have reached $1 trillion. Such nations have been hit hard by falling commodity prices. Few expect their debts ever to be repaid. Although the ten largest U.S. commercial banks continue to carry these loans on their books at full value, analysts estimate their true value to be 20–50 percent less. The banks' loans to six nations—Brazil, Mexico, Argentina, Venezuela, Chile, and the Philippines—represent 150 percent of their stockholders' equity.[5]

The general public-policy response to the mounting debt problem has been to try to sweep the problem under the generational carpet. "It comes down to 'peace in our time,'" suggested a vice president of T. Rowe Price Associates, an investment firm. "We've got a bunch of Neville Chamberlains running the financial system." Reminiscent of practices a half century ago, government increasingly has resorted to "debt warehousing," or transferring uncollectible debt to dummy corporations, in order to postpone the day of reckoning.[6] Corporate raiders raise money for their ventures by selling "junk bonds," high-interest debt securities issued by organizations set up solely for the purpose of acquiring an existing business, dismembering it, and profitably selling off assets to repay the debt. Senior-level executives arrange "leveraged buyout" deals to purchase with borrowed funds the very firms they currently manage. More investment capital is raised from bank borrowings, and less from selling stock. All must go according to schedule to keep the financial structure afloat.

Adam Smith observed in *Wealth of Nations*:

When national debts have once been accumulated to a certain degree, there is scarce, I believe, a single instance of their having been fairly and completely paid. The liberation of the public revenue, if it has ever been brought at all, has always been brought about by a bankruptcy; sometimes by an avowed one but always by a real one, though frequently by a pretended payment. The raising of the denomination of the coin has been the most usual expedient by which a real public bankruptcy has been disguised under the appearance of a pretended payment.[7]

Thanks to Paul Volcker and associates, inflation appears for the time being to have been subdued; and, with this, one of Adam Smith's debt-eroding measures has become unavailable. That leaves two other possible outcomes. The first, what Smith called a "real public bankruptcy," would involve debt repudiation and, in turn, public disillusionment with the economic and political system. The other possibility is that the economy can forever "outgrow" its multiplying burden of debt.

GROW OR COLLAPSE

Therefore, growth—in financial rather than physical terms—is the nation's chief economic policy. We need this not so that people can live better but so that government can postpone the inevitable crisis and save face. Growth covers a multitude of sins. With it, the pressure is eased to make difficult choices in allocating limited economic resources. There is no need to pick and choose between items in the budget; you can have everything. Unfortunately, public finances have deteriorated to the point that the U.S. economy must grow fast to meet past obligations now coming due. The recourse to deficit spending in good and bad times alike has produced a debt whose annual interest payments have grown from $19 billion to $179 billion between 1970 and 1985.[8] The mechanism of compound interest dictates that the economy must grow at a certain rate each year to cover its increased financial claims. If it does not, the U.S. Treasury might at some point be unable to fund the outstanding public debt.

Shorter workweeks, or any form of unfunded leisure, are most unwelcome in this regard. Whether the American people might live happier lives, or there might be closer family ties or less unemployment or crime, is of less urgent concern from a policy standpoint than that an undiminished stream of dollars continues to flow into the U.S. Treasury. The surly insistence upon such priorities resembles the attitude of an embezzler trying to maintain a check-kiting scheme. Government is far from neutral regarding the "choice" that the nation's workers allegedly make between increased pay or improved leisure. Workers *must* choose higher pay because that choice would furnish needed tax dollars while increased leisure would not. If the American people were allowed more time off from work, many of them would use the extra time to engage in "do-it-yourself" repair projects and other kinds of useful work, which would deprive commercial establishments of the opportunity to perform the same service for pay. The "underground economy," which cuts out the IRS through unreported cash transactions, might grow out of control.

DEBT, CAPITAL, AND TAXATION

But now fears of debts and deficits seem to have gone the way of the herpes scare. These fears are no longer emphasized, if mentioned, in the evening television news. The same attitude prevails in Washington. President Reagan in his first inaugural address spoke of how "for decades we have piled deficit upon deficit, mortgaging our future and our children's future for the temporary convenience of the present." Nowadays he seems less and less concerned about the national debt, or at least the $900 billion increase that has occurred in his seven years in office. This is not altogether surprising in this president, whose mind seems to live in certain clearings within the thickets of reality. They are historical, intellectual, and economic clearings, and are isolated, as though on separate movie sets—isolated not only from current reality but even from his own previous views. His view apparently is that there is sunlight in the clearings, at least in the distant ones, so why worry about the surrounding jungle?

International businessmen, bankers, and other traditional capitalists of our system seem only slightly disturbed over conditions that used to keep them awake at night. Some even see virtue in current and prospective deficiencies. The same is true of publications like the *Wall Street Journal* and *Forbes* magazine. Preoccupation with advancing the interests of capital is manifest in the current attitude of the business and financial community toward the national debt and deficits. One can fairly ask, "Why?" What are the reasons they give for their apparent change of position? For their new confidence, their tolerance of conditions they once held to be intolerable, the reasons are mixed.

First, they noted that most general economic indicators were positive. They especially liked the rising stock market. They observed that inflation has gone down from the inordinately high rate of 13 percent a year at the end of the Carter administration. They said that inflation could be worse. It could be. It is now about 4 percent, a rate considered intolerable in the 1950s and 1960s. They pointed out that interest rates have come down, again, from the high of the Carter period. Rates have come down, but they are still high for many borrowers. Then, they pointed to the fact that foreign money continued to flow into the United States, to the point that in November 1985 foreign holdings in marketable United States securities exceeded 200 billion dollars, and exceeded U.S. investments in foreign countries. They said, echoing Walter Wriston, the former chairman of Citicorp, that this was evidence that we live in a "global economy." They saw the inflow as a sign of confidence in the United States.

That it is, in any absolute way, a sign of confidence in the American political-economic situation must be doubted. The stronger case can be made that foreign capital is coming here because of uncertainty in other parts of the world. The potential for secure and profitable investment in Third World and developing nations seems to be exhausted. Some of these nations are defaulting on loans made in previous years. Political instability and the threat of socialization, even in countries such as France, Britain, and Italy, have discouraged investors in these countries. Germany and Japan are producing their own capital for investment, and have reached the point of domestic saturation. Yet investors are reassured by the continued popularity of President Reagan and his supporters. The ship of state may be losing way, and settling slowly in the water, but the deck appears to be level and there is no water in the first-class cabins.

These explanations are superficial—they are finding deeper, ideological satisfactions in things that are happening in the shadow of deficit and debt.

A major advantage, as the capitalists (of the "land, labor and capital" classification system) see it, is that, under pressure of the budget deficits and mounting debt, political liberals are in retreat, and domestic programs are being cut back. The capitalists find satisfaction in other developments not so directly related to the deficit-debt reality. These are developments bearing directly on giving advantages, relative or absolute, to the capital factor of production.

First, capital, or those who control it and profit from it, see a growing advantage over the labor factor. Unemployment hovers at about 7 percent, a point at which some labor analysts say that management can effectively control wages and worker benefits. The trend of wages, in recent years, has been downward. Average weekly wages of private non-agricultural workers in the United States were, in 1977, $189 a week. Measured in 1977 dollars, the value of those weekly wages in 1985 fell to a little over $171.00 a week, a decline of $17 a week. This is a decline of 9 percent in average weekly wages in less than a decade.[9]

Downward economic pressure on U.S. labor is further intensified by the importation of foreign labor, legal and illegal, and by bringing in both raw materials and manufactures produced by low-wage workers in countries such as Taiwan, Korea, and China. A recent news program showed steelworkers in India who were earning one dollar a day producing manhole covers for Baltimore, Maryland. Goods are also coming in from countries such as Germany and Japan, which have a built-in indirect subsidy in that their costs do not include costs of the magnitude of taxes paid by American workers and industry for defense, much of it committed to the protection of these very same countries. The pressure on American labor is further increased by competition from new equipment and automated machinery developed, built, and put in place with the aid of investment credits, tax-exempt industrial bonds, and other subsidies from federal, state, and local governments.

Capital also has an advantage, currently, over the second of the classic factors of production, namely land, or natural resources. Agricultural prices generally are depressed. In the United States, farm prices, set against prices with 1977 as the index base, are at an index number of 79. The prices of most industrial minerals, iron ore and copper for example, are depressed. Oil continues under severe downward pressure, despite the military uncertainties in the Persian Gulf.

Perhaps more important to capital's dominance is the fact that, within the political system itself, certain special, integral advantages were given to capital and to income from it. Until this year, capital gains in the United States were given a progressively preferred position as against other forms of income, to the point that capital gains, at least for tax purposes, had a status bordering on that of the sacred monies of the temples in ancient times. Capital was also developing its own theological and philosophical support. Established religions found that they could accommodate capitalism to their moral doctrines.

The changes in the amount, and in the percentage, of income taxes collected from the corporations, as against that collected from individuals, give a rough indication of what has happened. In 1960 approximately $67 billion was collected through income taxes: $45 billion from personal income taxes and $22 billion from corporate income taxes, a ratio of 2 to 1. In 1970, the total tax collected from the two sources was roughly $139 billion, with $104 bilion coming from individuals and $35 billion coming from corporations. The ratio had become 3 to 1. By 1980 the amount collected was $360 billion, of which $287 billion was levied on individuals and $72 billion on corporations. The ratio was almost 4 to 1. In 1985, $397 billion was collected in individual income taxes, and $77 billion from corporations, a ratio exceeding 5 to 1. The ratio between individual and corporate taxes was 3 to 2 in 1950, barely more than a generation ago.[10]

Even after tax reform, capital gains continue to get special treatment in rates, holding period, and sequestration. Pressure continues for further reduction of corporate income tax rates, for the continuation of special exemptions, and for the extension of special treatment of corporate income through depletion allowances, depreciation, investment credit, and retention of earnings. Dividend and interest income are given partial exemption from income taxes and protected in trusts and foundations even beyond the fourth generation of biblical note, as well as in corporate financial structures.

Finally, capitalists see good in the national debt. A large, more or less permanent, national debt will not in its effects run contrary to the trend toward concentration of control over capital, and its special treatment. In fact, the transfer of control over capital will be significantly enhanced by the increase of the national debt. If, as anticipated, the total national debt by the year 2000 will be close to four trillion dollars, about three-fourths of that will be held by individuals of some wealth (foreigners and Americans), by financial institutions, and by corporations. The other one-fourth will be held by government agencies and by state and local governments and their agencies.

The annual cost of servicing the three-fourths of the debt that is in nongovernmental control will come to close to $300 billion a year by 2000. The federal government will then be, as it is now in a lesser measure, the instrument through which taxes (largely levied on earned income, that is, on wages and salaries) will be collected and then transferred. More than that, these taxes will be transformed into capital, producing capital gains and other tax-privileged forms of income. Thus taxation will contribute to the increased and continuing concentration of wealth, and of power over wealth, and of wealth production. Meanwhile the president, and his Republican would-be successors, talk of selling off government assets, such as the national forests and possibly the PXs. The most popular investment in the U.S. today is in future tax collections of the U.S. government.

The state of our Republic, although existing in a different historical context, substantively is not unlike that described as marking the Roman Republic. In Sallust's observation of Roman civilization in the first century B.C., he noted that it was then marked by unequal distribution of wealth, depopulation of the countryside, exorbitant veteran's demands, high unemployment, widespread slave labor, bread and circuses for the poor, debt-ridden farmers, costly military ventures, oppressive taxes levied on some, and a government controlled by wealth, unprepared to comprehend the magnitude of the Roman state or its innumerable problems.

THE CONSUMPTION STANDARD

The great commercial and financial empire created in the United States has lately come under powerful attack from foreigners. As an indication of the serious deterioration in the economic strength of our nation we have a persistent and growing trade deficit. Financial journals, commentators, and the business sections of most major newspapers currently are giving heavy emphasis to this problem. Solemnly they note its threat to orderly trade among the more or less free trade nations. The *Wall Street Journal*, for example, proclaimed the trade deficit to have displaced the global debt crisis as the "number one" threat to the world economy. In response to the financial crisis, new quasi-ethical concepts have been developed, telling people how they ought to behave. Though absurd from a common sense standpoint, such behavior is urgently needed to keep the financial bubble growing.

It is generally agreed, both by advocates of protection and by advocates of free trade, that the old standards of judgment are in trouble. In determining whether trade is fair or not, certain formerly required considerations are either not being applied, or are no longer relevant. The useful life of concepts such as subsidies, direct and indirect; exploitation of labor; tax preferences; environment damage and depletion of finite resources, and so on, may have been superceded, however, by new and somewhat dubious views of global neighborliness.

If international trade is to be "fair" obviously there is a need to find other standards of judgment. Almost every day the press carries articles and editorials suggesting what those standards should be. The *Wall Street*

Journal has reported that, to the dismay of U.S. officials, some Europeans, and especially the Germans, are resisting our urgings that they spend more. The case of a German automobile owner is given as an example of the resistance. This German's Volkswagen Beetle recently failed to pass a federal automobile inspection, but the man stubbornly refused to consider borrowing to buy a car. "Better to walk than to borrow," he said.

Washington meanwhile continues to urge Germany and other European governments to give their citizens more pocket money, through lower interest rates and tax cuts. The hope is that Europeans will spend more on consumer goods. Americans want Europeans to go even beyond buying their own nationally produced goods and begin to "buy American" as Bob Hope in television ads has urged. Yet Germans, it would seem, are not even "buying German." Americans meanwhile are urged to do their part in bolstering the automobile market. We are implored even to buy German cars. In fact we are doing so, as the number of new BMWs, Mercedes, Audis, and Volkswagens competing for parking spaces near formerly convenient shops attests.

The Japanese, like the Germans, are also uncooperative on the consumption side. In their case, it is not so much automobiles as it is food. Jim Fallows in *The Atlantic* reported that most Japanese are thin. Fallows noted that the average American ingests 800 calories a day more than the average Japanese does: 3,393 calories to 2,593. Allowing for some natural differences in size, this is still a significant difference and may explain why the average American is approximately 15 pounds overweight. Meanwhile the Japanese market for American rice and soybeans is much too restricted. Fallows disclosed that the average life expectancy for Japanese women is now more than eighty years; for men it is in the mid-seventies. "Why aren't there any fat people here [in Japan]?" Fallows' son asked.[11]

Being fat has, of course, historical significance. Tribal chieftains in some countries were expected to be persons of great size and weight. Queens were under similar expectations as well, as Captain Cook discovered on reaching Hawaii. When the British navy ruled the waves and the pound sterling ruled the land, the British middle class—bankers, merchants and the like—were expected to have prominent stomachs, high blood pressure, and gout. Pork and beef were their staple foods. Overeating and being overweight have been democratized in the case of the United States. The protruberant belly is no longer the sign of wealth or aristocracy. We are the greatest popular over-eaters and over-consumers in the history of the world.

Only two possible exceptions exists: the Ik, and the Romans. The Ik are an African mountain tribe who, by report, gorge themselves on a good day's kill without thought for other people, or for their own tomorrow. And the Romans over-consumed, but did not put on weight, by providing the vomitorium as an adjunct to the dining room. (Sales of emetics, over-the-counter, are increasing in the United States).

Today the American people, as noted by President Reagan in his 1986 State of the Union message, make up five percent of the world's population, yet we consume twenty-five percent of the world's production of fossil fuel. Overall annual consumption of material resources by the United States is more than twice that of Western Europe, and four times that of Eastern Europe. Aside from the industrialized and industrializing world, the U.S. rate and quantity of consumption cannot even be realistically compared to that of other countries and areas of the world, ours being so large.

We have five percent of the world's population, and we have fifty percent of its automobiles. Approximately 15–20 percent of our material production is used to pay for the construction and maintenance of these automobiles, and 15 percent of the world's annual production of petroleum is used each year to fuel them. In an eight hour day, the average American works more than an hour to support his or her automobile. We are also consuming more defense than any other country of the free world. We spend about six percent of our Gross National Product on defense; the Germans spend a little over two percent; and the Japanese, less than one percent.

The world is evidently not satisfied with our performance. We are being asked to consume more. Arab oil producers want us to use more oil in order to stabilize the Middle East. Japanese and German automobile producers urge more of their cars upon us, even accepting American parts as a sales aid. Argentinians and Australians ask us to consume more beef and mutton. Brazilians and Columbians urge more coffee consumption on us. South American, Central American, Caribbean, and Pacific sugar producers would have us use more sugar. Asian, Mid-Eastern, and South American producers of drugs continue to supply the American market. Production overcapacity abounds in most areas.

How can we creatively respond to this challenge? Maybe we can impose on other nations standards of economic behavior that have already been foisted upon our own people. For instance: Countries exporting goods to the U.S. might be required to have their populations be overweight in roughly the same percentage as we are. That would provide a market for American agricultural products. Failing the will, or the ability, to adjust their domestic consumption upward to American levels, those exporting countries could be made to pay a monetary penalty for their self (or government) discipline.

Similarly, if our highways are overcrowded and dangerous, those of nations exporting to the U.S. should also be as crowded and dangerous as ours are. If there is insufficient space for highways, as in Japan,

Japanese could be required to buy cars in any case until their car-to-person ratio approaches ours. The Japanese already run in place because there is too little room for jogging. There is no reason why the principle could not be extended to automobiles. Perhaps they could produce a car that runs in place. Falling short of that, they should pay a duty on any of their cars exported to the United States. Also our duty on imports should reflect the differential between the percent of GNP spent on defense by the United States and that spent by the other countries. If we have to be over-defended, then so should they. They should certainly bear their share of the cost of the over-defense.

Our basic posture in the United States as regards the economy requires us to act like true imperialists: to have trade which is "fair" by U.S. standards, we must force on the rest of the world U.S. standards of production and of consumption. If those other nations will not consume their share of world over-production, they must not then throw overseas the excess created by their under-consumption or non-consumption. Their excess either should be excluded from the U.S. market; or, if we are to consume this surplus of the world, we should be paid to do so, especially if such consumption involves a threat to the personal health and safety of our citizens. After all, as it would seem that men and women were put on this continent to do their economic duty, so the other peoples of the earth will need eventually to make some investment in us, their prime consumer market.

9
MICRO AND MACRO EFFECTS OF REDUCED HOURS

If money is not the true reality, time, in some sense, is. Time too involves a standard, but the standard is imposed upon nature. The rhythm of life is governed by it. Unlike dollars, which can be created with the stroke of a pen, the time that each person is permitted to spend on this earth is fixed within natural limits. This life is our most precious resource. We would not want to waste the resource with too many senseless activities.

A proper balance in time between work and leisure is characteristic of a well-ordered and prosperous life. Balance between consumption and production is important to economic stability. The hours that a person is required to spend at work by an employer are not a natural requirement but the product of a conscious decision. On a microeconomic level, work hours are set by the employer as part of an employment offering, or, perhaps, through a collective-bargaining between the employer and an organized group of employees. On a macroeconomic level, legislation such as the Fair Labor Standards Act creates financial incentives for a certain schedule of hours. The impetus for this arrangement would be political will guided by perceptions of human decency.

Because the number of hours per day, or week, or year, required to be worked is set by conscious deliberation, it becomes an appropriate issue of public policy. Economic and social well-being are at stake. Some raise questions concerning the employment consequences if work hours are reduced. Discussions of this topic usually center on the effectiveness of reduced hours in bringing down the unemployment rate. Such questions involve speculation about the economy as a whole, or its macroeconomic dimension. Whatever happens at the level of the national or international economy will, of course, have corresponding activities on the level of a particular firm. Work hours are an important factor in any economic undertaking. Let us, therefore, consider a microeconomic model first, before moving on to some of the broader issues.

In our model, the labor market consists of people who are employed for a certain period of time by enterprises that produce particular goods or services. The weekly period of their employment would be determined, in part, by economic factors, and also, in part, by noneconomic or political factors. Businesses have a certain life cycle, which may affect their attitude toward work hours and other elements of production cost. At the beginning, an enterprise focuses more on the development and marketing of products. Its open-ended prospects permit a somewhat looser control of the production factors, so long as cash flow and profit margins appear adequate. Later, as an organization matures and sales volume reaches the upper limits of its market, the financial health of the firm increasingly depends on effective control of costs. Its managers take a closer look at the various elements of cost—labor is usually a prime target—and, if they find a way to economize, they take it.

A MICROECONOMIC MODEL

Our microeconomic model assumes, therefore, a going concern, which has an established market share and a settled routine of production. Let us suppose that the firm is engaged in manufacturing. Its managers are charged with maximizing profits. One day, let us suppose, the production manager brings to top management a proposal to buy a machine that will perform certain production operations, tended by one employee. The same operations currently require the full-time services of five employees. Even if the firm has to borrow to buy the machine, it can probably save money each month by avoiding the wages and benefits of the four unneeded employees. After determining that the project has an attractive payback period, top management might decide to go ahead with it. The new machine, installed in the plant, would increase labor productivity, or the ratio between production volume and the worker-hours of labor input. If the costs of production were lowered, the firm would improve its profit margin, assuming that product volume and price stayed the same. The increased profits, in turn, would trigger events in other areas. Let us see what might happen in the case of a publicly held corporation.

With higher profits, the price of the company's stock might rise, benefitting the current shareholders. Dividends paid on that stock might be raised. Then, because the shareholders are happy, the top-level managers might feel more confident and secure in their jobs. Feeling more confident, they might seek additional compensation for themselves. The greater profit margins might also allow the firm to cut the price of its product. Such a decision would be expected to gain increased sales volume either by capturing a larger share of the market or by market expansion through lower prices. Although the margins of profit would be immediately reduced, per-unit production costs would again drop if sales volume rose. Profits would also rise. Management could then apply the money from the additional profits to further capital investment, debt reduction, sales-promotion activities, and so forth. The initial improvement in productivity and profits would make numerous good things happen—except for those four employees who were laid off.

Labor, however, would not long be denied. Because corporate profits were higher and top management had rewarded itself accordingly, other employees might feel justified in seeking higher pay and more benefits. The union would become more ambitious in its demands. Non-union employees, too, would expect a more generous reward. Labor costs would tend to rise at all levels to fill the financial space created by the increased profits. This cost increase, in turn, would generate further pressure to cut the wage bill through improved productivity. As the hourly cost of labor increased, more investment decisions would swing toward proposals to purchase "labor-saving" equipment. A vicious cycle would develop—increased productivity followed by improved wages followed by further increase in productivity and then more wage improvements—as employment levels progressively declined relative to production volume.

It is important to recognize that this upward spiral of productivity, profits, and wages would work to the advantage of the incumbent stockholders, managers, and workers only. Clearly, the former employees, whose termination brought the higher profits, would not benefit. Also, the improved productivity would tend to reduce the need for new employees to be hired in the future. In the short run at least, this would be a game with definite winners and losers. The top-level managers would consistently win. Since productivity improvements apply mainly to production processes, their managerial jobs would not be threatened. Instead, their incomes would tend to rise with the increased profits. Because those would be the people making the investment decisions, one can be sure that the firm would continue to push for productivity improvements. On the other hand, the jobs of production workers would be put in jeopardy by the same processes. For them, it would become a question of which persons should be thrown to the wolves.

Such a question can be answered in several ways. An obvious method to reduce employment would be for a firm to lay off the particular people whose labor it no longer needs. In some cases it might identify them by their type of occupation. The firm could also ask the layoff candidates to draw straws, or it might make a selection on the basis of individual job performance. A more common method, though, would be to eliminate the employee with less seniority. Some employers, carrying this method a step further, will promise not to lay off any employee, but instead achieve the desired reductions through attrition; this has also been called the "silent firing." Persons who quit the firm, or who die or retire, or are promoted, would not be replaced. Their positions would instead be eliminated. Although this method is considered to be a humane way to reduce staff, it also introduces a generational bias into the process. It shifts the burden of unemployment from the current job-holders to persons who might be seeking a job in the future. The opportunities for employment that would normally open up from time to time fail to occur.

There is an alternative. Suppose it was decided that, with increased profits, the company could afford to put employees on a shorter work schedule without reducing their pay. This reduced schedule of hours might take the form of a shorter work day, a 4-day workweek, longer vacations or more holidays, or some other arrangement. Regardless of its form, the reduction in hours would put increased pressure on the firm to produce the required volume of product with its present crew of workers. Their productive efficiency would tend to rise, both because of the more challenging production target and the increased incentive for management to streamline operations or invest in additional equipment. To the extent that the employees working more efficiently for shorter periods of time could not produce the volume of product that the market required, then the firm might feel a need to hire more workers. Otherwise, it would risk losing market share in failing to supply product that could be profitably sold. If the firm does decide to hire additional employees, the per-unit cost of production would tend to rise. In the long run, output as well would tend to rise because of stronger consumer demand for products. That would bring per-unit production costs back down again.

Some suggest that the choice confronting a worker is whether the worker personally prefers additional income with which to purchase additional goods and services or additional leisure time in order to relax or pursue other interests. This is only partly true. Another issue is how many employees will continue to be employed at the firm. If workers collectively decide to seek shorter work hours, they will be sparing certain of their colleagues the ordeal of being laid off as well as preserving future job opportunities. On the other hand, if they collectively decide to keep hours the same and pursue higher income, then jobs will continue to be eliminated as productivity improves. Therefore, the question of hours involves the question of social responsibility as well as personal preference. There is a tradeoff between work hours and employment, not just between income and leisure.

LEISURE AS AN AID TO ECONOMIC GROWTH

So far we have looked only at the production side of economic activity. The consumption side is also affected by decisions concerning hours. Not even the most dogmatic opponent of shorter hours can deny that some workers will lose their jobs as technology transforms production processes. However, a typical response to this visible displacement of labor is: What if some workers lose their jobs? They will find other jobs in other sectors of the economy. A dynamic economy such as ours is continually shedding certain kinds of jobs while creating others. The prudent strategy in such circumstances would not be to cling to the present arrangements, but rather to go with the flow of progress.

"Going with the flow of progress" has a nice, ringing sound to it, until one examines what "progress" brings. A new job does not automatically arise elsewhere in the economy because a job in automobile manufacturing, for instance, has been eliminated. The great seedbed of new jobs in a free-enterprise economy is what we call the "consumer market." Employment must be built around a product that people who have money want to buy. Alternatively, it can be tied to a public service financed through taxation. In the absence of a saleable product, or a compulsory funded service that dictates someone be hired to provide it, unemployed persons would be reduced to such marginal free-enterprising routines as hustling shoe shines or selling flowers on the street corner.

Some contend that the economy can generate an endless quantity and variety of useful products. Such products as the automobile, telephone, and television have become household necessities, although they did not exist a century ago. Why cannot such new products regularly appear, catering to humanity's boundless desires? Would they not become a sufficient source of new employment? The answer is that such products do appear, but they do not always bring enough new jobs. Why not? In the first place, many would-be purchasers of a consumer product lack the money to buy it. In the second place, the people who have money may lack the time to devote to the product, which would make its purchase worthwhile. For example, a person might enjoy sailing, and would consider buying a sailboat of his own for that reason. Upon second thought, however, he might decide against its purchase after considering the extra work involved in storing and maintaining the boat, especially if it were likely that it would receive only occasional weekend use. If he had more free time to devote to this product, his decision might be different. So consumer desire, in theory boundless, runs up against a certain natural limit: people's capacity usefully to consume products. That limit is pushed back—consumer capacity is enlarged—by the amount of free time that people can spend in the consuming process.

Many economists today seem to have forgotten this fact. Leisure is not, as they suppose, a drain on the economy, but a lubricant. Leisure is like the rain that nourishes abundant consumer crops. It is obvious that if people literally do not have the time to use a product, they will have no need to buy it; and that, in turn, makes them less likely actually to buy it. "The industry of this country could not long exist if factories generally went back to the 10-hour day, because the people would not have the time to consume the goods produced," Henry Ford once said. Ford noted specifically that "a workman would have little use for an automobile if he had to be in the shops from dawn until dusk."[1]

Technologically advanced products are not "free" with respect to a consumer's personal time. They carry with their purchase an implied commitment of that time to learn and arrange for their proper use. If a person buys an automatic dishwasher to cut down on household chores, for example, he will first need to invest hours of free time in shopping for the appliance, in arranging for its delivery and installation, and in reading the instruction manual. If the dishwasher breaks down, he can either invest more time in trying to fix it himself, or else call the repairman. Consumer products of this sort require knowledge. Acquiring that knowledge requires time. Part of a product's "convenience" is offset by additional problems that uninformed consumers unknowingly incur when they try to cope with its increased technological complexity.

Years ago, Ralph Waldo Emerson recommended a life of manual labor as a means of retaining knowledge and control of one's personal possessions. "A man who supplies his own want," Emerson wrote, "who builds a raft or a boat to go a fishing, finds it easy to caulk it, or put in a thole-pin, or mend the rudder. What he gets only as fast as he wants for his own ends, does not embarrass him, or take away his sleep with looking after. But when he comes to give all the goods he has year after year collected, in one estate to his son . . . the son finds his hands full—not to use these things—but to look after them. . . . To him they are not means, but masters. . . . [He] is made anxious by all that endangers those possessions, and is forced to spend so much time in guarding them, that he has quite lost sight of their original use."[2]

In this respect, services differ from goods as a type of consumer product. Services save the time that would be required to gain knowledge. Instead of tinkering with a gadget to make it work, one engages the services of a repairman who has the knowledge already to accomplish that purpose. One hires an attorney, a tax-return preparer, or psychiatrist to perform a function that one, though theoretically free to perform the function oneself, anticipates will be professionally handled in less time and with fewer mistakes. Maybe the shortage of personal free time in our society has played a part in shifting economic growth from the goods-producing sector to the services-providing sector. Because of their greater convenience or use to consumers with respect to saving time, services tend to have a more elastic demand than goods. The services-providing industries are growing faster than the goods-producing industries, both in volume of output and employment.

On the other hand, jobs in the expanding services industries generally do not pay as well as ones in the shrinking industries of goods production did. Why not? It is largely because the services industries are labor-intensive, and, therefore, the opportunities for improving productivity and profits through capital investment are less. If service-sector employers could save money by investing in equipment and laying off people while maintaining the level of service to customers, they could then afford to pay higher wages to the remaining employees. Almost by definition, though, services require the direct involvement of people in the productive work. Human labor in this sector is less easily replaced by machines.

Some services are, of course, well-compensated. An attorney, doctor, or certified public accountant may charge $100 an hour or more to perform a particular service for clients. The high fee is often justified by the more difficult or extensive knowledge required to provide the service; and to acquire this knowledge, a professional worker must spend more time and money for education. However, that is only part of the reason for the high fees. For $100 an hour, the free market could supply any number of persons with the knowledge to be able and willing to perform most services. But the market for professional services is not free. State licensing procedures, effectively controlled by the profession itself, have created a quasi-monopolistic market that protects high incomes by restricting labor supply. Typically, the profession's "code of professional ethics" prohibits the more aggressive kinds of marketing activities. The phenomenon of the lucrative professions is, therefore, less an illustration of the economics of the services sector than of its politics.

EFFECT OF HOURS LEGISLATION

Now let us look at the macroeconomic events in reducing work time. On an economy-wide level, such a change might be put into effect through legislation. In the United States, the main law governing work hours is the Fair Labor Standards Act (FLSA) of 1938. Reductions in work hours would be made through amendment of this law. Rep. John Conyers of Michigan has introduced bills to that effect in the last several sessions of Congress. None of these bills has yet passed.

The bill that Rep. John Conyers has most recently introduced would amend, or update, the FLSA of 1938 in several respects. First, it would reduce the standard workweek in stages from 40 to 32 hours over an eight-year period. Second, it would increase the rate of penalty pay for overtime from time-and-a-half to double-time. Third, it would prohibit mandatory-overtime clauses in labor contracts. Organized labor has traditionally supported measures of this sort.

The idea of reducing the workweek through legislation is, of course, not new. Neither would Rep. Conyers' bill establish a new law. The proposed legislation would merely bring existing law up to date with economic changes that have taken place during the almost half century since the FLSA was originally enacted. The time-and-a-half overtime premium has become an ineffective deterrent as the cost of fringe benefits and of hiring and training new employees has increased relative to that of the extra half-time pay. The 40-hour workweek for human beings is no longer required in production processes that have loaded much of the work on machines. (Professor Wassily Leontief goes so far as to compare human workers today with the work horse, which was replaced by tractors and trucks in the early part of this century.[3]) Yet the legal mechanism to reduce work hours through economic disincentives rather than coercion would allow flexibility in making the change to shorter hours.

No employer would be required to change the schedule of work hours in response to enactment of this law. What would be required is that the employer pay a higher hourly wage during the overtime period (i.e., time worked beyond the weekly standard). If it is financially advantageous or necessary to do so, the employer can continue to schedule long hours. If not, the employer might want to cut the work schedule to avoid the higher costs. Such a provision is found in Section 7(a)1 of the FLSA, which reads as follows: "Except as otherwise provided in this section, no employer shall employ any of his employees who in any workweek is engaged in commerce or in the production of goods for commerce, or is employed in an enterprise engaged in commerce or in the production of goods for commerce, for a workweek longer than forty hours unless such employee receives compensation for his employment in excess of the hours above specified at a rate not less than one and one-half times the regular rate at which he is employed."[4]

How would wages be affected? Nothing in the law requires that a particular adjustment be made in workers' hourly or weekly wages, as the workweek is reduced. Still, if working hours were reduced gradually, employees would likely receive at least the same weekly wages (and increased hourly wages) for two reasons: First, the reduction in hours would take place not only in periods of recession, when employers can ill afford to give raises, but also in periods of economic expansion. Normal year-to-year increases in productivity would finance part of the gain. Society, and indirectly employers, would also reap the benefit of cost savings in unemployment compensation, welfare, and early retirement.

Second, to shorten the workweek would ease the supply of labor relative to demand. With lower unemployment, fewer people would be chasing jobs, so that employers would have to offer higher wages to attract and retain needed workers. In other words, balance would be restored in the supply and demand for labor, tending to firm up wages.

Lest it appear that shorter hours would work to the disadvantage of employers, one should recognize that from the employer's standpoint, the additional wages paid to newly hired workers represent not only higher labor costs but also an extra dose of consumer purchasing power. Those wages are not lost, but are recycled through the economy in the form of dollars saved for investment, taxed by the government, or spent for various goods and services. Instead of the pittance that unemployed workers and welfare recipients have to spend on consumer products, the employed workers would presumably be paid a living wage. Their additional input, both as producers and consumers, would expand the volume of economic activity beyond what it would have been, had they remained without a job. As the economy expands, businesses of all kinds would enjoy increased sales revenues and profits. Ultimately, production costs might be lowered because the fixed-cost component of a product's cost would be covered by a larger number of produced units, tending to offset the initial increase in direct-labor costs.

SOME INTERNATIONAL EXPERIENCES

All this may be a bit too theoretical. Experiences differ, of course, between employers, as between different national economies and different periods in time. With respect to the employment consequences, which are the primary policy concern, the record is complicated by a variety of factors. Generally the evidence points to increased employment, but the number of new jobs created or old ones saved may be reduced by productivity improvements through greater capital investment or elimination of nonproductive functions.

A campaign by the Australian trade unions in the late 1970s brought a reduction in work schedules from 40 hours to 38 or 35 hours in a number of industries, sometimes in the form of "rostered" schedules— for example, a 38-hour week consisting of 19 work days followed by 1 extra day off over a 4-week cycle. Productivity "offsets," guaranteed to the employer, were sometimes included in the agreement for reduced hours. A case study by an Australian government agency of firms that reduced hours found that changes in employment depend on "the relative strength of the reductions in man hours and in standard hours" as against increases in planned capital stock, as well as on adaptations made in the area of work schedules or rules. One firm at the Altona petrochemical complex in Victoria, which adopted a 35-hour week, increased its employment of production workers by 25 percent and total employment by 7 percent as a result of adding a fifth shift. Another was able to avoid employment increases by working out an agreement with the union to reduce production shift teams from 5 to 4 persons.

The Australian government report, issued in 1984, observed that

in none of the case studies, including those where productivity increased, did employment fall over the short term. However, over the longer term it is possible that in some cases employment levels will be allowed to fall through natural wastage. It was also observed that where productivity offsets take the form of reduced manning levels per shift, there is less of a need to increase employment over the short term so as to maintain output. The key question here, though, is whether the net effect of these lower manning levels, along with any other sustained productivity offsets, will be strong enough to increase both a firm's desired level of output and its demand for labour services. In some cases, the transition from a desired to an actual increase in output could take a longer period than covered by the case studies. There is also the more general point that improved productivity in one firm can assist those which it supplies to contain their costs. This can be expected to have a generally beneficial effect on employment. Perhaps the most interesting case study observation was that increased employment can sometimes be a *prior* condition for achieving productivity offsets, e.g., where there is an increase in machine running time during current operating hours.[5]

European studies also suggest that jobs can be created or saved when weekly work schedules are shortened. Rolande Cuvillier's book, *The Reduction of Working Time,* published by the International Labor Office in 1984, reports the following:

In the Federal Republic of Germany, it is estimated that in spite of gains in productivity, reductions in normal weekly working hours made it possible to provide the equivalent of 200,000 jobs, with almost the same number coming as a result of lengthening annual leave.... In Austria the Council for Economic and Social Affairs estimated that reduction in working time brought about a 60 percent increase in employment between 1959 and 1975, after allowing for gains in productivity and leaving economic fluctuations out of account. During this period weekly working hours fell to 40 from between 45 and 48 and annual leave increased first to three weeks and then to four. In France an annual fall of 30 minutes in average weekly working between 1967 and 1976 is said to have resulted in the creation of 50,000 jobs a year, despite gains in productivity and leaving out of account the effects of economic growth. According to another estimate, any jobs that were created in France in the 1970s were due entirely to reduction in average working time, since productivity and output have risen only very slowly since 1973.[6]

HOW WOULD SHORTER WORK HOURS AFFECT WASTE?

One can also raise the more general question of how a reduction in work hours might affect the kinds of products and activities brought forth in the economy. In particular, how might it affect an economy of waste? It is clear that, if waste is the main element being eliminated in economic activity, there can be little objection to reducing worktime. The economy can certainly afford to do that, if the price to be paid is to keep fewer people in prisons, prepare for less war, be exposed to fewer commercial advertisements, and so forth. At the same time one cannot predict with any degree of confidence that waste will beat a graceful retreat if its economic necessity disappears. It may be, for instance, that the legal system will continue mercilessly to insist on its privileges and, in effect, mandate a continuation in that form of waste. Such problems would have to be addressed by other means.

Because the situation is rather unprecedented, no one knows for sure how or if waste might contract with a change in economic conditions. The following discussion will take a stab at such a prediction. In general it would seem that, if average work hours were cut, one might expect that the economy would produce less waste. Reduced production would put additional pressure on the economy to furnish necessities, which people, by definition, need. Under this additional pressure to produce necessities, labor would shift back into the productive sectors of industry, and away from the sectors of waste. A shortage of food, for instance, would drive up the price of food, and that would draw additional resources to its production. The comparatively inelastic demand for necessities relative to the demand for discretionary products makes their price more sensitive to fluctuations in supply. Predictably, then, marketplace forces would draw labor away from waste and toward useful production, reversing the trend of recent years.

Of course, such predictions are pure speculation. We have never experienced this kind of situation before. The experience of the two world wars comes closest, perhaps, to demonstrating the shift in resources when a sudden scarcity of labor is created. It seems safer to suppose that, had the workweek been reduced ten or twenty years ago, the U.S. economy might not have developed its present tendencies to waste, than to predict their disappearance if working hours are cut in the future. Manpower might have stayed where it was, having never been displaced. Waste, once created, develops self-perpetuating constituencies. Livelihoods and career interests are at stake. When waste becomes a large part of the system, it attracts the defensive efforts of some people, regardless of merit.

Part of the reason that the U.S. economy tolerates waste to the extent that it does may be simply that people need jobs, which the productive sectors of industry are unable to furnish. There is therefore less moral resistance to waste than otherwise. If, on the other hand, the economy could provide enough jobs in the productive sector, there would be no purpose in keeping unneeded functions alive. That is not to say that persons or groups with a vested interest in waste would give up without a fight. They certainly would not. However, the economy would develop new opportunities, and, perhaps, inspire other priorities. A smaller economic surplus could well bring a smaller tolerance of waste.

Shorter work hours might themselves allow a reduction in certain kinds of waste. For instance, if one accepts the argument that reduced work schedules would create more jobs and that less unemployment tends to reduce crime, then one would anticipate that the economy might rid itself of certain crime-related functions and costs. More and better-paying jobs for teenagers could mean that fewer of them would be lured into street crime, prostitution, or drug dealing. A better balance in the supply of jobs relative to demand might ease the competition among working people to acquire unreasonably advanced academic credentials. They would have little stomach for job-training programs without a future. Reduced unemployment might also ease certain of the psychological and social problems that have been linked to joblessness, including alcoholism, domestic abuse, and mental or physical illness. Nations would no longer have to go to war to create jobs. The mania to export products (and unemployment) to foreign countries might subside. Workers frustrated in a career would have real alternatives. Ultimately that might produce a revitalized and happier workforce.

Increased leisure, too, might reduce the stress and strain of daily living, which, in turn, could ease the demand for health-care services of various kinds. If parents spent more time at home with their children and with each other, the children presumably would receive better parental supervision, which could reduce the caseload of social workers and clear the juvenile-court docket. More people with leisure would have more time for volunteer services in the community. The elderly might be visited more often by younger relatives. More free time might advance the quality of leisure-related activity beyond casual beer drinking, television viewing, and spectator sports. Houses might be kept in better repair. Schools might attract more students out of real interest in the course materials. More inventions might be hatched in garage or basement workshops. If a person spends most of his waking hours at work, his time away from work will be spent mainly in sleeping, eating, and attending to other of life's basic needs. His most ambitious recreational idea will be to sit in front of a television set, sipping beer or soft drinks. More free time frees up more time for purposes beyond rest and recuperation.

There is no reason, in fact, why "free" time cannot become additional time for work. The work, however, would more likely be self-directed. Such work would allow fuller pursuit of one's own dreams in time once devoted to serving institutional agendas. Some pundits have suggested that the average American worker lacks the capacity for self-direction. We disagree. The greatness of our nation has always been found in its opportunities for individual endeavors, and not in enforcing conformity to bureaucratic plans. If U.S. society is to make a successful adjustment to the challenge of our times, we must, to paraphrase yesterday's conservatives, "get government (and economic concerns generally) off peoples' backs." Increased leisure, not producing more money and taxes, points the way to our more hopeful future as a full-functioning democracy.

10
INTERNATIONAL
WORK-SHARING

The conventional wisdom holds that the U.S. economy cannot afford to reduce hours at this time because of the nation's continuing problems with trade competition. There is an argument that runs like this: If the standard workweek were cut from 40 to 35 hours and workers received the same weekly pay as before, it would amount to a 14.3 percent increase in their hourly wage, assuming that actual hours followed the standard. This would mean a large increase in labor costs, which the employer would have to absorb in some way. With moderate profit margins, a likely outcome would be that the employer would raise the price of products. Higher prices would bring reduced product demand. Domestically, the competitive impact of this change would be a wash, because all suppliers of a product would be subject to the same hours regulations. Internationally, the effect would be different. If work hours were reduced in the United States but not in the nations that are our principal trade rivals, then U.S.-made goods would compete at a disadvantage in international markets because of their higher labor costs and prices. The effect would be a loss of market share to foreign imports, which in turn, would bring reduced domestic production and employment.

EVIDENCE BEARING ON THIS QUESTION

The trouble with this type of argument is its lack of an empirical reference. In a theoretical discussion, one can always select particular aspects of a situation which favor one's own theories and pretend that the others have no bearing. Unfortunately, the debate about the shorter

Table 10.1
Manufacturing Workweek and Merchandise Trade Balance for Several
Industrialized Nations, 1955–1984: Countries with Trade Surpluses (trade
balance in millions of U.S. dollars)

Year	Canada mfg. work= week	Canada trade balance	Japan mfg. work= week	Japan trade balance	West Germany mfg. work= week	West Germany trade balance
1955	41.0	(240)	45.7	(460)	48.8	342
1960	40.4	(96)	47.8	(436)	45.6	1,311
1965	41.1	134	44.3	283	44.1	420
1970	39.7	2,868	43.3	437	43.8	4,375
1971	39.7	2,203	42.6	4,307	43.0	4,699
1972	40.0	1,481	42.3	5,121	42.7	6,292
1973	39.6	2,096	42.0	(1,383)	42.8	12,649
1974	38.9	749	40.0	(6,582)	41.9	19,664
1975	38.6	(2,445)	38.8	(2,040)	40.4	15,240
1976	38.7	953	40.2	2,427	41.4	13,741
1977	38.7	2,222	40.3	9,696	41.7	16,618
1978	38.8	3,081	40.6	18,204	41.6	20,703
1979	38.8	2,770	41.1	(7,626)	41.8	12,181
1980	38.5	6,690	41.2	(10,711)	41.6	4,929
1981	38.5	4,330	41.0	8,729	41.1	12,109
1982	37.7	16,679	40.9	6,979	40.7	20,572
1983	38.4	15,377	41.1	20,276	40.5	18,145
1984	38.5	16,654	41.7	33,640	41.0	18,538

*Source:*Prepared by the author.

workweek and its economic consequences has been dominated by academic and other experts who merely assert a conclusion and are believed. We will insist that the discussion of work hours and trade include some examination of facts.

In Tables 10.1 and 10.2, the average manufacturing workweeks of several nations are compared with the merchandise trade balances for the same nations in certain years. Three of the nations—Japan, Canada, and West Germany—have achieved large surpluses in their trading with the United States. These nations, especially Japan and West Germany, also happen to show relatively large reductions in their manufacturing workweeks since the 1950s. The United States, South Korea, and South Africa stand out for their longer workweeks or lack of progress in shortening hours. All three show a negative balance of trade. The United States, in particular, has progressed from trade surpluses in the early years to enormous deficits. Its manufacturing workers received virtually no improvement in hours during that period. West Germany, on the

Table 10.2
Manufacturing Workweek and Merchandise Trade Balance for Several Industrialized Nations, 1955–1984: Countries with Trade Deficits (trade balance in millions of U.S. dollars)

Year	United States mfg. work=week	United States trade balance	South Korea mfg. work=week	South Korea trade balance	South Africa mfg. work=week	South Africa trade balance
1955	40.7	3,988	–	(323)	–	(224)
1960	39.7	5,537	–	(311)	45.0	(231)
1965	41.2	6,101	57.0	(288)	46.1	(697)
1970	39.8	2,834	52.3	(1,148)	47.1	(1,275)
1971	39.9	(2,018)	51.9	(1,326)	47.1	(1,630)
1972	40.6	(6,323)	51.6	(898)	46.5	(885)
1973	40.7	1,590	51.3	(1,015)	47.5	(1,188)
1974	40.0	(9,968)	50.0	(2,392)	48.5	(2,327)
1975	39.5	2,233	50.5	(2,193)	46.6	(2,137)
1976	40.1	(17,085)	52.5	(1,059)	46.1	(1,527)
1977	40.3	(39,118)	52.9	(763)	46.5	675
1978	40.4	(42,278)	53.0	(2,261)	47.0	1,080
1979	40.2	(40,203)	52.0	(5,283)	47.7	(1,095)
1980	39.7	(36,198)	53.1	(4,787)	48.4	(4,606)
1981	39.8	(39,613)	53.7	(4,877)	48.2	(8,835)
1982	38.9	(42,609)	53.7	(2,397)	47.1	(7,950)
1983	40.1	(69,340)	54.4	(1,747)	46.2	(5,450)
1984	40.5	(94,599)	54.3	(1,386)	46.5	(5,622)

Source: Prepared by the author.

other hand, has enjoyed widening trade surpluses, even while its average manufacturing workweek has dropped.

An article on work-sharing in *Monthly Labor Review* pointed out that "short-time compensation probably helped German manufacturers in the mechanical engineering industry to compete with U.S. manufacturers in the nonelectrical machinery industry during the 1974–75 period. As demand declined, the Germans could muster both heavy work sharing and some reduction in force to maintain productivity, allowing them to retain skilled personnel without adding to the unemployment insurance taxes. U.S. manufacturers not only faced higher unemployment taxes for whatever layoffs occurred, but also had less flexibility to maintain productivity through work sharing as a supplemental labor adjustment tool."[1]

In Japan's case, the manufacturing workweek has come down almost as fast as in West Germany. In the late 1960s, the Japanese Ministry of Labor launched a campaign to encourage the larger manufacturing firms to convert from a 6-day week to a 5-day week, mainly to counter the "sweatshop" image of Japanese manufactured goods. This change did not seem to hurt Japan's competitive position. An article in the *Wall Street Journal* on January 18, 1973, reported:

The Japanese five-day week would seem like good news for U.S. companies battling tough Japanese competition. After all, a shorter workweek should mean less production. It should—but it doesn't. For the Japanese are working harder than ever, and companies that have cut the workweek say that, if anything, production is rising.... One reason Japan succeeds in world business is that it works hard, analysts say. But how hard it works seems to have little to do with how long it works. Average weekly working hours in Japan have been falling steadily for years. Employees were at the job 45.8 hours a week in 1967; by the end of 1971, this had decreased to 42.5 hours.... "And in just that period, productivity has been rising, wages have been rising, and they're still selling to us like mad," the U.S. labor economist says.[2]

Australia is a country that lately has taken the lead in reducing work-time. An agency of the Australian government, the Bureau of Industry Economics, studied the impact of hours reductions during the 1980–1982 period on that nation's economy. Its report, issued in 1984, concluded that "the recent decline in standard hours in Australia has probably not, in itself, contributed significantly to a weakening in the competitiveness of Australian products on international markets over the past decade." A principal finding of the study was that "productivity offsets" had compensated for a large part of the potentially higher labor costs incurred through shorter hours. In some cases, such as the agreement for a 35-hour week at the Altona petrochemical complex near Melbourne, these offsets were written into the labor contract. The study further found that "firms can be paying for a considerable amount of unproductive man hours. A reduction in the standard workweek can then be partly accommodated by some reduction in unproductive time."[3]

Studies that attempt to correlate changes in average work hours with changes in trade positions are speculative at best. A nation's competitive strength in international markets involves many economic variables, of which the length of the workweek may be relatively unimportant. There are some particular difficulties in analyzing trade results from an hours perspective. First, the fact that business managers are not ideologically neutral toward the length of work hours may influence patterns of investment and location of jobs. Many would associate employees' willingness to work long hours with a favorable business climate, and so would tend to move business operations to areas which tolerate such conditions. Second, nations with rapidly developing national economies characteristically run trade deficits in the early years. These change to surpluses as the industries mature. Their workweeks start out long and later come down. So there would seem to be a correlation between trade surpluses and shorter hours, but actually not. Third, it is difficult to correlate changes in hours and trade balances on a year-to-year basis. If shorter workweeks "cause" higher labor costs and loss of trade competitiveness, the deleterious effect might not appear immediately but several years later. Both trade balances and the level of work hours are strongly influenced by swings in the business cycle. The cumulative effect of reduced hours on labor costs and prices may be overshadowed by more immediate fluctuations in the economy.

If shorter hours hurt trade competitiveness via their impact on labor costs, then another set of figures might be helpful. Table 10.3 shows the average annual percentage change in average work hours, hourly compensation, and unit labor costs, expressed both in national currencies and in U.S. dollars, for the United States, Canada, Japan, and nine European countries in the period 1960–1984. U.S. manufacturing industries reduced their workweek by a smaller amount than in any other country between 1960 and 1984, and also gave production workers the smallest increase in hourly compensation. On the other hand, the U.S. industries' annual increases in per-unit labor costs, expressed in U.S. dollars, were the smallest of the twelve industrialized countries. This is surprising in view of arguments that rising labor costs adversely affect a nation's balance of trade. The United States moved from regular trade surpluses to large trade deficits during the same period when its manufacturing industries were burdened with relatively small increases in per-unit labor costs. Japan, on the other hand, moved from trade deficits to surpluses, despite large annual increases in labor costs. Such statistics also tend to refute arguments concerning a tradeoff between shorter hours and higher pay.

The best-informed opinon on this subject is that concerns (that reduced work hours will jeopardize a nation's trade position) have a real foundation, but are often exaggerated. During the 1930s, when the 40-hour week was debated in regards to high unemployment, the International Labor Organization (ILO) investigated the trade implications. "Can one say that countries which make efforts to regulate labor supply ... are ipso facto at a disadvantage in international competition?" a 1931 study asked. "Experience appears to show that the countries with the most advanced labor legislations are by no means the least successful in the competition for world markets. ... It is difficult to establish a definite connection of cause and effect in this subject, and the conclusions advanced on both sides are necessarily in the nature of conjectures."[4]

A 1975 ILO publication, *Hours of Work in Industrialised Countries* by Archibald A. Evans, treats the trade question in the following manner:

Table 10.3
**Average Annual Percentage Change in Average Hours, Hourly
Compensation, Unit Labor Costs in Local Currency, and Unit Labor Costs
in U.S. Dollars for Manufacturing Industries in Several Countries, 1960–
1984**

Country	Average Annual Percentage Change, 1960-1984			
	Average Weekly Hours	Hourly Compensation	Unit Labor Costs in Local Currency	Unit Labor Costs in U.S. Dollars
United States	-0.1%	7.2%	4.7%	4.7%
Canada	-0.3%	9.2%	5.6%	4.9%
Japan	-0.7%	13.6%	4.9%	7.5%
France	-0.8%	12.7%	6.7%	5.7%
West Germany	-0.9%	9.7%	4.6%	8.1%
Italy	-1.4%	16.8%	10.7%	7.0%
United Kingdom	-0.7%	13.6%	9.8%	7.0%
Denmark	-1.1%	12.8%	6.8%	6.6%
Netherlands	-1.1%	12.0%	5.0%	7.3%
Norway	-1.1%	11.6%	7.7%	8.8%
Belgium	-1.3%	12.3%	4.8%	6.1%
Sweden	-1.3%	11.8%	6.8%	6.4%

*Source:*Prepared by the author.

International competition has also been constantly advanced as an argument
against reducing hours of work in one country if competing countries did not
carry through a similar reduction at more or less the same time. In practice, it
would appear that the dangers of increased competition, though they are certainly real up to a point, have been overrated. Costs in the country reducing
hours of work are not likely to be proportionately increased and there are often
many other factors of greater importance affecting competition, including levels
of productivity, the existence or absence of tariffs and other obstacles to international trade, marketing difficulties and exchange rate fluctuations. Reductions
of working hours have also tended to follow similar trends in large groups of
industrial countries, even if some of them were somewhat ahead or behind
others.[5]

WOULD A U.S. HOURS REDUCTION BE UNILATERAL?

The last sentence in the quotation above leads to another point, which is worth noting. Arguments that shorter work hours would hurt trade competitiveness assume that a nation is alone in implementing the hours reduction. Obviously, if the manufacturing workweek is reduced simultaneously and at the same rate in two nations that are trade rivals, whatever impact the change might have on labor costs would affect both nations the same. Neither would derive a competitive advantage from the hours change. Table 10.4 gives the changes in average manufacturing hours in a number of countries in recent years. The countries are listed in descending order by the magnitude of their workweek declines, measured in annual percentage change over the period shown. It is certainly foolish to be worrying that the U.S. economy might be competitively hurt from unilateral reductions in the workweek. In reality, most other nations were unilaterally reducing their workweeks relative to those in the United States.

What assurance have we in the United States that other nations would follow our lead if the U.S. government enacted shorter-workweek legislation? If we negotiated multinational agreements or treaties to that effect, the assurance would be quite strong. Even if we did not, the evidence of recent years points to a real possibility that other industrialized countries might consider hours reductions to address their own domestic problems. The United States would not have to educate or exhort others to reduce hours; we are the laggards. With the least recent experience of reduced hours, U.S. policymakers are the most convinced that such a move might harm the economy.

In the United States, the 40-hour week has been the legal standard for such a long time that we are apt to forget that the struggle to reduce work hours is a part of contemporary history; not so in Europe, where Saturday work was the norm in the years immediately following World War II. Americans believe that working hours are a matter to be negotiated between particular unions and employers, or, secondarily, for organized labor to seek in special-interest legislation. In western Europe, more emphasis is put on cooperative discussions between labor, management, and government in what is sometimes called a "tripartite" decision-making process. Typically government ratifies, through law, agreements reached between the other two social partners. The policy-seeking dialogue can take place within particular industries at the national level or, lately, at a supranational level in such bodies as the European Parliament or the European Community (EEC).

By now, the 40-hour week is the standard in most Western industrialized countries. While the U.S. economy continues to coast on schedules of work largely unchanged in the past 30 years, the Europeans retain a

Table 10.4
Average Manufacturing Workweek in Several Industrialized Nations, 1955–1985

Nation	1955	1960	1965	1970	1975	1980	1985
Finland	44.0	44.4	44.0	38.3	33.8	33.2	32.3
Belgium			40.8	37.9	34.8	33.4	33.1
Denmark			39.7	36.2	33.1	32.6	32.5
Hungary m	186	181	179	165	162	161	145
Poland m			177	172	163	159	153
Netherlands *	48.8	48.8	46.1	44.2	40.9	40.8	40.3
Spain		43.5	44.4	44.1	42.7	41.3	38.6
Greece		44.2	43.8	44.6	42.7	40.7	39.3
West Germany *	48.8	45.6	44.1	43.8	40.4	41.6	40.7
France	44.9	45.7	45.6	44.8	41.7	40.7	38.6
Czechoslovakia		48.1	47.7	43.8	43.6	43.5	43.1
Japan	45.7	47.8	44.3	43.3	38.8	41.2	41.5
United Kingdom- men		47.4	46.1	44.9	42.7	41.9	43.0
United Kingdom- women		40.4	38.6	37.7	36.8	37.3	38.1
Switzerland	47.7	46.1	44.9	44.7	44.5	43.8	42.9
Israel *		41.9	41.9	42.1	40.3	38.3	38.7
Ireland	45.1	45.4	44.0	42.7	41.5	41.1	41.1
Cyprus *	45	43	46	45	43	41	41
Portugal			44.8	44.8	41.8	39.0	38.1
Canada	41.0	40.4	41.1	39.7	38.6	38.5	38.8
Soviet Union		42.1	40.2	40.6	40.7	40.5	40.3 #
United States *	40.7	39.7	41.2	39.8	39.5	39.7	40.5
New Zealand		40.4	40.7	40.4	40.8	39.6	40.2
Puerto Rico	35.8	36.4	36.9	36.6	37.0	38.0	38.4
South Africa		45.0	46.1	47.1	46.6	48.4	46.2
Mexico		46.3	45.5	45.1	45.6	46.6	46.4 #
Peru		45.3	48.4	–	46.1	45.6	44.8
Guatemala *	45.4	45.6	46.1	45.9	47.2	45.1	46.5 #
Singapore	47.7	46.4	47.2	48.7	48.4	48.6	47.0
South Korea *			57.0	52.3	50.5	53.1	53.8

* hours paid for
m hours per month
reported for 1984 instead of 1985

Source: Prepared by the author.

sense of forward momentum. Thus the first moves to crack the 40-hour barrier have been made on the other side of the Atlantic. In France, the socialist government of François Mitterrand came to power in May 1981 with a campaign platform that featured the 35-hour week. Legally the French workweek is 39 hours, and efforts are underway to chop off more hours. The French government has encouraged employers and workers to negotiate "contracts of solidarity," which would combine reduced hours with new jobs for the unemployed. Reduced social security contributions were offered as an incentive. "If organized labor wants to remain a force of social change... it must become a medium for new work patterns and life styles," said Edmond Maire, general secretary of the French Democratic Confederation of Labor (CFDT). "From now on, the utilization of leisure time is a social preoccupation of the first order."[6]

In Denmark, the legal workweek has recently been reduced from 40 to 39 hours as the result of a compromise agreement reached by the national government when it intervened in labor negotiations two years earlier. In Sweden, where 40-hour workweeks are combined with 5-week minimum annual vacations, 9-month maternity or paternity leave, phased retirement, and other types of leisure, workers' actual time worked per year averages about 1500 hours, compared with 1900 hours in the United States.[7] Belgium and the Netherlands are two other European countries that have made great progress toward shorter hours. Collective-bargaining agreements in Belgium, for instance, have reduced workweeks to 36–39 hours for a majority of workers, although the legal standard remains 40 hours.[8]

In July 1984, I.G. Metall, the world's largest free trade union, won an agreement for a 38.5-hour workweek for West Germany's steel and automobile workers after a seven-week strike. Herman Rebhan, general secretary of the International Metalworkers Federation, proudly declared: "The 40-hour week is now in the dustbin of industrial history. Over the next few years we shall see working time continually nibbled at and reduced. By the late 1980s most of the industrialised world will be on 35 hours or less, and in a decade we shall see the first 30-hour agreements."[9]

An active campaign to achieve shorter hours has been waged as well at the supranational level. In May 1979, the European Trade Union Confederation, a principal force behind this campaign, resolved to seek an immediate 10 percent reduction in total worktime per worker without loss of wages by various means, including a 35-hour workweek, 6-week annual paid vacation, retirement at age 60, and extended education and career training. Discussions have been held between European employers and trade unionists, under the auspices of the European Commission, seeking a consensus on the level of hours reduction.[10] While the Europeans are sensitive to the dangers of trade competition, they also recognize the socially damaging result of allowing unemployment to remain high. The current president of the European Trade Union Confederation, Georges Debunne, has said: "The ETUC feels that as a start [toward shorter hours] must be made somewhere—and soon—Europe is the ideal point of departure. A Pan-European solution would have a better chance of success than either individual national plans, which would be complicated by competitiveness between countries, or a world plan which would entail a long wait, with neither a short- nor medium-term solution."[11]

Both the Commission of the European Communities and the European Parliament have officially taken positions in favor of reducing worktime to fight unemployment. "The case for seeking to maintain and create jobs through the reduction of working time rests principally on the desirability of achieving greater [social] equity at a time of very high and rising unemployment," suggested a Commission memorandum. "It is important to avoid the hardening of two distinct groups in society—those with stable employment and those without—a development which would have disruptive social consequences and would endanger the very foundations of our democratic societies in the longer run."[12]

In its recommendation to the European Council in September 1983, the Commission invited member states "to reaffirm the need for a strategy at the Community level to combat the problem of unemployment, and within that framework, for a common approach to the reduction and reorganization of working time, as an instrument of economic and social policy; to acknowledge as the principal policy aims of such a common approach: to bring about a reduction in individual working time, combined with its reorganization, sufficiently substantial to support the positive development of employment, under conditions which safeguard competitivity as well as basic social rights; to limit more strictly systematic overtime and increasingly to compensate necessary overtime by time off in lieu rather than by additional [wage] payments."[13] The European Parliament has declared its support of Community measures that "guarantee in the short term a significant reduction in daily, weekly, and/or yearly working hours and in working life, in order significantly to slow down and subsequently halt the trend towards growing unemployment."[14]

At the world level, the ILO serves as a clearinghouse for information about working hours in all nations, and has set international labor standards in many areas. Although its most advanced workweek standard remains 40 hours, the ILO continues to encourage further improvements. The ILO's director-general, Francis Blanchard, has suggested that

substantial progress can be made to shorten working hours if it is based on three considerations. The first is that the economic difficulties point clearly to the need to tackle the problem in a regional and international framework so as to reduce the effect on inflation and balance of payments. The second is that rather than pursue a uniform reduction to 35 hours, realism and wisdom point to a diversified approach by branch of activity and exploring all ways of regulating working time. Thirdly, it is essential to rely to the maximum degree possible on employers' and workers' organizations to advance solutions through negotiations. These should be encouraged by governments and, if need be, helped. The ILO stands ready to contribute its expertise and assistance.[15]

The long workweeks prevalent in South Korea, Singapore, China, Latin America, and other Third World areas obviously pose an inhibiting barrier to further improvements in the industrialized countries. Japan, on the other hand, has moved a considerable distance toward worldclass treatment of labor. The Japanese Ministry of Labor has actively promoted the conversion of industry from a 6-day week to what it calls the "two-holidays system." Recognizing the political dangers of an unbalanced economy, the Japanese government has encouraged policy discussions aimed at increasing leisure time, which put pressure on employers in particular industries to close on weekends. Motoyuki Miyano, managing director of the Leisure Development Center, states that the issue "is nothing less than better trade relations between the U.S. and Japan," a *Wall Street Journal* article reported. "If the Japanese worked less and played more, he says, Japanese competitiveness might drop just a bit, lessening trade frictions with the U.S. and Europe. 'How do we do this? We're hoping to decrease working hours per year to 1,500 hours from 2,100 hours, and increase leisure time by almost 40%,' he says. More leisure also would stimulate Japan's service sector and overall economy, he adds, satisfying critics both in the U.S. and in Japan."[16]

Japan's former prime minister, Yasuhiro Nakasone, endorsed this type of argument, saying that "the time has come for Japan to make a historical transformation in its traditional policies on economic management and the nation's lifestyle." He was responding to a report of an advisory committee that called on the Japanese people to work less, save less, and have more free time. Unless these changes were made, Nakasone said, there could be "no further development for Japan." While the report aroused a certain controversy among those who doubted that Japan could afford to relax its competitive efforts, the conclusion was that Japan had to develop a different style of living and working in order to keep its place in a stable world economy. "We are not telling people to give up the traditional virtue of diligence," said Haruo Mayekawa, a former Bank of Japan governor, who chaired the advisory committee; but he added: "I think it is simply miserable that a large number of Japanese continue to live in small homes so far from work, where they toil long hours, leaving insufficient time for rest and leisure."[17]

On May 23, 1988, the Economic Council of Japan published its New Economic Five Year Plan, covering the period from 1988 to 1992. The plan called for the nation's real economic growth rate to rise by 3¾ percent annually, and for annual working hours to decline to a level "as close as possible to 1,800 hours." If fully implemented, this recommendation would give Japanese workers more leisure than their counterparts in the United States. Meanwhile, the Japanese government has made arrangements for the increased use of leisure by developing recreational and cultural programs and constructing new facilities. The "Law of Building Resort," enacted in May 1987, provides for three new resort centers to be constructed in Japan, which would accommodate several million visitors each year. In addition, a council has been established and placed within the Leisure Development Center to prepare for increased travel to foreign countries. Thus the new financial capability of Japan is being matched by a commitment to more enjoyable lives for its workers.[18]

While the Japanese example is often cited as a reason to deprive U.S. workers of additional leisure, it in fact suggests a hopeful path for the less developed nations to follow as they become industrialized. Industrial growth and development in a nation brings rising labor expectations, and the emergence of trade unions to attain them. Before long, wages rise, work hours fall, and the sharp differences in labor standards found there and in the industrialized countries are reduced to a tolerable level. It is in the interest of earlier-generation industrial powers, such as the United States, to hasten the maturation process in those developing nations, if only to minimize their own period of painful exposure to the cost differentials. If Japan can attain civilized standards of labor treatment, then so eventually can South Korea, Taiwan, Brazil, Indonesia, or Pakistan. As their economies grow and mature, their trade competition becomes less virulent. The world becomes economically a safer place for us Americans. The process, however, takes time.

LABOR NEEDS IN DEVELOPED AND DEVELOPING COUNTRIES

Too often economic development in Third World countries takes a course less friendly to labor. In Indonesia, for example, hulling the rice crop by hand used to provide employment for numerous rural women. In the early 1970s rice producers began importing mechanical hullers from Japan, which increased their profits but, at the same time, eliminated an estimated 133 million work days and $50 million in annual income for manual laborers. In Pakistan, the use of tractors has likewise caused the loss of 200,000 rural jobs. An UN study in the late 1970s found that more than $70 billion of investment in developing nations by multinational enterprise, half from the United States, provided employment for only about 4 million persons.[19] Although some additional spin-off jobs were also created from this investment, the study concluded that "the impact of both direct and indirect MNE employment in developing nations may not necessarily be positive."[20]

Another problem is that foreign governments have helped multinational corporations to build profitable export businesses that offer poor wages and working conditions to their employees. The newly industrialized countries of the Far East such as Singapore and South Korea have achieved much of their economic growth by establishing "Export Processing Zones." These are special areas within the country where the multinationals are allowed to produce goods for export in a duty-free environment. An ILO study of such operations in the Far East found that the typical employee was a young single female who worked in the factories for a few years until marriage. The pay was low, turnover was high, and the workweek averaged between 45 and 48 hours. To cut costs further, some employers hired workers as apprentices at less than the regular wage but routinely laid them off just before the period of apprenticeship ended.[21]

A similar arrangement is found in the border region between Mexico and the southwestern part of the United States under the Maquiladora Program, begun in 1965. This program allows raw materials and intermediate manufactured products to cross the border with no import duty on the Mexican side and only a value-added tax on the Mexican content levied by the United States. An article in *Monthly Labor Review* describes the operations as follows: "In general, twin Mexican and U.S. plants exist, each responsible for different parts of the production process. The Mexican operations, which on average have a production work force of 75 to 80 percent women between 19 and 23 years old, perform the less skilled, more labor-intensive tasks, while the U.S. plants perform more capital-intensive jobs requiring higher skill levels. . . . Mexico's proximity to the U.S. market makes its wage structure competitive with the low wage levels found in Hong Kong, Taiwan, and South Korea. For example, at the October 1983 exchange rate, an average compensation of 90 cents per hour was paid to workers in maquiladora firms."[22]

The transfer of jobs from the developed nations has come mainly at the expense of American workers. Japan has contributed little; neither have the nations of Western Europe. The relatively wide-open U.S. market has become a dumping ground for other nations' unemployment. Financially, the United States cannot afford to play that role much longer. Even though some employment must leak to other countries, the process should not be allowed to happen too quickly. Otherwise, it would gut the U.S. industrial base. The owners of foreign businesses would reap enormous profits without helping foreign workers that much. There needs to be, instead, a controlled leak of jobs to the developing nations, which allows enough time for living standards there to rise along with a local consumer market. Other developed nations besides the United States should give up industrial jobs to the Third World countries.

It is possible to imagine a U.S. trade program designed to accelerate the rise in labor standards around the world, which would at the same time protect American workers from the immediately punishing effects of trade competition. It would seem the two objectives are incompatible, for the U.S. economy would be required at once to give more freely and to conserve jobs and money. The solution lies in a shift from the economic to the political. The world economy cannot continue without damage to function in a purely economic manner, with the strong pushing out the weak.

The political approach would be for the strong, observing a global ethical consensus, to direct more economic resources to the weak. It would also make sure that in any international transfers of wealth, labor gets its share. In the developing world are an estimated 500 million persons who are unemployed or substantially underemployed, compared with 30 million such persons in the developed world.[23] It is therefore urgent that economic growth and jobs be targeted to the developing nations, even if this costs the developed nations something. Ideally, a political solution to world trade problems would seek long-term equalization of economic development by lifting up the nations that have fallen behind while hurting workers in the more advanced countries as little as possible.

World political opinion has been moving in that direction. The 1976 World Employment Conference and subsequent UN gatherings have provided a forum for ideas of this sort to be expressed. One theme that has emerged from such discussions has been the need for a "New International Economic Order," which would bring the developing nations into the world's economic mainstream. The Lima Declaration and Program of Action called for the developing nations' share of industrial production to be increased to 25 percent of the world total by the year 2000. To accomplish that goal, the developed nations would have to import more manufactured goods from developing nations, which could mean phasing out certain of their own industries.[24]

The developing countries suffer from two special problems that directly block their economic advancement. One is the low market prices for primary commodities such as minerals or agricultural produce. The other is the heavy burden of debt owed to foreign banks. Both problems call for treatment within the framework of a more general political solution. The foreign debt was often incurred to undertake development projects; but, once the facilities were in place, low prices and insufficient markets for products did not allow enough operating margin to handle debt payments. Global production overcapacity was the root cause of the inadequate return on investment. In addition, corrupt public officials spirited much-needed cash from the developing countries for personal investments abroad. An international body or an effective alliance of national producers is needed to maintain adequate price levels by limiting supplies or directly setting the price. If commodity prices are not high enough, then it would be necessary to apply political remedies as well to the world debt problem.

PRODUCTION OVERSUPPLY

Indeed, the root of much that is wrong with the global economy lies in production oversupply relative to consumer demand. The *Wall Street Journal* has acknowledged, in an article dated March 9, 1987:

[A]ll this emphasis on what is wrong in the U.S. and in its relations with trading partners—especially Japan, with its mercantilist drive to export—tends to obscure a world-wide problem: Many major industries, all around the globe, are burdened with far too much capacity. "Overcapacity is a world-wide problem, and it's getting worse," says Lester Thurow.... "We're still investing as if the world economy were growing at 4% a year instead of the actual rate of 2%." While a lot of automated capacity has been added, effective demand has been sluggish....

Roger Vincent, an expert at Bankers Trust Co., estimates that world automotive demand stands in the "low 30 millions" of vehicles annually, while capacity "is in the low to mid–40s." By 1990, capacity should rise to the mid–40s, he says, and demand won't grow very much.... [In the steel industry] most economists calculate the annual global overcapacity at 75 million to 200 million metric tons. ... Although no figures on the [computer] industry's capacity use are published, most computer makers are clearly being plagued with overcapacity. The problem is reflected in declining orders and intense competition.... Makers of farm and construction equipment are buried in overcapacity, but, surprisingly, some countries, especially South Korea, are nonetheless believed to be planning more plants.... In the textile industry, cheap-labor foreign competition is causing the howls. Overcapacity lingers on as more and more mills are built in less developed nations, with more and more mills in the U.S. thus turned into surplus capacity.[25]

In all this, one sees the need for a global strategy to ease production supply and bolster demand. This gets back to Henry Ford's idea of the worker-as-consumer. Labor is basically in oversupply, and labor is a prime ingredient of whatever commodities or manufactured products have value on world markets. The reason for its oversupply is technology, whose progress appears irreversible. Advancing technology has spread havoc in the world's labor markets. It has uprooted human beings from lifelong patterns of employment and, causing an oversupply of labor, driven down its price. The developing nations, harder pressed, threaten to take jobs away from the developed. Yet, for every job lost to imports from the Third World, five jobs are lost to productivity growth through technology, an ILO study claims.[26]

The appropriate and effective remedy for job loss through technological advancement is a politically induced reduction in worktime. Only this can attack the destabilizing element at its source. Efforts to save jobs by trade protection pass unemployment back and forth between nations, but accomplish nothing in total. To solve the global unemployment problem, hours reductions and trade policies should be combined in a way that promotes orderly and humane progress in living standards. The developed countries, which offer their people a better material life already, can afford to cut work schedules first, and should. The developing countries should then be allowed to fill the vacated capacity in labor supply, so that living standards there would rise more rapidly. Thus a political solution to global unemployment and poverty would involve a certain allocation of work based on relative needs and opportunities.

A global policy consensus would be required to make this work. The world's people, putting their collective mind to the task, can solve economic problems of oversupply. Through a two-pronged policy, the nations can regulate their own employment levels. One prong of the policy would address job loss from advancing technology; it would find a remedy in reduced work hours. The other prong of the policy would address job loss from imported products, and find a remedy in trade protection. In the second case, however, the degree of protection allowed each nation would depend on the policy consensus reached at an international level. Fair or responsible trade policies would be internationally acceptable, and invite no retaliation.

Responsible employment policy in the developed nations should include the willingness to make fundamental changes in the work routine in response to technological developments that threaten the position of labor. A nation that moves ahead with reduced work hours would be giving evidence to the world community that it is prepared to act responsibly to combat unemployment. On the other hand, an irresponsible or politically unacceptable policy would be for a nation simply to export its unemployment to other nations without attempting to restructure work schedules. A nation guilty of such unfair practices might attract just retaliation against its products through import restrictions. As for the developing nations, which are economically more vulnerable, the world community should make special trade allowances to encourage their growth and development. As part of the deal, such nations should be required to upgrade their labor standards, and permit trade unions to organize freely.

A PROPOSAL TO ENCOURAGE HIGHER LABOR STANDARDS WORLDWIDE

The immediate reality, of course, is that the world community lacks such a consensus on trade questions. The political association among nations is weak. That is why multinational corporations, which have outgrown political institutions in their scope of operation, exercise such leverage to the detriment of labor. Trade policy rests primarily in the hands of national governments, some of which are inclined to press their national advantage as far as it will go. All governments have the power to control trade across their national borders, and, specifically, to restrict it by various means. The challenge is to control trade in a way which is harmonious with the needs of the international community yet protects national interests.

For national governments (though not for trade lawyers and lobbyists), tariffs provide a better means of regulating trade than quotas or voluntary restraints. They are flexible yet systematic, and have the additional advantage of bringing needed tax revenues into the coffers of government. Their main drawback would be an ill-reputed association with economic nationalism. It might be possible, however, to develop a tariff system that is compatible with international policy objectives. Among those objectives should be to promote the worldwide advancement of labor standards. Rising labor standards in one country are not a threat to the citizens of another: on the contrary, they represent expanding consumer markets, which benefit workers and businesses in foreign countries as well as in their own.

It is in the interest of all humanity that labor standards should rise in all countries. Workers should receive from their employment increasing amounts of pay and benefits, and reduced schedules of hours. They should have a safe and reasonably pleasant work environment. They should enjoy the rights of free association and collective bargaining with employers. There should be prohibition of slave labor and restrictions on child labor. Adequate attention should be given to workers' needs regarding personal sickness, parental responsibilities, old-age retirement, human rights, and job security. A tariff system, designed to promote more humane treatment of labor, would give employers, regardless of nationality, a financial incentive to produce goods under higher-standard conditions of employment, which would at least partially offset their present incentive to shortchange labor.

In such a scheme, sketched here in broad outlines, the amount of the tariff levied on imported products might depend on the level of labor standards in the country from which the goods were exported. Higher labor standards would bring lower protective tariffs; lower labor standards would bring higher tariffs. The tariff rates might be set by means of an index, in which various factors representing elements of labor treatment were combined by a weighting formula. The chief factor or component of such an index might be the prevailing level of wages and hours where the exported goods were produced. In addition, the governments of the importing nations might, if they wished, develop other kinds of criteria to enforce other policy objectives. Although such a system might not have been practical in past years, computers are today able to make a quick and accurate calculation of weighted elements to determine an index of this kind and administer the operation on a large scale.

The index could be applied to types of imported products, industries, national economies, or specific enterprises where the exported goods were produced. It would not matter whether the foreign producer was a foreign-owned business or an American business operating abroad; all would be subject to the same criteria in setting tariff rates. The purpose of such a system would be to create an incentive for foreign producers to upgrade wages and reduce hours by allowing them cheaper access to the U.S. market. In this way, foreign nations need not fear economic nationalism on the part of the United States, and they should have no cause to retaliate against U.S. products. Labor in all developed nations is threatened by excessive hours and low wages in the developing world. All have an interest in seeing the dangerous disparities in labor costs disappear as quickly as possible.

In conclusion, government has indeed a moral responsibility to spread income-producing opportunities to persons in need of them. When for reasons of personal ambition or status the society's wealth becomes unreasonably concentrated in a few hands, government has a right and a duty to intervene to disperse the concentration. There is no "economic merit" to justify perpetuating extreme differences of wealth. Socialist revolutions confiscate wealth. Welfare states compulsorily redistribute it by taxation and government spending. Worksharing also involves a form of income redistribution, but it is a more mild form than that to which we are already accustomed. If people are poor, let them work their way out of poverty. Is that not the American way? On the world scene, the same kinds of economic disparities exist, and they, too, need correction by political means.

II
HISTORICAL
AND
THEOLOGICAL
VIEWS

11
A SHORT HISTORY OF
WORKING HOURS

A history of unemployment cannot fail to record that, during most of the recorded human lifetime on the planet, the concept of unemployment, and concern over it, did not exist. In hunter-gatherer, subsistence agricultural, surplus agricultural, and mercantile societies, a span taking us from 30,000 years ago up to 200 years ago, the idea of unemployment had no applicability. In part, this is because of the restricted role that work played in society, as well as the insignificance of what we nowadays call "the economy."

Work we have always had with us; its intensity is what has varied. As translated in *Cross Currents,* French sociologist Jacques Ellul observes:

Primitive human beings are habitually regarded as living in perpetual famine, as spending all their time trying to survive.... However, more and more studies demonstrate the contrary. Economists studying primitive culture, ethnographers, and historians of ancient civilizations now argue that those in prehistoric times, like people in many traditional societies, lived in a certain natural abundance.... Not only was survival not precarious, but the work was light. It was in this way that traditional societies were sustained throughout history....On the whole, people in primitive societies were not permanently threatened by famine. Marx's conception of the human being as above all a worker, obligated to work for survival, merely reflects the belief of his own time.... [1]

From prehistory until industrialization, there was no concern with the hours of labor. Labor was, for one thing, not a commodity separable from the rest of life, but just another normal activity. Social, personal, and political interactions surrounded, and gave meaning to, the activity of labor, which was, in any case, limited by the presence of sunlight, the rigors of the seasons, and the necessity for prayer. Religious, secular, and natural powers all collaborated to save people from excessive work.

RELIGIOUS REST

The Babylonians anticipated the Hebrews in setting aside the seventh day as a day of rest during which, even if natural conditions were favorable to laboring, labor was forbidden to occur. Passed on to Christians and Moslems, the custom of the recurring weekly holiday formed the first recognition that reasons other than exhaustion or the unsuitability of natural conditions might suspend labor.

Moses began his religious career as one so filled with outrage at the excessive hours of work required of his fellow Hebrews that he murdered an Egyptian foreman. Returning from a sojourn in the desert, Moses and his brother Aaron approached the Pharaoh with this demand: "These are the words of the Lord the God of Israel: 'Let my people go so that they may keep my pilgrim-feast in the wilderness.'" Pharaoh's response reflects an attitude in keeping with the tone of hardheaded managers today: "Moses and Aaron, what do you mean by distracting the people from their work. Back to your labors!" Pharaoh called the Hebrews a "lazy people," and ordered them not to reduce their daily production of bricks.[2] It took five plagues and several other "miracles" for Moses to persuade the Pharaoh to reconsider his position, and then three more plagues and a parting of the Red Sea waters for the Hebrew people to escape the work-obsessed Egyptian society and begin their journey to the promised land.

The institution of the sabbath was among the Commandments of God delivered to Moses during the Hebrews' flight from Egypt: "Remember to keep the Sabbath day holy. You have six days to labor and to do all your work. But the seven day is a sabbath of the Lord your God; that day you shall not do any work."[3] From a secular standpoint, this could be seen as the beginning of the shorter-workweek movement. In the context of religion, the Commandment expresses a distinction between the sacred and secular spheres of life or, in Jesus' words, between "what is due to Caesar" and "what is due to God."[4] Working for a secular employer is clearly perceived to be within man's secular domain, so that working on the Sabbath, God's reserved time, was considered to be a sin. The "spirit" of the Fourth Commandment is that the dividing line between hours of work and hours of leisure should be drawn on the basis of one's priorities—whether to prefer material things or "things of the spirit."

WORK HOURS IN ROMAN AND MEDIEVAL TIMES

From an economic and historical standpoint, we often assume that the amount of worktime relative to leisure is determined by a society's stage of technological achievement. This is true only up to a point. Otherwise we would have to believe that life in primitive societies is filled with back-breaking labor from dawn to dusk on most days of the year, and that the modern increase in leisure coincides with advancements in labor-saving technology. In fact, Harold Wilensky has pointed out, "In the perspective of several centuries, time at work increased before it de-creased. The secular decline in hours and days of work is greatly ex-aggerated by the usual comparison of gross daily or weekly averages with those of the 'take off' period of rapid economic growth in England, France, and America—a time of horrendous working schedules and conditions. Estimates of annual hours and days of work for populations of earlier times yield less confidence in great progress."[5]

Workers in the late Roman empire worked an annual schedule of hours not significantly greater than our own, although the distribution was different. Contemporary American workers have more time off on weekends and during the evenings, but the Romans made up for that with their greater number of holidays. Professor Wilensky writes: "In the old Roman calendar, out of 355 days, nearly one third (109) were marked as . . . unlawful for judicial and political business. In the last two centuries of the republic, festival days were stretched to accommodate more spectacles and public games. The Roman passion for holidays reached its climax in the middle of the fourth century when days off numbered 175. If we assume a 12-hour day, which is probably on the high side, total working time would be only about 2,160 hours a year."[6]

Europeans worked roughly 48 hours per week during the early Middle Ages. This saying was attributed to King Alfred the Great: "Eight hours work, eight hours sleep, eight hours play, make a just and healthy day."[7] The religious day of rest limited the workweek to six days, while the absence of effective lighting arrangements limited the daily hours of work to the period between sun-up and sun-down. That meant that working hours were longer during the summer than other seasons in the year. The medieval guilds regulated hours worked in urban occu-pations, while in the country peasants worked the land under various sharecropping arrangements with the nobility. There was a generous number of holidays.

Again, Wilensky estimates that preindustrial European workers did not endure a significantly more burdensome schedule of annual work hours than workers today. Parisian wire-drawers in the 13th century worked 16 hours a day during the "summer" six months and 8 hours a day during the "winter" six months. However, they also received a 30-day annual vacation in addition to another 141 days off during the year, which leaves 194 working days during the year. Their 2,328 annual average hours of work compares with the 1,914 hours that U.S. manufacturing workers averaged in 1977. A book of work rules in 13th century France prohibited night work, Sunday work, and work after Saturday vespers (4–5 p.m.), except for certain highly skilled artisans. Tapestry makers in Beauvais worked 12 hours a day during the summer, which included a one-hour lunch break and another half-hour break in the morning. On the other hand, it is estimated that agricultural workers in medieval Europe put in 3500 to 4000 hours of work per year.[8]

According to Wladimir Woytinsky, work hours began to lengthen in the late middle ages, as the number of holidays declined and restrictions on Sunday work were not so strictly observed. In 1495, King Henry VII of England decreed that summer work hours be increased to the period between 5 a.m. and 7–8 p.m., with two hours of rest. His granddaughter, Elizabeth I, confirmed this schedule in 1563, but allowed 2½ hours of daily rest. Meanwhile, Thomas More, in *Utopia*, imagined a society in which people would work only six hours a day. That was not to be. At the close of the 17th century, an Englishman typically worked a 10-hour day. The work was done over a 12-hour span, with two hours of rest. A century later, the 14-hour day was customary, and in some cases it ranged upwards to 16–18 hours. Not just adult men, but also women and children, worked this ghastly schedule of daily hours.[9]

In such circumstances, writes Woytinsky, "little resistance could be expected from the workers; in the absence of protective legislation and organization for the protection of their status they were forced by mass unemployment to accept work under almost any conditions. Handicraftsmen too were driven to the utmost of their endurance by the fear of succumbing to factory competition."[10]

BEGINNING OF THE HOURS STRUGGLE IN BRITAIN AND AMERICA

Historically, one might say that the modern effort to reduce work time began in the year 1800. The industrial revolution, spurred by James Watt's development of the steam engine 30 years earlier, was rapidly converting British industry from handicrafts to large-scale manufacturing. A number of inventions made it cheaper to produce textiles and other goods in factories than in the home. Relatively unskilled labor was needed to tend the machines. The factory owners offered an attractive wage, but workers gradually fell at their mercy as alternative opportunities for employment vanished. More than low wages, it was the excessive hours worked in the mills, especially by women and children, which attracted attention as an abuse. Because the workers were powerless, the moral impetus of legislation to protect them from abusive work schedules had to come from the economically and politically enfranchised classes. Almost as soon as the workday was stretched beyond its traditional, preindustrial length, opposition developed to the practice. The struggle to confine laboring time to sustainable levels was focused, at first, on women and children; but many recognized that this was only the first step toward more thorough reform.

Robert Owen is the key figure in this early struggle to reduce hours. Self-educated, Owen went into the textile business at the age of ten. In 1800, he bought his father-in-law's cotton mills at New Lanark, Scotland. There Owen established a model industrial community, in which the company's 2500 employees enjoyed superior housing and sanitation, stores with low prices, and schools for their children. The workday there was 10½ hours, compared with 13–14 hours in competitors' textile mills. The business prospered, and Owen's reputation as a progressive businessman spread. In later years, Owen attempted to establish a utopian agricultural/industrial community in the state of Indiana.

The hours issue was of central importance to Owen's scheme of progress for industrial workers. Besides setting an example in his own business, Owen was the principal figure behind the Factory Act of 1819, which attempted to limit the hours of women and children. In 1833, he presented agruments for an 8-hour day to the Society for Promoting National Regeneration, which suggested that "if the right to exist be granted to the weak as well as the strong, then 8 hours constitutes on the average the longest period of physical exertion of which a human being is capable without impairing health, intelligence, the sense of moral values and happiness, the maintenance of which is in the true interest of every human being.... [N]o human being has the right to demand that others work more than is needed for the good of humanity in general merely for the purpose of enriching himself by impoverishing others."[11] Like Henry Ford a century later, Robert Owen combined humanitarian appeals with a recitation of hardheaded economic logic. Some businessmen supported his proposal for a shorter workday on the grounds that long hours were causing overproduction and a drop in prices.

The proposal for shorter work hours was advanced as an issue of social reform in Britain during the period 1800–1850, aided by public-spirited men of influence and means. After 1850, the trade unions continued the fight from a position of economic and political power. The Factory Act of 1819 was first in a series of measures advanced in Parliament to improve working conditions for manufacturing production workers. In 1833, Parliament passed a bill prohibiting the employment of children under nine in factories, limiting the workweek of children under thirteen to 48 hours, and limiting the workweek of persons thirteen to eighteen years of age to 69 hours. While these laws were an improvement over the previous arrangement, the real object of workers' agitation in the 1830s and 1840s was to pass a 10-hour bill that would apply to all workers. A high-minded member of Parliament, Lord Ashley, later the Earl of Shaftesbury, was recruited by a clergyman representing the workers' "short-time committees" to introduce such legislation on their behalf.

Lord Ashley's bill, first offered in 1833, was waylaid by the appointment of a Royal Commission "to collect information in the manufacturing districts with respect to employment of children in factories."[12] This led to the enactment of a government-sponsored bill, the previously mentioned Factory Act of 1833, which was regarded as a compromise measure. Ashley later led a campaign to limit the work of women and children in coal mines. The Chartist movement of the 1840s brought continuing pressure on Parliament to pass a general 10-hours bill, and in 1848 it was done. The bill that Parliament passed that year produced a monumental economic change. From a perspective twelve years later, Karl Marx declared that its results were "a rise in the money wages of factory operatives, despite the curtailing of the working day, a great increase in the number of factory hands employed, a continuous fall in the prices of their products, a marvelous development in the productive powers of their labor, an unheard-of progressive expansion of the markets for their commodities."[13] The law's evident success encouraged labor on both sides of the Atlantic to press for further hours reductions.

In the United States, agitation for shorter hours began as early as 1791, when carpenters in Philadelphia struck for the 10-hour day. The issue came alive during the 1820s in several large cities along the eastern seaboard. In 1825, several hundred journeymen carpenters in Boston went on strike for a 10-hour day, but the strike was lost. Two years later, the country's first central labor body, the Mechanics Union of Trade Associations, was organized in Philadelphia. The 10-hour day was its principal concern. In New York City, where workers already had a 10-hour day, employers in 1829 tried to raise the daily schedule of work to 11 hours. This precipitated a meeting of 5000 workers to protest the move. A political party called the New York Working Men's Party was formed, which ran candidates for the state assembly.

The 1830s brought gains in this area for government workers. In 1835, trade unionists in Philadelphia called the nation's first general strike to demand higher wages and a 10-hour day. The strike was successful. Philadelphia's city government agreed to a "6 to 6" daily work schedule in the summer, which allowed two hours off for lunch. In 1836, a trade-union committee persuaded President Andrew Jackson to establish a 10-hour day in the Philadelphia Navy Yard. A more sweeping concession was made four years later by Jackson's successor, Martin Van Buren. On March 31, 1840, President Van Buren signed an executive order limiting the work of all mechanics and laborers employed in the executive branch "to the number of hours prescribed by the 10-hour system."[14]

The 10-hour movement was an attempt to reduce daily work hours by imposing a uniform schedule of hours throughout the year. Under the old system, workers were kept on the job from "sun up" to "sun down," which meant that their daily schedules varied from 7½ hours during the winter to 12 hours during the summer. In 1836, Congress passed a law requiring federal offices to be kept open for public business at least eight hours a day from October through March and ten hours a day from April through September. In 1840, the building-trades unions were able to negotiate a 6-day, 60-hour week in a number of cities.

In the decade of the 1840s, labor looked increasingly to the state legislatures to win the 10-hour day, especially in New England where daily work schedules remained in the 12–14-hours range. The theory behind this strategy was that, because state governments had chartered the corporations, they had the power to regulate corporate conduct. In 1842, a group of female workers from the textile mills in Lowell, Massachusetts, brought a petition for the 10-hour day to the Massachusetts legislature. This had a certain irony, considering that the "Lowell girls" had been widely portrayed as "cheerful" employees having ample opportunities for recreation and spiritual improvement, despite their 11–13-hour days.

Indeed, the 10-hours campaign in New England was accomplished by extensive moral posturing on both sides. A mill owner said: "Yes, I verily believe that there are a large number of operatives in our cotton mills who have too much time to spare now," adding that more leisure "would increase crime, suffering, wickedness, and pauperism."[15] On the other hand, a resolution adopted at the 1852 Ten Hours State Convention in Boston made it clear that workers, too, believed God was on their side. It read: "We believe it is the intention of the Great Creator to shorten the time of man's toil, and to extend the opportunities for moral, social, and intellectual improvement, by the introduction of labor-saving machinery, and by the powers and mechanical uses of water, steam and electricity.... If it be God's will to abridge man's daily labor to eight, six, or even less hours, we ought cheerfully to submit and say—'Thy will be done.'"[16]

The New Hampshire legislature acceded to workers' demands in 1847. The state law, which went into effect in September 15th of that year, provided that "in all contracts related to labor, ten hours shall be taken to be a day's work unless otherwise agreed by the parties." The law proved ineffectual, though, as employers quickly found a way to evade its requirements. The main loophole was contained in the words "unless otherwise agreed by the parties." Before the law was to take effect, many New Hampshire employers forced their employees to sign agreements permitting longer hours. Those who refused to sign were fired and then blacklisted.

Even so, progress toward a 10-hour day continued during the 1850s. Labor was gradually building a network of local organizations around this issue, which provided the basis for a national federation in subsequent decades. In 1851, a shoemaker from Trenton, New Jersey, was elected to Congress on a 10-hour plank. In 1853, the New York state assembly passed a law requiring a 10-hour schedule in public works. The California legislature passed a 10-hour law in the same year. By the time of the Civil War, most skilled mechanics in the United States worked a 10-hour schedule, although other factory workers continued to work 11–12-hour days or longer. It was not until 1874, however, that the first state law for a 10-hour day was passed that did not make an exception for contractual agreements between workers and employers.

STRUGGLE FOR THE 8-HOUR DAY

Meanwhile, a new issue was taking form: the 8-hour day. Ships carpenters and caulkers in New York City had received this schedule for repair work in 1849. Boston caulkers in 1854 became the first union to win an 8-hour day. However, the movement really began in 1859 when a Boston machinist named Ira Steward presented a demand for an 8-hour day for all workers at the convention of the National Union of Machinists and Blacksmiths in Philadelphia. Called "father of the eight-hour day" by his friends and "that eight-hour monomaniac" by his detractors, Steward was a man driven by a cause. During the early 1860s, he built a national movement by his tireless proselytizing and a coherent economic philosophy. If employers granted workers an 8-hour day with no reduction in pay, Steward suggested, the general standard of living would improve. "Men who labor excessively are robbed of all ambition to ask for anything more than will satisfy their bodily necessities," he argued.[17] Workers might achieve the 8-hour day simply by refusing to work longer hours, or else through legislation.

In 1863, Steward's union, the National Union of Machinists and Blacksmiths, endorsed the concept of an 8-hour day, as did the Boston Trades' Assembly. In the following year, Steward founded the Workingmen's Convention of Boston to promote it. The first of a series of eight-hour organizations, the Grand Eight-Hour League of Massachusetts, was established in 1865. Others were quickly formed throughout the land. As

Civil War soldiers returned home to face high unemployment, Steward's idea found a fertile reception.

Eight-hour bills were introduced in the U.S. Congress in 1865 and 1866, but failed to pass. In 1866, the representatives of more than 60,000 workers engaged in 8-hour leagues and local unions met in Baltimore to form a national organization called the National Labor Union. Within three years, its membership had grown to 600,000 workers. A delegation from this group presented a petition for the 8-hour day to President Andrew Johnson. Congress passed an 8-hour law in 1868, which applied to laborers, mechanics and other workers employed by the federal government. It was signed by President Ulysses S. Grant. Illinois became the first of six states to enact similar legislation. However, these laws again contained clauses allowing employers to evade their requirements. The organizing committee of the 8-hour leagues complained that "for all practical intents and purposes they [the 8-hour laws] might as well have never been placed on the statute books, and can only be described as frauds on the labouring class."[18] In 1870, the U.S. Supreme Court ruled that the federal government did not have to observe its own 8-hour law.

Organized labor went through a period of instability during the 1870s, as it groped for a formula to deal with the nation's economic problems. On the local level, workers continued to fight vigorously for the 8-hour day. A wave of 8-hour strikes occurred in the summer of 1872. In New York City 100,000 workers, concentrated in the construction industry, struck for three months to win the 8-hour day. Because of the large number of foreign-born workers who took part in the strike, one employer was moved to comment: "I see behind all this the spectre of communism." An editorial in the *New York Times* asked, referring to the strikers' victory parade: "What proportion of that long column of strikers were thoroughly American?"[19] On a national level, organized labor became involved in other issues, such as the Greenback issue, which some believe fatally weakened the National Labor Union.

A severe recession, brought on by the 1873 collapse of the banking firm of Jay Cooke & Co., afflicted the nation's economy for six years. By 1877, one fifth of American workers had been laid off. Less than half held regular full-time jobs. Some employers used the occasion to bring back the 10-hour day. The National Labor Union collapsed in 1872, and efforts to reconstruct a nationwide labor organization failed in the following year. A part of the labor movement went into secretive, violence-prone groups, such as the "Molly Maguires." Another part formed around a fraternal order, known as the Knights of Labor, which, eschewing strikes of violence, pursued an idealistic program of building workers' cooperatives. Its principal leader, Terence V. Powderly, took a dignified and moderate approach toward advancing the working class.

Membership in the Knights of Labor rose from 5000 in 1875 to 700,000 in 1886, but declined rapidly in the 1890s.

The forerunner of the present national labor organization, a group known as the Federation of Organized Trades and Labor Unions of the United States and Canada, was established at a convention in Pittsburgh in November 1881. Labor was hoping to recover what it had lost during the depressed decade of the 1870s, especially in regards to the 8-hour day. At its 1884 convention, the new organization adopted a resolution that read: "Resolved by the Federation of Organized Trades and Labor Unions of the United States and Canada that eight hours shall constitute a legal day's labor from May First, 1886, and that we recommend to labor organizations throughout their jurisdiction that they so direct their laws as to conform to this resolution by the time named."[20]

This resolution is the origin of the May Day labor holiday, now celebrated throughout the world. At the time of its adoption, the Federation of Organized Trades and Labor Unions had a membership of 50,000. The Knights of Labor had 200,000 members. The two organizations cooperated in preparation for a general strike, planned for May 1, 1866. Both grew rapidly in the preceding year. The goal of an 8-hour day had a galvanizing effect on American workers, who, Philip S. Foner reports,

smoked "Eight-Hour Tobacco," purchased "Eight-Hour Shoes," and sang the "Eight-Hour Song":

We mean to make things over; we're tired of toil for naught

But bare enough to live on; never an hour for thought.

We want to feel the sunshine; we want to smell the flowers;

We're sure that God has willed it; and we mean to have eight hours.

We're summoning our forces from shipyard, shop, and mill.

Eight hours for work, eight hours for rest, eight hours for what we will.[21]

On May 1, 1886, an estimated 350,000 American workers went out on strike for the 8-hour day. More than 11,000 business establishments were affected. The stockyards and railroads in Chicago were completely shut down. In New York City 25,000 striking workers marched in a torchlight parade. Workers in many other cities across the country also took part in the general strike. As a result, more than 50,000 workers received the 8-hour day, and another 150,000 workers received it without striking.

Despite its success in gaining shorter hours, the May Day strike is best known for an incident that happened three days afterward in Chicago.

The strike precipitated an attack by police on striking employees of the McCormack Reaper Works, in which six workers were killed. On May 4th, a mass meeting was held in Haymarket Square to protest police brutality. It was at this meeting that an unidentified person threw a bomb into the crowd, killing a police sergeant. Four workers and seven other policemen were killed in the ensuing melee. The leaders of the anarchist group that had sponsored the rally were brought to trial. Four were convicted of inciting violence, and were hanged. Seven others were imprisoned. The biased manner in which the trial was conducted gained worldwide notoriety, and gave the labor movement a set of martyrs: Engel, Fischer, Parsons, and Spies.

Later that year, the American Federation of Labor was organized in Columbus, Ohio. Its goal was to stake a position apart from the Knights of Labor, whose mass of unskilled workers threatened the skilled craftsmen, as well as from the Marxist socialists. The American Federation of Labor steered clear of general strikes and political programs or ideologies. Instead, it preferred to work within the system to achieve immediate economic gains for the members. "We have no ultimate ends," said Adolf Strasser, a union spokesman. "We are all practical men.... We are going on from day to day."[22] In the matter of the 8-hour day, though, the American Federation of Labor remained firmly on labor's traditional course. "The displacement of labor by machinery in the past few years has exceeded that of any period in our history," observed the AFL's first president, Samuel Gompers. "So long as there is one man who seeks employment and cannot obtain it, the hours of labor are too long."[23]

Shortly after its formation, the American Federation of Labor made plans for another May Day strike. A decision was made at its 1888 convention in St. Louis to conduct the strike on May 1, 1890. Instead of a general strike, the federation selected one of its constituent unions, the Carpenters and Joiners, to carry on the fight for the 8-hour day. On Washington's birthday, 1889, mass meetings were held in 240 cities, where 8-hour resolutions were adopted. Others were held on the 4th of July. On May 1, 1890, the carpenters struck. Again there were large demonstrations in Chicago, New York, and other American cities. When the dust had settled, more than 23,000 carpenters in 36 cities had won the 8-hour day. Another 32,000 received a 9-hour day. The success of this venture led the American Federation of Labor to call May Day strikes in subsequent years, each featuring a different union. The United Mine Workers, International Typographical Union, and bakers union were some who participated in these strikes for the 8-hour day.

The May Day strike of 1890 brought a brief convergence between the American labor movement and its more radical counterpart in Europe, which was inclined toward Marxist socialism. The two ran in parallel in the quarter-century following the American Civil War. In *Das Kapital,* Karl Marx noted with approval how the American eight-hour movement "ran with express speed from the Atlantic to the Pacific, from New England to California" in the late 1860s.[24] The International Working-men's Association, otherwise known as the Socialist "First International," which Marx and his associates founded in London in 1864, embraced the goal of the 8-hour day in 1866, the same year it was adopted by the National Labor Union in the United States. Though it never officially joined Marx's organization, the National Labor Union sent a delegate to its international congress in Basle in 1869, and pledged adherence to its principles in the following year. Samuel Gompers, an immigrant from the Netherlands, had been a youthful admirer of Karl Marx, but later came to detest socialism. The American Federation of Labor, under Gompers' leadership, became a "meat and potatoes" organization, fo-cusing on limited economist goals, while the European socialists took a more apocalyptic view of the capitalist system.

In the 1890s, the European and American labor movements joined forces to seek an 8-hour day. American delegates to the organizing conference of the socialist Second International in 1889 brought news of plans for the May Day strike in the following year. The socialists therefore adopted this resolution:

The Congress decides to organize a great international demonstration, so that in all countries and in all cities on one appointed day the toiling masses shall demand of the state authorities the legal reduction of the working day to eight hours.... Since a similar demonstration has already been decided upon for May 1, 1890, by the American Federation of Labor at its convention in St. Louis, December, 1888, this day is accepted for the international demonstration.[25]

The European trade unions, unlike the American Federation of Labor, retained the general strike in their observance of May Day. Otherwise, the event was carried out with equal spirit and success on both sides of the Atlantic. On May 1, 1890, workers in the United States, Canada, Germany, France, and other nations demonstrated en masse for the 8-hour day. The aging revolutionary, Frederick Engels, wrote ecstatically in the preface to a new edition of the *Communist Manifesto*: "As I write these lines, the proletariat of Europe and America is holding a review of its forces; it is mobilized for the first time in One army, One flag, and fighting One immediate aim: an eight-hour working day, established by legal enactment.... The spectacle we are now witnessing will make the capitalists and landowners in all lands realize that today the proletarians are, indeed, united. If only Marx were with me to see it with his own eyes!"[26]

The thirty-year period following the 1890 May Day strike marks the final countdown in the struggle for the 8-hour day. Labor had its sights firmly fixed on that goal, but employers were not ready to concede. The fight grew bloody. In 1905, a Russian Orthodox priest named Father Gapon led a large but peaceful delegation of trade unionists to petition the Czar for an 8-hour day among other things, at his Winter Palace in St. Petersburg. Troops opened fire on the crowd, killing many. This incident generated such public outrage, including a general strike and other unrest, that the Czar felt obliged to offer his nation a limited form of parliamentary democracy.

In the American West, some of the 8-hour strikes were also violent. One of the worst occurred in the Colorado mining camps at Cripple Creek and Telluride. The turmoil began in 1901 when the Colorado Supreme Court declared the state's 8-hour law unconstitutional. Labor groups succeeded in passing a referendum that made it legal, but the mine owners refused to abandon the current work schedules, calling for a 7-day, 84-hour workweek. When the miners struck, troops were summoned. Instead of enforcing the state's 8-hour law, the soldiers drove thousands of strikers from their homes at bayonet point. They loaded many in railroad box cars and shipped them out of the area. Over a 15-month period of violence, the soldiers killed 42 strikers, wounded 1112 others, and arrested 1300. The strikers, led by Charles Moyer and William ("Big Bill") Haywood, fought back, and eventually obtained an 8-hour day and a $3/day minimum wage. In other incidents, 39 persons were killed during a 1907 strike by San Francisco trolley car workers who demanded an 8-hour day. In 1916, a strike by lumber workers in Everett, Washington, brought five deaths, before this goal was won.

In the late 19th century, American workers generally worked more hours a week than their counterparts in Britain, but about as many as workers in France and Germany. It is estimated that in 1840 the average workweek was 69 hours in England, 78 hours in the United States and France, and 83 hours in Germany. By 1880 the British workweek had been reduced to 52 hours, while 60-hour weeks prevailed in the United States, Germany, and France. Italian and Russian workers had 72-hour workweeks. The average work time came down rapidly in most industrialized nations during the 1890s. In Britain there was a rush toward shorter hours after the turn of the century. More than one million British workers had their hours reduced in 1902, compared with 5000 who suffered increases. In Germany, workers generally had 9- or 9½ hour days in the years before World War I. In the United States, the average workweek dropped from 58.4 hours in 1890 to 57.3 hours in 1900, to 54.9 hours in 1909, and to 53.8 hours in 1913.

The American struggle for shorter hours was dealt a setback by a 1905 ruling of the U.S. Supreme Court, which overturned a New York statute limiting work in bakeries and confectionery shops to 10 hours a day. The majority held in Lochner vs. New York that "statutes of the nature of that under review, limiting hours in which grown and intelligent men may labor to earn their living are mere meddlesome interferences with the rights of an individual."[27] On the other hand, the same court in 1908 upheld an Oregon statute restricting the work hours of women. In the United States, the legal variations among the states allowed employers to shop around for less restrictive arrangements. Therefore, the best way to reduce hours, where this could be done constitutionally, was through federal legislation. The Eight-Hour Law, which Congress enacted in 1892, prescribed an 8-hour day for federal laborers and mechanics employed in public works. Its coverage was broadened in 1912 to include the work done by federal contractors and subcontractors on jobs exceeding $2000. Another important federal law was the 1916 Adamson Act, which set a standard 8-hour work day for railroad workers.

The drive for an 8-hour day picked up steam during the period of World War I. Henry Ford offered this to his employees in the automobile plants at the time he instituted the $5/day minimum wage. In 1916, he urged President Wilson to make the 8-hour day an issue in that year's presidential campaign. Instead, the Wilson administration jailed Bill Haywood and other leading "Wobblies" on wartime charges of sedition. Out West, the Wobbly-led lumbermen of the Pacific northwest pursued a novel method of winning the 8-hour day: they hired on for ten hours of work, but left two hours early.

An equally tumultuous situation developed in the 1919 steel strike. In an industry that still scheduled workweeks of 72 hours, the 365,000 striking steel workers demanded an 8-hour day, one day's rest in seven, an end to 24-hour shifts, union recognition, and overtime pay. Judge Elbert Gary, president of U.S. Steel, regarded these proposals as an attempt to "sovietize the steel industry."[28] Employer violence against the strikers claimed 18 lives. In the Pittsburgh area, thousands of deputy sheriffs, state troopers, vigilantes, and so on harrassed union members. In Gary, Indiana, the regular army was brought in. The U.S. Department of Justice detained hundreds of foreign-born workers, and ordered many deported. In the end, the strike was broken.

The brutality used to crush the strike backfired. It aroused the conscience of leading citizens, who became aware of abuses practiced in the steel industry. A Commission of Inquiry of the Interchurch World Movement issued a "Report on the Steel Strike of 1919," criticizing the industry, and especially U.S. Steel, in these words: "The 12-hour day is the most iniquitous of the byproducts of the corporation's labor policy which is to get cheap labor and keep it cheap."[29] The commission's report attracted attention in government. In particular, the secretary of Commerce, Herbert Hoover, was moved by the report. He believed that the long hours in steel were a "black spot on American industry" and ordered a department study. The secretary of Labor declared: "The 12-hour day and the 7-day week in American industry must go.... Society cannot afford to permit any industry to unmake men in order to manufacture any product."[30]

President Harding's aid was enlisted. The president drafted a letter to Judge Gary suggesting that it "would have a tremendously helpful effect throughout the country" if he would cooperate in reducing work hours.[31] That was not quite enough to persuade the judge. President Harding next invited top steel executives to a dinner at the White House to discuss the matter. For more than a year thereafter, the president, members of the Cabinet, and assorted clergymen wheedled, badgered, and cajoled executives of the steel companies to end the long hours. Finally, on August 23, 1923, in the same issue that headlined the untimely death of President Warren G. Harding, the *New York Times* carried an announcement on an inside page to the effect that directors of the American Iron and Steel Institute had approved plans for the "total elimination" of the 12-hour day in their industry.

Worldwide, arrangements for the 8-hour day were falling into place. With the new League of Nations, an International Labor Organization was established to monitor work conditions. When the ILO's constitution was drafted, "the adoption of the 8-hour day or a 48-hour week as the standard to be attained" was declared to be "of special and urgent importance."[32] An international conference was held for that purpose in Washington, D.C., in October 1919. From it came the "Hours of Work Convention" (ILO Convention No. 1), which established the standard of an 8- or 9-hour day and 48-hour week for industrial firms.

Although several leading nations refused to ratify this convention, its standard generally prevailed. In the period between the armistice of November 1918 and August 1919, when the conference report was prepared, 8-hour laws were adopted in Austria, Czechoslovakia, Denmark, France, Italy (for railroad workers), the Netherlands, Poland, Spain, and Switzerland. The provisional government introduced the 8-hour day in Russia in March 1917, which the Bolsheviks later affirmed. In the United States, the number of workers receiving 8-hour days under collective-bargaining agreements increased from 172,000 in 1915 to 1,440,000 in June 1918. Postwar legislation brought the 8-hour day to Belgium, Bulgaria, Latvia, Yugoslavia, and Sweden. By 1922, the 48-hour workweek was standard in Europe, Australia, and New Zealand, as well as in most American industries.

British employers lengthened the work day during the 1920s, particularly in the coal-mining industry after the 1926 strike was defeated. In Germany, where the economy was subject to especially large swings in the business cycle, part-time work greatly increased during a recession in 1926, as again in the 1930s. The U.S. economy enjoyed brisk and stable growth after an early recession, and its workweek was generally unchanged. In the Soviet Union, whose government sought to demonstrate the advantages of socialism over the capitalistic system, a manifesto was issued on the tenth anniversary of the October 1917 revolution, announcing a 7-hour work day. Belgium and France both had 48-hour workweeks as a result of legislation enacted in 1921 and 1919, respectively. It should be understood that average hours in Japan, China, India, and other less advanced industrialized countries were then at a level that the Europeans had experienced a half century or more earlier.

THE 40-HOUR WORKWEEK

The 5-day week appears to have originated in certain New York City department stores at the time of World War I. By the mid–1920s it had spread to industries such as clothing, laundries, paper-box manufacturing, newspaper printing, and the building trades. A survey conducted by the Bureau of Labor Statistics (BLS) in 1926 found that 4.7 percent of the workers in union trades had a 5-day week. In the men's garment industry the proportion was 32.3 percent. A 17-week strike by fur workers in New York City in the spring of 1926 produced the first negotiated contract for a 5-day, 40-hour workweek. Additionally, this contract provided for a 10 percent wage increase, seven paid holidays, and limited overtime. The transition from a 6-day to a 5-day week was sometimes made in partial steps. For instance, there would be a half day of work on Saturdays or shortened hours during the summer months only.

A notable step was Henry Ford's decision in 1926 to introduce a 5-day week at the Ford Motor Company. Ford made this announcement:

The country is ready for the 5-day week. It is bound to come through all industry. ... The short week is bound to come, because without it the country will not be able to absorb its production and stay prosperous. The harder we crowd business for time the more efficient it becomes. The more well-paid leisure workmen get the greater become their wants. These wants soon become needs. Well-managed business pays high wages and sells at low prices. Its workmen have the leisure to enjoy life and the wherewithal with which to finance that enjoyment. The industry of this country could not long exist if factories generally went back to the 10-hour day, because the people would not have the time to consume the goods produced. ... Just as the 8-hour day opened our way to prosperity, so the 5-day week will open our way to a still greater prosperity.[33]

Henry Ford's views were generally not shared by his peers in the business community, who opposed the 5-day week on the grounds that it might lead working men into more drunkenness, laziness, crime, and "loose living." References to Rome's decline because of its many holidays were frequent. U.S. Steel's tight-fisted president, Judge Gary, brought religious arguments to bear against the 5-day scheme: "The Commandment says: 'Six days shalt thou labor and do all thy work.' The reason it didn't say seven days is that the seventh is a day of rest, and that's enough."[34] Economic objections to the 5-day workweek included predictions of higher labor costs and increased foreign competition, an alleged technical inability to make the change, expected labor shortages, the absurdity of paying workers six days' wages for five days' work, and so forth.

The Great Depression of the 1930s preempted whatever plans anyone might have had constructively to change working hours. Hours went down in a spiral of insufficient work opportunities. For economic reasons, the average workweek in manufacturing declined from 44.2 hours to 38.2 hours—a 13 percent drop—between 1929 and 1932. It was down to 34.6 hours in 1934. That was not the kind of "progress" anyone wished to see, but no one knew how to regain control. Henry Ford vainly announced the $7/day minimum wage. John D. Rockefeller let it be known that he and his son were again buying common stocks. President Hoover, among other things, publicly advocated that workers' hours be cut in preference to layoffs. At his request, the president of Standard Oil of New Jersey (now Exxon) toured the country to recommend shorter hours—with reduced pay, of course. While most labor leaders were not philosophically opposed to that, the proposal left a bitter taste in the mouths of rank-and-file union members: it was "sharing the misery" as much as work-sharing.

Nevertheless, organized labor went ahead with legislative plans for a reduced workweek. In 1930, the American Federation of Labor developed a 5-day-week proposal, urged by its Metal Trades Department, which soon turned into one calling for a 5-day, 30-hour week with no reduction in pay. Labor for the first time favored legislation rather than collective bargaining as the means of cutting hours. In December 1932, Senator Hugo Black of Alabama introduced a 30-hour bill in Congress. This bill would have prohibited circulating in foreign or interstate commerce goods produced by firms "in which any person was employed or permitted to work more than five days in any week or more than six hours in any day."[35] Black's bill came to a vote in the special session of Congress called by the incoming President, Franklin D. Roosevelt. It easily passed the Senate on April 6, 1933, but then encountered unexpected opposition from the administration, which caused the bill to be buried in the House Rules Committee.

President Roosevelt intended to incorporate hours reductions in a broader package of economic legislation designed to protect workers' purchasing power. The National Industrial Recovery Act, passed in 1933, regulated hours and wages by means of industrial codes. In each industry, management and labor were supposed to work out an agreement to establish voluntary codes of fair practice, which would stabilize employment. Hopefully, workers who felt more secure about their jobs and income would spend more freely for consumer products, and so the economy would improve. The 40-hour week became the standard in most industries under the NRA, as the program's administrative arm, the National Recovery Administration, was known. In the automobile and clothing industries, however, a 35-hour week was selected. A 44-hour week was standard in the retail trade. In general, the NRA codes set hours slightly below the current average so that additional employment would be generated.

The program came to an abrupt end in May 1935, when the U.S. Supreme Court ruled the law unconstitutional in the case Schechter Poultry Corp. vs. United States. The court found that the NRA code in the poultry industry did not fit the category of regulating interstate commerce, and also that the Executive branch had improperly assumed legislative powers. Roosevelt was furious. This ruling led to his ill-fated attempt in 1937 to obtain a more compliant court by "packing" it with replacements for the aging justices. Despite the legal setback, the NRA codes of hours and wages largely continued to be observed. His hand strengthened politically by the 1936 election, Franklin Roosevelt was determined to pass employment legislation that would meet the constitutional test.

The two enduring pieces of hours legislation enacted under Roosevelt are the Walsh-Healy Public Contracts Act of 1936 and the Fair Labor Standards Act of 1938. The Walsh-Healy Act prescribed a 40-hour work-week for all businesses that furnished more than $10,000 a year in materials, supplies, articles, or equipment to the federal government, and it required the payment of "time and one half" overtime wages when weekly hours exceeded that level. It also required overtime to be paid for work beyond 8 hours in a day, and, to date, remains the chief federal law regulating daily hours. Further provisions had to do with minimum wages, restrictions on child and convict labor, and health and safety protection.

The Fair Labor Standards Act (FLSA), passed two years later, sought the broader, but legally more tenuous, coverage of firms engaged in interstate commerce. Its constitutionality was tied to the clause in Article I, Section 8 of the U.S. Constitution, which gives Congress the power "to regulate commerce with foreign nations, and among the several states, and with the Indian tribes"—the so-called "interstate commerce clause." The bill was carefully drafted by lawyers at the U.S. Department of Labor under the direction of Secretary Frances Perkins. Enacted into law in June 1938, the Fair Labor Standards Act applied mainly to production workers in mining and manufacturing. It provided for the new standard to be phased in over a 2-year period. The standard became 44 hours in the first year, and then dropped to 40 hours, starting in October 1940. Numerous occupations were specifically "exempt" from coverage, including newspaper delivery boys, family farmers, and radio announcers. Perhaps the most important exemption pertains to an employee who is "employed in a bona fide executive, administrative, or professional capacity."

Over the years, workers in other industries not originally included have come under coverage of the FLSA through amendments. These include workers in retail trade, services, and construction (1961); farm and other workers (1966); state and local government workers (1974); and hotel, motel, and restaurant workers (1977). In the 1985 case of Garcia vs. San Antonio Metropolitan Transit Authority, the U.S. Supreme Court affirmed coverage for municipal bus drivers. When the law was passed in 1938, it applied to about one third of all U.S. wage-and-salary workers. In 1979, more than sixty percent of these workers, or 54 million people, were covered.

PROSPECT FOR FURTHER IMPROVEMENTS

Early on, it was recognized that the higher pay for overtime work constituted a perverse incentive for people to work longer hours. The research director of the International Brotherhood of Pulp, Sulphite, and Paper Mill Workers commented at a 1956 conference on work hours: "Aside from the workers' desire for their paid holidays and paid vacations, there is no evidence in recent experiences that workers want shorter daily or weekly hours. The evidence is all on the other side. Hundreds of local and International officials have testified that the most numerous and persistent grievances are disputes over the sharing of overtime work. The issue is not that someone has been made to work, but that he has been deprived of a chance to make overtime pay."[36] Although employers were supposed to find overtime financially disadvantageous, it has become less so as the cost of hiring additional employees and paying fringe benefits has increased relative to the cost of the half-time premium. Some employers have used overtime as a motivating benefit or built it into their compensation structure in lieu of higher straight-time pay.

Another reason for the weakening of labor support for shorter hours has been the unions' domination by their older members. Most union contracts contain a provision for layoffs by seniority. That means that in ordinary economic circumstances a majority of union members can feel reasonably safe in their jobs, knowing that a cushion of less-senior workers stands between themselves and the unemployment lines. Having little personally to fear, they tend to lose sympathy for their jobless peers and even become personally indignant at the thought of giving up income to help younger people by sharing the work. Other bargaining issues, such as improved pensions and health-insurance benefits, may appeal more to this influential group of workers.

The unemployment problem is, of course, a concern for the entire community, and not just for labor and management as they negotiate at the bargaining table. For this reason, the legislative route to hours reductions would appear to be more appropriate than bilateral labor agreements. Shorter-workweek bills, usually supported by organized labor, have gained the support of other political constituencies affected by high unemployment. They would include, among others, racial minorities, the young, and the poor.

In the 1960s, Rep. Adam Clayton Powell, who represented the Harlem district in New York City, introduced a bill in Congress for a 32-hour workweek and an increase in the minimum wage. The Johnson administration supported his proposal to raise the overtime premium to double-time pay, but did not favor a lower standard. Nevertheless, no change was made in the law. In the 1970s and 1980s, Rep. John Conyers of Detroit has introduced similar legislation proposing to amend the Fair Labor Standards Act. An earlier version of his bill called for the standard workweek to be reduced in stages from 40 to 35 hours over a 4-year period. A later version has sought a 32-hour workweek, phased in over eight years. Both versions have included, as well, provisions to raise the overtime-pay rate from time-and-one-half to double-time and to prohibit mandatory-overtime clauses in labor contracts. The Conyers bill, H.R. 1784, is the focus of most contemporary efforts to reduce the workweek legislatively in the United States.

The prospects of passing legislation of this sort have never been good; a swarm of business lobbyists and academic experts has always been on hand to testify against it. In October 1979, the Conyers bill, co-sponsored by thirteen other members of Congress, received three days of hearings in the Labor Standards subcommittee of the House Education and Labor Committee. The bill was never reported out of committee, and it failed to attract a Senate sponsor. Several others bills introduced by Rep. Conyers, most recently in April 1985, have received even less support in the Congress. (Interestingly, another bill of which Rep. Conyers was the chief sponsor, making Martin Luther King's birthday a national holiday, passed the Congress and was signed into law by President Reagan after many years of effort. Political attitudes, for various reasons, quickly change.)

Yet it may be seen as parochial, and unduly pessimistic, to end our short history of shorter working hours on the current situation in the United States. Seldom have the prospects for reduced work hours seemed less promising. The most memorable event of the decade was the attempt in 1981 to gain a 32-hour workweek by members of the Professional Air-Traffic Controllers Association (PATCO), which prompted President Reagan to fire the union's striking members. Give-backs by labor, not further hours reduction, have been the rule. One should understand, however, that, when the issue is seen from a global perspective, the picture brightens considerably. While Washington fiddles, the mantle of leadership in this area has passed to other countries. With our complacent labor practices, the United States has become, to an alarming degree, an economic and social backwater, as newer and more progressive ideas are hatched in such places as Tokyo, Brussels, and Paris.

While working hours in the United States have shown little change in the postwar period, the nations of western Europe, in particular, have taken great strides forward. The momentum they have achieved in bringing the workweek down to 40 hours has, in some cases, carried on to reductions below that level. The world's largest free trade union, I.G. Metall, took on both the national government and the employers' associations in West Germany in 1984 and, after a seven-week strike, won an impressive victory for a 38.5-hour week in the automobile industry. Now, a union official claims, "the trade union demand [for shorter hours] is much more popular [in 1987] than three years ago. It is therefore much easier to mobilize the workers for this demand."[37] Elsewhere, in Australia, France, the Netherlands, and several of the Scandinavian countries, progress has been made during the 1980s in establishing workweeks shorter than 40 hours.

In summary, the hours issue, though dormant in the United States, is alive and well in other parts of the world. Where the spirit of progress is, there will likely be found also an effort to reduce worktime and provide additional leisure.

12
WORK, LEISURE, PHILOSOPHY, IDEOLOGY, AND THEIR PERVERSIONS

Viewed in economics as the conversion of human energy and skill into goods and services, work has always been with us. Whether in Eden by the banks of the Euphrates or at Tomorrowland in Anaheim, the fourth inevitability of human life (before death, along with taxes, and while enduring the counsel of bores), remains the requirement to labor. Yet work is rarely investigated, or analyzed philosophically, by the economist. The production of things, the offering of services, engage the economist's attention. Likewise the rewards of labor in the form of income are of economic concern.

Economists are at once too inclusive and too exclusive in their view of work. The discipline of economics defines certain activities right out of the labor statistics. For instance, the effort of running a household—provisioning it, cleaning it, and providing transportation for its younger members—is never measured by economists. Conversely, economists do measure activities involving no worthwhile effort, such as takeovers of one corporation by another. Philosophers have attempted, with somewhat greater success than economists, to wrestle with the concept of work. The ancients asserted work's place in the human scheme without exaggerating its importance. Theologians from the beginning held that work was neither a duty nor a calling but a simple necessity. Protestants elevated work into a badge of divine favor. Marx, following the encyclopedists and the utilitarians, transmuted work into the index of human value.

Work is itself the major source of economic provision afforded by a majority of citizens. Without jobs, most of us cannot survive in the mainstream of society. The stream of income gained by daily effort pays for most housing, food, education, services, and government. No work, no pay, no life: this is the rule to which most persons are subject. In the industrialized, and allegedly post-industrial, worlds, work occurs whenever a person sells the use of his or her time to someone else. Within that time, the employer directs the performance of certain tasks that are aimed, in theory, at the production of goods or the distribution of services. In trade for his or her time, the worker receives income.

Thus generalized, work in the modern world is presumed to be connected with activity; but what is measured is its connection with time. In traditional societies, often miscalled primitive, where monetary units are insufficiently widespread to enable comprehensive monitoring of economic activity, the connection between work and production is stronger; but that between work and time remains undiminished. Work is therefore, together with language, one of the principal distinguishing characteristics of the human species.

In the biological evolution of organisms, the rate of change of any part is governed by the rate of change of the whole. Changes do not take place piecemeal. In organisms such as the human body, when growth of a part outdistances the whole, the vitality of the whole is threatened. The general name for such a disorder is cancer.

By analogy, the physical, emotional, and spiritual dimensions of the total person are interdependent. The integrity, the wholeness of the person can be disturbed and even destroyed unless each of these functions properly in relation to the others. Losing weight or gaining weight—anorexia or overeating—are physical responses to spiritual disturbances. Thinking and feeling and working are natural and complementary activities that comprise the integrated functioning of the whole person. The individual who for whatever reason develops one area without proper regard for the others experiences inner disturbances that are externalized in overeating or overworking or oversleeping or overreacting or some other disorderly behavior.

In the organic view of human society, a culture is a set of generally accepted guidelines or norms controlling individual behavior in a social context. Economic behavior, which in the case of the U.S. society is concerned with getting and spending money, produces results that we measure in the "gross national product" or GNP. Economic growth is measured by increases in GNP, as reported by the U.S. Department of Commerce. A percentage increase in GNP from one date to another is currently accepted as evidence that things are getting better.

Carrying this biological analogy one step further, we can say that the GNP measure is too simplistic, just as gaining more pounds is an unreliable measure of the progress and health of an overweight person. The broader view of the biological analogy would say that the healthy vitality of the whole society requires that the rate of change of any part should bear a healthy relation to changes in other parts. It is in this context that the large discrepancies between the "haves" and the "have nots," within our nation and among nations, appear as a social cancer. The technologies of production outdistance the ethics of distribution.

Our society is morally dominated by the work ethic. We measure human progress by investments that increase the annual sales of fast foods, fast horses, and fast bombers. This was not always the accepted view.

WORK IN ANCIENT TIMES

Jacques Ellul makes the point that the biblical text most often cited to prove that work is part of the human nature actually includes none of the known attributes of work. In Genesis 2, Adam is told to "cultivate" and to "guard" Eden. Yet

this original notion includes none of the characteristics of work! True, cultivation is required, but it has little utility, because the Garden already flourishes on its own without any particular human help. Also ... from whom [is the Garden to be guarded]? There is no enemy there, no "principle of evil," no Satan. There is only the serpent, not a mythical or metaphysical serpent, just a simple animal. Nevertheless, Adam is told to cultivate and to guard, to concern himself with functions perfectly useless and unnecessary. This is neither law, constraint, nor necessity. At the same time the distinction between these activities and play does not yet exist. One is not able to speak of *work* in the ordinary sense.

After the break between God and humanity work as such appears, that is, as something necessary and harsh.... It is not a "natural law" but a constraint of the precarious condition in which human beings find themselves.... And what of Paul's famous words—"Those who do not work should not eat" (2 Thess. 3:10)—which are always triumphantly cited to prove the excellence of work? This is exactly a necessity: to eat, it is necessary to work. That is the point. No virtue, no value is involved.... The biblical teaching is radical: You should work. Simply that. And God, if he wants, will grant the rewards, the results. The product of work is always a *gift*, freely given, not obligatory, coming from God alone. And it is on this condition that all of the sacrifices and offerings are made. Work remains, therefore, chancy and uncertain; it is not automatically gratifying.[1]

In his discussion of the condition of work in the Roman Empire, Ellul is equally incisive:

In the most general terms, the ideal human life involved the total absence of work. Work was not invested with any moral value. On the contrary, it was the mark of an inferior condition, of degradation (in that it was negation of liberty, being of the order of necessity!). The ideal of the free Roman, not just of the patrician, or the rich, but of all citizens, was leisure—not laziness or rest, but a certain conception of life. Leisure (*otium*) is not an emptiness but involves human relations, conversation, discussion of political issues, participation in numerous assemblies, societies and associations—therefore, a life dedicated to the social and political, not absorbed by work. Work was a negative quality—a "non-leisure" (*neg-otium*), the absence of leisure, the absence of a free life. This idea of work as harsh, difficult, and degrading we find over and over again, in varying degrees, in different times and places. No society was ever dedicated to work. Of course, work was an ever-present reality. But work did not cease to appear heavy and unbalanced until the town grew to be of great importance. With the development of urban life, work becomes more indispensible and, ironically, less and less rewarding.[2]

In considering the place of work in life and in society, Ellul notes that in former times work played a different role than it does at present, when it serves to define, and even to give value to, most people's lives.

Slaves in antiquity had nothing in common with the blacks of the West Indies in the 17th and 18th centuries, whose condition was atrocious. By contrast, Greek and Roman slaves were not weighted down with work. Their chores were generally light, and they had a great deal of leisure time. Slavery was more a condition of the deprivation of liberty or citizenship than of work. Considering the number of slaves needed to work a piece of land, it is easy to understand the low productivity. Further, current scholarship emphasizes that slaves, since they represented capital, were used carefully and sparingly. And many slaves practiced important professions (lawyers, doctors, teachers, businessmen) and had access to upper administrative levels.... It is enough to emphasize that slaves were not crushed with work, any more than were free artisans. The "average" work difference between those who did nothing and slaves was negligible in ancient societies. Of course, there were exceptional cases like galley slaves and slaves in the mines...but it must be remembered that these slaves were condemned criminals and that it was only as offenders that they carried out dangerous or exhausting work.[3]

TRADITIONAL CATHOLIC TEACHINGS

By the Middle Ages, ancient forms of slavery had been replaced by serfdom; but restrictions on overworking one's dependents applied as strongly as did the rest of the moral code. As Ellul wrote of the Scholastics:

Of course, among the numerous theologians, one is able to find texts praising work. But I do not believe these are typical or that they express the common viewpoint. It seems that work was habitually considered from two points of view. First, there is the idea that humanity has been sentenced to work which preserves the traditional judgment (harsh, enslaving, etc.), but as a just condemnation from God. Therefore, it is necessary to work in order to accept the human condition decreed by God, that is the natural condition. Further, this is written into the theology of suffering, of the mystical union with the suffering of Christ and the redemptive value of human suffering. It is, essentially, from this perspective that work is considered something positive. It is painful, prostrating, exhausting, and *the cause of this* must be received positively because, just like sickness, infirmity, etc., it is an occasion to be in communion with the suffering of Jesus and a way for a person to work out his salvation. When examining theological texts favorable to work, it is necessary to remember such a dimension.

The other aspect suggests that, in all cases, lowly work may be ennobled if it is offered directly to God. And if people are put to work constructing cathedrals or in monasteries by rules imposing work on all, this is nevertheless a suffering that one accepts for the glory of God. In other words, when work is considered *in itself,* in its natural reality, it is always something evil, to be suffered, disagreeable. But as part of a total life before God, it is invested with a value external to itself and was able to take on a positive role in the Christian life, in which all that we make is offered to the glory of God.[4]

When St. Thomas Aquinas considered the nature of work it was as an adjunct to his inquiry into whether members of religious orders were bound to work with their hands. In finding that the religious were not so bound, Aquinas notes that "the Apostle [Paul] ordered manual labor first of all in order to avoid theft . . . [s]econdly, to avoid the coveting of others' property . . . [t]hirdly, to avoid the discreditable pursuits whereby some seek a livelihood. . . . It must, however, be observed that under manual labour are comprised all those human occupations whereby man can lawfully gain a livelihood, whether by using his hands, his feet, or his tongue. For watchmen, couriers, and the like who live by their labor, are understood to live by their handiwork, because, since the hand is the organ or organs, handiwork denotes all kinds of work by which a man may lawfully gain a livelihood."

Having outlined the religious benefits of secular work, he specifies work's place within the natural law:

[N]ature has provided man with hands instead of arms and clothes with which she has provided other animals, in order that with his hands he may obtain these and other necessaries. From this it is clear that this precept [is] as all the precepts of the natural law. . . . Yet not everyone sins that works not with his hands, because those precepts of the natural law which regard the good of the many are not binding on each individual, but it suffices that one person apply himself to this business and another to that; for instance, that some be craftsmen, others husbandmen, others judges, and others teachers, and so forth, according to the words of the Apostle (I Cor. 12:17): "If the whole body were the eye, where would be the hearing? If the whole were the hearing, where would be the smelling?"[5]

The traditional Christian position on the nature of work has been restated by John Paul II in an encyclical early in his term. Probing the sense of work in classical times, the Pope remarked:

The ancient world introduced its own typical differentiation of people into classes according to the type of work done. Work which demanded from the worker the exercise of physical strength, the work of muscles and hands, was considered unworthy of free men and was therefore given to slaves. By broadening certain aspects that already belonged to the Old Testament, Christianity brought about a fundamental change of ideas in this field, taking the whole content of the gospel message as its point of departure, especially the fact that the one who, while being God, became like us in all things, devoted most of the years of his life on earth to manual work at the carpenter's bench. This circumstance constitutes in itself the most eloquent "gospel of work," showing that the basis for determining the value of human work is not primarily the kind of work being done, but the fact that the one who is doing it is a person. The sources of the dignity of work are to be sought primarily in the subjective dimension, not in the objective one.

Such a concept practically does away with the very basis of the ancient differentiation of people into classes according to the kind of work done. This does not mean that from the objective point of view human work cannot and must not be rated and qualified in any way. It only means that the primary basis of the value of work is man himself, who is its subject. This leads immediately to a very important conclusion of an ethical nature: However true it may be that man is destined for work and called to it, in the first place work is "for man" and not man "for work." Through this conclusion one rightly comes to recognize the pre-eminence of the subjective meaning of work over the objective one. Given this way of understanding things and presupposing that different sorts of work that people do can have greater or lesser objective value, let us try nevertheless to show that each sort is judged above all by the measure of the dignity of the subject of work, that is to say, the person, the individual who carries it out. On the other hand, independent of the work that every man does, and presupposing that this work constitutes a purpose—at times a very demanding one—of his activity, this purpose does not possess a definite meaning in itself. In fact, in the final analysis it is always man who is the purpose of the work, whatever work it is that is done by man—even if the common scale of values rates it as the merest "service," as the most monotonous, even the most alienating work.[6]

Proceeding to the 19th century view of work, John Paul suggests that the scientific materialism of Marx is morally indistinguishable from the "economistic thought" of capitalists:

For certain supporters of such ideas, work was understood and treated as a sort of "merchandise" that the worker—especially the industrial worker—sells to the employer, who at the same time is the possessor of the capital, that is to say, of all the working tools and means that make production possible. This way of looking at work was widespread especially in the first half of the 19th century. Since then explicit expressions of this sort have almost disappeared and have given way to more human ways of thinking about work and evaluating it. The interaction between the worker and the tools and means of production has given rise to the development of various forms of capitalism—parallel with various forms of collectivism—into which other socioeconomic elements have entered as a consequence of new concrete circumstances, of the activity of workers' associations and public authorities, and of the emergence of large transnational enterprises. Nevertheless, the danger of treating work as a special kind of "merchandise" or as an impersonal "force" needed for production (the expression "work force" is in fact in common use) always exists, especially when the whole way of looking at the question of economics is marked by the premises of materialistic economism.

A systematic opportunity for thinking and evaluating in this way, and in a certain sense a stimulus for doing so, is provided by the quickening process of the development of a one-sidedly materialistic civilization, which gives prime importance to the objective dimension of work, while the subjective dimension—everything in direct or indirect relationship with the subject of work—remains on a secondary level. In all cases of this sort, in every social situation of this type, there is a confusion or even a reversal of the order laid down from the beginning by the words of the Book of Genesis: Man is treated as an instrument of production, whereas he—he alone, independent of the work he does—ought to be treated as the effective subject of work and its true maker and creator. Precisely this reversal of order, whatever the program or name under which it occurs, should rightly be called "capitalism"—in the sense more fully explained below. ... [C]apitalism has a definite historical meaning as a system, an economic and social system, opposed to "socialism" or "communism." But in the light of the analysis of the fundamental reality of the whole economic process—first and foremost of the production structure that work is—it should be recognized that the error of early capitalism can be repeated wherever man is in a way treated on the same level as the whole complex of material means of production, as an instrument and not in accordance with the true dignity of his work—that is to say, where he is not treated as subject and maker, and for this very reason as the true purpose of the whole process of production.[7]

Work, by which material is converted to the use of mankind, is therefore seen in Christian terms not as an absolute value, but as subordinate to people's lives and spirits. Reviewing Christian teaching, John Paul continues,

[W]e must first of all recall a principle that has always been taught by the church: the principle of the priority of labor over capital. This principle directly concerns the process of production: In this process labor is always a primary efficient cause, while capital, the whole collection of means of production, remains a mere instrument of instrumental cause. This principle is an evident truth that emerges from the whole of man's historical experience.

When we read in the first chapter of the Bible that man is to subdue the earth, we know that these words refer to all the resources contained in the visible world and placed at man's disposal. However, these resources can serve man only through work. From the beginning there is also linked with work the question of ownership, for the only means that man has for causing the resources hidden in nature to serve himself and others is his work. And to be able through his work to make these resources bear fruit, man takes over ownership of small parts of the various riches of nature: those beneath the ground, those in the sea, on land or in space. He takes over all these things by making them his workbench. He takes them over through work and for work.... [8]

Further consideration of this question should confirm our conviction of the priority of human labor over what in the course of time we have grown accustomed to calling capital. Since the concept of capital includes not only the natural resources placed at man's disposal, but also the whole collective means by which man appropriates natural resources and transforms them in accordance with his needs (and thus in a sense humanizes them), it must immediately be noted that all these means are the result of their historical heritage of human labor. All the means of production, from the most primitive to the ultramodern ones—it is man that has gradually developed them: man's experience and intellect. In this way there have appeared not only the simplest instruments for cultivating the earth, but also through adequate progress in science and technology, the more modern and complex ones: machines, factories, laboratories and computers. Thus everything that is at the service of work, everything that in the present state of technology constitutes its every more highly perfected "instrument," is the result of work. This gigantic and powerful instrument—the whole collection of means of production that in a sense are considered synonymous with "capital"—is the result of work and bears the signs of human labor.... [9]

This truth, which is part of the abiding heritage of the church's teaching, must always be emphasized with reference to the question of the labor system and with regard to the whole socioeconomic system. We must emphasize and give prominence to the primacy of man in the production process, the primacy of man over things. Everything contained in the concept of capital in the strict sense is only a collection of things. Man, as the subject of work and independent of the work he does—man alone is a person. This truth has important and decisive consequences.

Opposition between labor and capital does not spring from the structure of the production process or from the structure of the economic process. In general the latter process demonstrates that labor and what we are accustomed to call capital are intermingled; it shows that they are inseparably linked. Working at any workbench, whether a relatively primitive or an ultramodern one, a man can easily see that through his work he enters into two inheritances: the inheritance of what is given to the whole of humanity in the resources of nature and the inheritance of what others have already developed on the basis of those resources, primarily by developing technology, that is to say, by producing a whole collection of increasingly perfect instruments for work. In working, man also "enters into the labor of others." Guided both by our intelligence and by the faith that draws light from the word of God, we have no difficulty in accepting this image of the sphere and process of man's labor. It is a consistent image, one that is humanistic as well as theological. In it man is the master of the creatures placed at his disposal in the visible world. If some dependence is discovered in the work process, it is dependence on the Giver of all the resources of creating and also on other human beings, those to whose work and initiative we owe the perfected and increased possibilities of our own work. All that we can say of everything in the production process which constitutes a whole collection of "things," the instruments, the capital, is that it conditions man's work; we cannot assert that it constitutes as it were an impersonal "subject" putting man and man's work into a position of dependence.

This consistent image, in which the principle of the primacy of person over things is strictly preserved, was broken up in human thought, sometimes after a long period of incubation in practical living. The break occurred in such a way that labor was separated from capital and set in opposition to it, and capital was set in opposition to labor, as though they were two impersonal forces, two production factors juxtaposed in the same "economistic" perspective. This way of stating the issue contained a fundamental error, what we can call the error of economism, that of considering human labor solely according to its economic purpose. This fundamental error of thought can and must be called an error of materialism, in that economism directly or indirectly includes a conviction of the primary and superiority of the material, and directly or indirectly places the spiritual and the personal (man's activity, moral values and such matters) in a position of subordination to material reality.... [10]

The same error, which is now part of history and which was connected with the period of primitive capitalism and liberalism, can nevertheless be repeated in other circumstances of time and place if people's thinking starts from the same theoretical or practical premises. The only chance there seems to be for radically overcoming this error is through adequate changes both in theory and in practice, changes in line with the definite conviction of the primacy of the person over things and of human labor over capital as a whole collection of means of production. [11]

THE PROTESTANT WORK ETHIC

The traditional view, then, called for work to find its place as an assistant to mankind, not a master. In the course of history, however, the Protestant transformation of Christian values gave rise to changes in the view of work. These alterations of traditional thought were explored in the early part of this century with some thoroughness by Max Weber, through whom the term "Protestant work ethic" became widely distributed. Citing American colonial history, Weber demonstrated the method by which the work came to take primacy over the person who does the work.

"For six pounds a year you may have the use of one hundred pounds.... He that spends a groat a day idly, spends idly above six pounds a year, which is the price for the use of one hundred pounds. He that idly wastes a groat's worth of his time per day, one day with another, wastes the privilege of using one hundred pounds each day. He that idly loses five shillings' worth of time, loses five shillings, and might as prudently throw five shillings into the sea. He that loses five shillings, not only loses that sum, but all the advantage that might be made by turning it in dealing, which by the time that a young man becomes old, will amount to a considerable sum of money."

It is Benjamin Franklin who preaches to us in these sentences, the same which Ferdinand Kurnberger satirizes in his clever and malicious *Picture of American Culture* as the supposed confession of faith of the Yankee. That it is the spirit of capitalism which here speaks in characteristic fashion, no one will doubt, however little we may wish to claim that everything which could be understood as pertaining to that spirit is contained in it. Let us pause a moment to consider this passage, the philosophy of which Kurnberger sums up in the words, "They make tallow out of cattle and money out of men." The peculiarity of this philosophy of avarice appears to be the ideal of the honest man of recognized credit, and above all the idea of a duty of the individual toward the increase of his capital, which is assumed as an end in itself. Truly what is here preached is not simply a means of making one's way in the world, but a peculiar ethic. The infraction of its rules is treated not as foolishness but as forgetfulness of duty. That is the essence of the matter. It is not mere business astuteness, that sort of thing is common enough, it is an ethos. *This* is the quality which interests us.[12]

Those who argue that having reached the Protestant work ethic stage is the best in thinking about the nature of work that we are likely ever to do could be right. However, associated with the explosion of goods of the last two hundred years, there is some possibility that the ethic has been surpassed both by technology and by human moral development. Even if they are right, however, certain functional problems with this mode of thought were pointed out by Weber.

[S]ince the interest of the employer in a speeding-up of harvesting increases with the increase of the results and the intensity of the work, the attempt has again and again been made, by increasing the piece-rates of the workmen, thereby giving them an opportunity to earn what is for them a very high wage, to interest them in increasing their own efficiency. But a peculiar difficulty has been met with surprising frequency: raising the piece-rates has often had the result that not more but less has been accomplished in the same time, because the worker reacted to the increase not by increasing but by decreasing the amount of his work. A man, for instance, who at the rate of 1 mark per acre mowed 2½ acres per day and earned 2½ marks, when the rate was raised to 1¼ mark per acre mowed, not 3 acres, as he might easily have done, thus earning 3¾ marks, but only 2 acres, so that he could still earn the 2½ marks to which he was accustomed. The opportunity of earning more was less attractive than that of working less. He did not ask: how much can I earn in a day if I do as much as possible? but: how much must I work in order to earn the wage 2½ marks, which I earned before and which take care of my traditional needs?

This is an example of what is here meant by traditionalism. A man does not "by nature" wish to earn more and more money, but simply to live as he is accustomed to live and to earn as much as is necessary for that purpose. Wherever modern capitalism has begun its work of increasing the productivity of human labour by increasing its intensity, it has encountered the immensely stubborn resistance of this leading trait of pre-capitalistic labour.[13]

Such resistance may have turned out to be something fully human, not merely pre-capitalistic. Possibly capitalism, and its modes of thought as well as its ideological antagonists, may prove to be the historical aberration rather than the norm. Even if not, the relationship between wages and work at the height of pure, unreformed capitalism was amply explored by Weber.

[S]ince the appeal to the acquisitive instinct through higher wage-rates failed, [another obvious possibility] would have been to try the opposite policy, to force the worker by reduction of his wage-rates to work harder to earn the same amount that he did before. Low wages and high profits seem even today to a superficial observer to stand in correlation; everything which is paid out in wages seems to involve a corresponding reduction of profits. That road capitalism has taken again and again since its beginning. For centuries it was an article of faith, that low wages were productive, i.e. that they increased the material results of labour so that, as Pieter de la Cour, on this point, as we shall see, quite in the spirit of the old Calvinism, said long ago, the people only work because and so long as they are poor.

But the effectiveness of this apparently so efficient method has its limits. Of course the presence of a surplus population which it can hire cheaply in the labour market is a necessity for the development of capitalism. But though too large a reserve army may in certain cases favour its quantitative expansion, it checks its qualitative development, especially the transition to types of enterprise which make more intensive use of labour. Low wages are by no means identical with cheap labour. From a purely quantitative point of view the efficiency of labour decreases with a wage which is physiologically insufficient, which may in the long run even mean a survival of the unfit. The present-day average Silesian mows, when he exerts himself to the full, little more than two-thirds as much land as the better paid and nourished Pomeranian or Mecklenburger, and the Pole, the further East he comes from, accomplishes progressively less than the German.

Low wages fail even from a purely business point of view wherever it is a question of producing goods which require any sort of skilled labour, or the use of expensive machinery which is easily damaged, or in general wherever any great amount of sharp attention or of initiative is required. Here low wages do not pay, and their effect is the opposite of what was intended. For not only is a developed sense of responsibility absolutely indispensable, but in general also an attitude which, at least during working hours, is freed from continual calculations of how the customary wage may be earned with a maximum of comfort and a minimum of exertion. Labour must, on the contrary, be performed as if it were an absolute end in itself, a calling. But such an attitude is by no means a product of nature. It cannot be evoked by low wages or high ones alone, but can only be the product of a long and arduous process of education. Today, capitalism, once in the saddle, can recruit its labouring force in all industrial countries with comparative ease. In the past this was in every case an extremely difficult problem.[14]

Recruitment of labor has proved to be extremely difficult even at the height of current development, despite the permanent unemployment rate. The saddle capitalism is in appears to be on a tiring horse. But it did not seem that it would ever tire in the days of Franklin.

In fact, the *summum bonum* of this ethic [is] the earning of more and more money, combined with the strict avoidance of all spontaneous enjoyment of life.... It is thought of so purely as an end in itself, that from the point of view of the happiness of, or utility to, the single individual, it appears entirely transcendental and absolutely irrational. Man is dominated by the making of money, by acquisition as the ultimate purpose of his life. Economic acquisition is no longer subordinated to man as the means for the satisfaction of his material needs.

This reversal of what we should call the natural relationship, so irrational from a naive point of view, is evidently as definitely a leading principle of capitalism as it is foreign to all peoples not under capitalistic influence. At the same time it expresses a type of feeling which is closely connected with certain religious ideas. If we thus ask, *why* should "money be made out of men," Benjamin Franklin himself, although he was a colourless deist, answers in his autobiography with a quotation from the Bible, which his strict Calvinistic father drummed into him again and again in his youth: "Seest thou a man diligent in his business? He shall stand before kings" (Prov. xxii. 29). The earning of money within the modern economic order is, so long as it is done legally, the result and expression of virtue and proficiency in a calling; and this virtue and proficiency are, as it is now not difficult to see, the real Alpha and Omega of Franklin's ethic, as expressed in the passages we have quoted, as well as in all his works without exception.[15]

Through the seventeenth to the nineteenth centuries, the power of religion was domesticated in the service of the economy, rather than ranging free over the sphere of all that is best in mankind. The work ethic is the culmination of this narrowing process, as R.H. Tawney observed:

The pioneers of the modern economic order were *parvenus*, who elbowed their way to success in the teeth of the established aristocracy of land and commerce. The tonic that braced them for the conflict was a new conception of religion, which taught them to regard the pursuit of wealth as, not merely an advantage, but a duty. This conception welded into a disciplined force the still feeble *bourgeoisie*, heightened its energies, and cast a halo of sanctification round its convenient vices. What is significant, in short, is not the strength of the motive of economic self-interest, which is the commonplace of all ages and demands no explanation. It is the change of moral standards which converted a natural frailty into an ornament of the spirit, and canonized as the economic virtues habits which in earlier ages had been denounced as vices. The forces which produced it was the creed associated with the name of Calvin. Capitalism was the social counterpart of Calvinist theology.[16]

THE CALVINIST VIEW OF LEISURE

Modern capitalist thought, which has had great difficulty advancing beyond Calvin, had therefore travelled a great distance from the situation described by Plato when he wrote, "But the Gods, taking pity on mankind, born to work, laid down the succession of recurring Feasts to restore them from their fatigue, and gave them the Muses, and Apollo their leader, and Dionysius, as companions in their Feasts, so that nourishing themselves in festive companionship with the Gods, they should again stand upright and erect."[17]

Simultaneous with the historical alteration in thinking about work, wherein work was changed from a necessity (having no inherent value), beyond a duty to a calling (the performance of which was a measure of human value), was a diminution in the merit assigned to leisure. Far from seeing work as the prerequisite of leisure, as traditional economies and Christian thought had done, the capitalistic work ethic, rooted in Calvinism, saw leisure as a distraction from work. Leisure in the work ethic is limited to recreation, in the sense of recuperation from previous work, and justified not on any human grounds but solely on the materialist principle of restoration of the human machine for the purpose of producing more work.

Josef Pieper stated the effects of this change in thought succinctly:

[I]t is essential to begin by reckoning with the fact that one of the foundations of Western culture is leisure. That much, at least, can be learnt from the first chapter of Aristotle's *Metaphysics*. And even the history of the word attests the fact: for leisure in Greek is *skole,* and in Latin *scola,* the English "school." The word used to designate the place where we educate and teach is derived from a word which means "leisure."[18]

Leisure.... [nowadays] appears as something wholly fortuitous and strange, without rhyme or reason, and, morally speaking, unseemly: another word for laziness, idleness and sloth. At the zenith of the Middle Ages, on the contrary, it was held that sloth and restlessness, "leisurelessness," the incapacity to enjoy leisure, were all closely connected.... Idleness, in the old sense of the word, so far from being synonymous with leisure, is more nearly the inner prerequisite which renders leisure impossible: it might be described as the utter absence of leisure, or the very opposite of leisure. Leisure is only possible when a man is at one with himself, when he acquiesces in his own being.... [19]

... [A]ll sham forms of leisure ... [have] a strong family resemblance to want of leisure and to sloth (in its old metaphysical and theological sense). The opportunity is given for the mere killing of time, and for boredom with its marked similarity to the inability to enjoy leisure.... And the counterpart to that is the fact that if real leisure is deprived of the support of genuine feast-days and holy-days, work itself becomes inhuman: whether endured brutishly or "heroically" work is naked toil and effort without hope.[20]

Sloth, or idleness, when seen in its active form, thus undermines the common understanding of it as a phenomenon of passiveness. Leisure, however, is not just the absence of work, but life's gift itself. While moral and religious sanction is often claimed for the requirement to work long hours to satisfy a "work ethic," proponents of that theory overlook a saying of Jesus which instead associates leisure with a life of godliness and faith: "Consider how the lilies grow in the fields; they do not work; they do not spin; and yet, I tell you, even Solomon in all his splendor was not attired like one of these. But if that is how God clothes the grass in the fields, which is there today, and tomorrow is thrown on the stove, will he not all the more clothe you? How little faith you have!"[21]

A contemporary affirmation of the positive role that leisure can play in life may be found in the concluding section of *Economic Justice for All*, a policy document prepared recently at the direction of U.S. Catholic bishops. The statement reads:

"Some of the difficulty in bringing Christian faith to economic life in the United States today results from the obstacles to establishing a balance of labor and leisure in daily life. Tedious and boring work leads some to look for fulfillment only during time off the job. Others have become 'workaholics,' people who work compulsively and without reflection on the deeper meaning of life and their actions. The quality and pace of work should be more human in scale enabling people to experience the dignity and value of their work and giving them time for other duties and obligations. This balance is vitally important for sustaining the social, political, educational, and cultural structures of society. The family, in particular, requires such balance. Without leisure there is too little time for nurturing marriages, for developing parent-child relationships, and for fulfilling commitments to other important groups: the extended family, the community of friends, the parish, the neighborhood, schools, and political organizations. Why is it one hears so little today about shortening the work week, especially if both parents are working? Such a change would give them more time for each other, for their children, and for their other social and political responsibilities."[22]

LEISURE IN AN ECONOMIC AGE

When human life, stripped of its communal tendencies, becomes reduced to an economically useful commodity, only labor seems to have any value. In this misunderstanding, the practical distinction between materialist Marxists and materialist capitalists is invisible. Inverting the virtues and vices, both ideologies begrudge leisure any place at all in working life, though capitalists permit some activities outside work that require the purchase of special sporting equipment. Both the *Wall Street Journal* and *Pravda* could run the same shocked editorial decrying anyone who nowadays proclaimed leisure to be central to the notion of ordinary life.

Another function of the *Journal*, other than voicing the attitudes which the possessors of most of the money wish that most of the people shared, is to rein in the more adventurous capitalist spirits whose pursuit of profit might lead them astray from the path of conventional labor practices. One such renegade, fortunately uninfluenced by those secular pieties, was Henry Ford. His conception of overpaying (by then current standards) his workers, and of limiting their working hours to the then radical figure of 40 hours per week, was not rooted in any wild beneficence. Ford noted that he couldn't sell many of his automobiles to his workers if they didn't make enough to afford them, and have some time off to use them. (In those days adequate provision of public transportation obviated the need for driving to work, a subsequent source of sales even Henry Ford could not foresee.)

Ford's conception of leisure was somewhat deformed in the sense that it allowed workers to purchase goods hitherto unthinkable except for the very rich, without fully imagining that workers might have a need for contemplation, civic activity, and worship—better things than driving a car. Consumption was the debased currency offered to workers in lieu of leisure; and, as it was the only thing on offer, it was duly accepted.

But the assembly line perfected the world of "total work," as cited by Pieper, and as developed from rationalists like Benjamin Franklin. Capitalism first propounded and then refined the vision of the world of total work, but Communism took a parallel line of development. Penetrating Communism even to the level of the visual arts, the mechanized farmer and the assembly line worker are the principal heroes.

The *New York Times* has reported that the Swedish automobile manufacturer Volvo has constructed a new plant in which teams of workers move with each vehicle throughout the factory and perform all the tasks associated with its assembly. This is intended to increase productivity as well as job satisfaction (and they are not unrelated concepts, despite the attitudes of the Simon Legree school of management). Given advances in robotics as well as the quality-circle concept in Japan, it may be, therefore, that the age of the assembly line is coming to an end within the same century that spawned it. However the diminution of the value of leisure required by the world of total work will not be reversed even should its most visible symbol, the assembly line, be replaced. For it cannot be everywhere replaced, and is in any case being exported to Taiwan and Yugoslavia and Haiti as manufacturing's weight in the industrialized economies continues its twenty year decline.

What is required is as simple in conception as it is difficult to muster the will to perform: namely, an increase in the amount of leisure time available to Americans. Just as the presumed value of work was enforced through an increase in the time devoted to it, as farmers became factory workers, so an increase in the socially assigned value of leisure can be enforced through an increase in the time devoted to it.

As presently organized, industrialized economies such as the United States restrict leisure largely to those years after mandatory retirement at the age of 65. A weekend is barely long enough to do the shopping, tend the lawn, and restore some of the sleep lost during the working week to tension. Those capable of extracting actual contemplative leisure from a weekend are swimming against the tide of the culture. What is necessary is that the tide be reversed, and that leisure for talking with one's friends, working with civic associations, and taking aimless journeys not be primarily restricted to an age which many of us do not live to reach, and at which many of the faculties of enjoyment have been blunted.

The enforced leisure of retirement is difficult to enjoy if one has for so long been out of practice. Leisure, like the faculty for music or the soil of one's garden, must be cultivated with practice over time, not in one sudden burst of activity. To take the bulk of ten years, on average, of life after retirement, and spread it over a working life of forty years, will not only improve the ability to enjoy leisure of its recipients, it may help to reduce unemployment as well.

The need for facing the problem of unemployment in other than piecemeal fashion is threefold: it is moral, political, and economic. As a nation we cannot survive in peace if we continue to abandon somewhere between a third and a quarter of the population to productive disutility, material scarcity, and moral hopelessness. The normal, permanent, structural rate of unemployment has more than doubled in forty years. It hits hardest at the young, both those actively seeking work and those whose education and stability are affected by their parents' unemployment. It perpetuates the bondage of an underclass of ill-educated, ill-housed, ill-nourished and ill-cared-for people whose potential contribution to national prosperity is thrown away. And it sows the seeds of future social and political instability.

Regularly we urge the redistribution of land in developing nations. The rationale is that the basis of production which, in agricultural societies, is land, must be shared if developing nations are to fulfill their promise for their people. But we shy away from proposals to redistribute work in the United States. Jobs are the basis of production in industrialized societies, and it is likewise proper to suggest that they be shared if the United States is to advance beyond permanent rising unemployment.

Shortening working time has economic, moral, and social justification. Shortened working time would spread income across social barriers, leading to lower taxation rates on any one segment of society because all segments would be contributing. Shortened working time would afford more people the dignity of a job, as well as the necessary spiritual refreshment of truly leisure time. And shortening working time, by diminishing unemployment, would diminish the strain on social cohesion that continued economic inequality renders dangerous.

Yet the opposition to the idea is not less formidable for being misguided. The philosophical case against redistributing work, though loudly presented, is faulty. When you hear that working defines a person's moral worth, and that the penalty of unemployment must be inevitable in order to weed out slackers, you know you are in the presence of unreconstructed Social Darwinists. Their philosophy of salvation by work alone runs contrary to the history of Western philosophy, and is an aberration of a hundred years ago whose survival is a tribute to the tenacity of conveniently incomplete thought.

The historical case against redistributing work is often misstated. The rise in Western prosperity since the Renaissance is not a function of people working more hours, but of more people working more productively. Wide distribution of work, not intensity of individual work, permitted the consumer society to develop; and restrictions on distribution of work, evidenced by rising structural unemployment, have coincided with the hiccoughs and pauses in continued prosperity that have marked the decades of the 1970s and 1980s both in the United States and the rest of the industrialized world.

The commercial and economic case against shortened working time is the least convincing, in that it is essentially shortsighted and primarily greed-motivated. Employers fear that hiring more workers, while lowering the working hours but not the compensation of existing workers, will raise their expenses without a concomitant rise in productivity and profits. The self-employed object because their chances of making more money than they would working for someone else depend on their being willing to work longer hours. Some workers would also object that by working fewer hours for the same pay so that others might have jobs, the viability of their industry might be threatened. No account is taken of the effect of the increased gross purchasing power if some proportion of the unemployed were working.

In sum, there are no surprises in the case made against shortening working time. Negative statements prevalent in the Middle Ages, the Industrial Revolution, and the Depression are recycled. Laziness, drunkenness, and similar proclivities to waste were assigned then, and are assigned now, as being the most probable outcomes of higher incomes and less unemployment for workers. Always it is the other fellow's laziness, drunkenness, and wasteful habits which must be avoided. For ourselves personally, more leisure and less work could be a positive thing.

NOTES

CHAPTER 1

1. David Hamilton, *The New Mexico Independent* (August 15, 1975).
2. Paul A. Samuelson, *Economics*, 5th edition (New York: McGraw-Hill, 1961), p. 620.
3. John Diebold testimony to Subcommittee on Automation and Energy Resources, Joint Economic Committee of Congress, 1960. Quoted in Marcia L. Greenbaum, *The Shorter Workweek*, Bulletin #50 (Ithaca: New York School of Industrial and Labor Relations, 1963), p. 2.

CHAPTER 2

1. "Employment by Industry, Selected Years, 1950–84," *Monthly Labor Review* (May 1985), Table 9, p. 61; *Monthly Labor Review* (June 1986), Table 13, p. 72.
2. *Wall Street Journal* (April 13, 1983). Also in Runzheimer report on cars and living costs, "Why the auto industry likes robots."
3. "Auto automation: To battle the Japanese, GM is pushing boldly into computerization," *Wall Street Journal* (July 9, 1984), p. 1.
4. "Tricky technology: auto makers discover 'factory of the future' is headache just now," *Wall Street Journal* (May 13, 1986), p. 1. Quotes Maryann Keller, auto analyst at Furman, Selz, Mayer, Dietz & Birney, Inc.
5. "The future of the automobile: the report of MIT's international automobile program," St. Paul *Pioneer Press* (August 8, 1984), p. 9D.
6. "Robots: next step for garment makers," *Wall Street Journal* (August 7, 1986).
7. *Business Week* (August 3, 1981): 62. Quotes Harvey L. Poppel, vice-president of Booz, Allen & Hamilton.
8. Minneapolis *Star and Tribune* (October 8, 1985). Quotes Prof. John Wil-

loughby of American University. See also *Wall Street Journal* (September 3, 1985), p. 1.

9. "Office automation of white-collar work may cost jobs, a report says," *Wall Street Journal* (January 14, 1986), p. 1.

10. "Special report: the speedup in automation," *Business Week* (August 3, 1981), pp. 58, 62.

11. International Labor Organization, *ILO Information* 15, No. 4 (October 1987), p. 4. Cites Karl H. Ebel and Erhard Ulrich, "The computer in design and manufacturing—a servant or master?"

12. Ibid., p. 4.

13. "Tricky techonology: auto makers discover 'factory of the future' is headache just now", *Wall Street Journal* (May 13, 1986), p. 1.

14. "High tech to the rescue; more than ever, industry is pinning its hopes on factory automation," *Business Week* (June 16, 1986); p. 102. Quotes Thomas G. Gunn, director of manufacturing consulting at Arthur Young.

15. Ibid., p. 101.

16. "Delayed future: upgrading of factories replaces the concept of total automation," *Wall Street Journal* (November 30, 1987), pp. 1, 8.

17. Robert W. Bednarzik, "The impact of microelectronics on employment: Japan's experience," *Monthly Labor Review* (September 1985); p. 46. Cites a study by the Japan Ministry of Labour, "The relationship between technical innovation and labor." See also: "Microelectronics (ME) age and its effect," *Focus Japan* (October 1983), p. 2.

18. *ILO Information* (October 1987), p. 5. Cites Dr. Raphael Kaplinsky, "Microelectronics and employment revisited: a review."

CHAPTER 3

1. *What is at stake in a shorter workweek?* New York: National Association of Manufacturers, 1964, p. 10.

2. Hal Sider and Cheryl Cole, "The changing composition of the military and the effect on labor force data," *Monthly Labor Review* (July 1984), pp. 10–13; Charles C. Killingsworth, "Structural unemployment without quotation marks," *Monthly Labor Review* (June 1979), p. 32; Robert A. Gordon, *Measuring Employment and Unemployment* (Washington, D.C.: U.S. Government Printing Office [hereafter GPO], 1962); *Handbook of Labor Statistics, 1980*, technical notes, p. 3.

3. Joanna Moy, "Recent trends in unemployment and the labor force, 10 countries," *Monthly Labor Review* (August 1985): Table 2, p. 13.

4. "Working like a log" (editorial), *The Wall Street Journal* (April 6, 1984).

5. "Fast-food employees getting difficult to find, survey finds," Minneapolis *Star and Tribune* (June 12, 1985), survey by the Bureau of National Affairs.

6. *Handbook of Labor Statistics, 1975*, Table 39, p. 105; *Monthly Labor Review* (May 1980): Table 8, p. 73, Table 14, p. 77; *Monthly Labor Review* (April 1984), p. 18.

7. Earl F. Mellor, "Investigating the differences in weekly earnings of women and men," *Monthly Labor Review* (June 1984), pp. 17–28.

8. *Amway—the Industry Leader* (Amway Corp., 1984); Amway, *A Business of*

Your Own, 1980. See also: Bureau of Labor Statistics, *Workers, Jobs and Statistics: Questions and Answers on Labor Force Statistics* (September 1983), pp. 6–7.

9. Barry Bluestone and Bennett Harrison, *The Great American Job Machine: The Proliferation of Low Wage Employment in the U.S. Economy* (Washington D.C.: Joint Economic Committee of Congress, 1986).

10. U.S. Department of Commerce, Bureau of Economic Analysis, *Business Conditions Digest* 27, No. 1 (January 1987): Chart C1, "Civilian labor force and major components," p. 51.

11. *Economic Report of the President* (Washington, D.C.: GPO, 1987); Table B–32, "Civilian employment and unemployment by sex and age, 1947–1986," p. 282; Table B–31, "Population and the labor force, 1929–1986," p. 280.

12. U.S. Department of Labor, Bureau of Labor Statistics (hereafter BLS), *Workers without Jobs: A Chartbook on Unemployment* (Washington, D.C.: GPO, 1983), pp. 6–58.

13. Bluestone and Harrison, *The Great American Job Machine,* pp. 21–44.

CHAPTER 4

1. Paul H. Douglas, *The Theory of Wages* (New York: Macmillan, 1934), pp. 295–314. See also Paul H. Douglas, *Real Wages in the United States, 1890–1926* (Boston: Houghton Mifflin,1930); Peter Henle, "Leisure and the long work-week," *Monthly Labor Review* (July 1966), pp. 724–25; Harold Wilensky, "The uneven distribution of leisure: the impact of economic growth on 'free time,'" *Social Problems* (January 1961), p. 32. The Wilensky article refers to an unpublished Ph.D. thesis by T.A. Finegan at the University of Chicago, updating Douglas' work.

2. See Bureau of Labor Statistics, *Employment and Earnings* (January 1988): "Explanatory Notes," pp. 229–38.

3. Janice Neipert Hedges, "Job commitment in America: Is it waxing or waning?" *Monthly Labor Review* (July 1983), p. 20.

4. Geoffrey H. Moore and Janice N. Hedges, "Trends in labor and leisure," *Monthly Labor Review* (February 1971): Table 2, "Hours worked by full-time workers, May 1955, 1960 and 1965–70," p. 5.

5. Peter Henle, *Monthly Labor Review* (July 1966): Table 2, "Hours worked by full-time nonagricultural wage and salary workers," p. 723; *Employment and Earnings* (January 1988): Table 32, "Persons at work in nonagricultural industries by class of worker and full- or part-time status," p. 196.

6. Henle, *Monthly Labor Review* (July 1966); pp. 721–727.

7. Peter Henle, "Recent growth of paid leisure for U.S. workers," *Monthly Labor Review* (March 1962), pp. 249–250; Peyton K. Elder and Heidi D. Miller, "The Fair Labor Standards Act: Changes of four decades," *Monthly Labor Review* (July 1979), p. 10; Daniel E. Taylor and Edward S. Sekscenski, "Workers on long schedules, single and multiple jobholders," *Monthly Labor Review* (May 1982), p. 49. See also *Monthly Labor Review* (July 1979): "Supreme Court case of National League of Cities v. Usery 426 U.S. 833," p. 12; Peyton K. Elder, "The 1977 amendments to the federal minimum wage law," *Monthly Labor Review* (January 1978); p. 11.

8. Peter Henle, *Monthly Labor Review* (March 1962): Table 2, "Full-time wage

and salary workers, by hours of work during the survey week and industry, May of 1948, 1952, 1956, and 1960," p. 251.

9. Henle, *Monthly Labor Review* (July 1966), p. 727.

10. *Employment and Earnings* (January 1988): Table 7, "Employed and Un-employed full- and part-time workers by sex, age, and race," p. 167; Table 32, "Persons at work in nonagricultural industries by class of worker and full- or part-time status," p. 196.

11. *Employment and Earnings* (January 1988): Table 30, "Persons at work by hours of work and type of industry," p. 195. Also: "Mean hours worked by all person at work, 1943–1976, annual averages" and "Percent distribution of hours worked by persons at work 35 hours and over and average hours, workers on full-time schedules, 1967–1976, annual average," unpublished tables compiled by the BLS.

12. See Joseph S. Zeisel, "The workweek in American industry 1850–1956," *Monthly Labor Review* (January 1958); pp. 23–29.

13. See John Zalusky, "Shorter Hours—the steady gain," *AFL-CIO American Federationist* (January 1978).

14. "Working and playing," *Wall Street Journal* (August 8, 1985); based upon data collected by Philip Morris, Inc.

15. Henle, *Monthly Labor Review* (March 1962), p. 253–54. See also *Monthly Labor Review* (July 1958); pp. 744–51.

16. Henle, *Monthly Labor Review* (March 1962), pp. 256, 258 (footnotes); Moore and Hedges, *Monthly Labor Review* (February 1971), p. 5; Janice N. Hedges and Daniel E. Taylor, "Recent trends in work time: hours edge downward," *Monthly Labor Review*, (March 1980), p. 9; *Monthly Labor Review* (July 1983): p. 20.

17. International Labor Organization, *Convention Concerning Annual Holidays with Pay* (revised), 1970 (Convention #132).

CHAPTER 5

1. "Critics say U.S. economic picture is blurred by reliance on bad data," *Wall Street Journal* (January 10, 1986).

2. "How to save taxpayers $100 million a year," *Readers Digest* (January 1984); *Wall Street Journal* (December 6, 1984, editorial).

3. "Report of the Committee on Recent Economic Changes," (New York, 1929), pp. xv, xviii, 52, 59, 80, 81, 574–578. Included in Benjamin Kline Hunnicut, "The end of shorter hours," *Labor History* (Summer 1984); p. 384.

4. Thorstein Veblen, *The Theory of the Leisure Class* (New York: New American Library, 1953); pp. 39, 43, 70, 78–79.

5. Letter to Benjamin Vaughan, July 26, 1784. Quoted in *A Benjamin Franklin Reader*, edited by Nathan G. Goodman (New York: Thomas Y. Crowell, 1945); pp. 791–92.

6. Adam Smith, *Wealth of Nations* (New York: The Modern Library, 1937); pp. lviii, 315.

7. *Wall Street Journal* (August 1, 1985); M. Shanken Communications "Diet soft drinks: too good to be true," *New York Times* (February 4, 1987), p. 14.

8. "Glamor of upscale frozen foods fades as buyers return to basics," *Wall Street Journal* (December 15, 1987).

9. "Driven down: despite strong sales, auto makers believe real booms are over," *Wall Street Journal* (May 3, 1984), p. 1.

10. "Home PC: People don't need it, but they fear life without it," *Wall Street Journal* (August 13, 1985).

CHAPTER 6

1. Smith, *Wealth of Nations*, p. 625.

2. "Baby-goods firms see direct mail as the perfect pitch for new moms," *Wall Street Journal* (January 29, 1986).

3. "Small business: Brace yourself—1,000 brokers will be after your business," *Wall Street Journal* (June 10, 1985), p. 21. See also: "Insurers forcing people to buy policy to qualify for student loan," *Wall Street Journal* (September 10, 1985).

4. "Going into hock: soaring levels of debt, national and private, cause rising worries," *Wall Street Journal* (May 9, 1985), pp. 1, 20.

5. "Saving time is worth more than money to grocery shoppers, survey finds," Minneapolis *Star and Tribune* (May 7, 1985), p. 9B. Based on a nationwide survey of 1200 supermarkets between December 1984 and February 1985.

6. "Bigger, shrewder and cheaper Cub leads food stores into the future," *Wall Street Journal* (August 26, 1985).

7. "The hidden persuaders: stores use subtle design factors to lure customers," St. Paul *Pioneer Press and Dispatch* (December 15, 1987), pp. 1c, 3c.

8. "Brand-name produce hits stores—but will it really taste better?" *Wall Street Journal* (September 23, 1985).

9. "Tylenol, the painkiller, gives rivals headaches in stores and in court," *Wall Street Journal* (September 2, 1982), p. 1.

10. "Nestlé ends 3rd world sales pitch," St. Paul *Pioneer Press* (January 27, 1984).

11. *Statistical Abstracts* (1988): Table 1327, p. 755; "U.S. International Transactions—Summary: 1960 to 1987." See also: *United States Trade: Performance in 1984 and Outlook* (Washington, D.C.: U.S. Department of Commerce, June 1985).

12. "Gillette Keys sales to third world tastes," *Wall Street Journal* (January 23, 1986), p. 1.

13. "Smoking section: Cigarette companies develop third world as growth market," *Wall Street Journal* (July 5, 1985), p. 1.

14. "Makers of plowshares are finding there's more of a market for swords," Minneapolis *Star and Tribune* (December 23, 1985), p. 1A.

15. "NASA clash: growing militarization of the space program worries U.S. scientists," *Wall Street Journal* (January 15, 1986), p. 1.

16. "Military families worried by proposed retirement pay cuts," Minneapolis *Star and Tribune* (February 12, 1985), p. 3A; "Stockman blasts military pension system," Minneapolis *Star and Tribune* (February 6, 1985), p. 3A.

17. "Pentagon prepared for World War IV," St. Paul *Pioneer Press* (January 12, 1984), p. 1.

18. Minneapolis *Star and Tribune* (February 4, 1985). Interview with Stephen Watson, president of Dayton-Hudson department stores.

19. "Stodgy old mass-merchandisers will spend billions upgrading to serve 'upwardly mobile,'" Minneapolis *Star and Tribune* (October 10, 1984), p. 1C.

20. "Spending surge fails to match retailers' hopes," *Wall Street Journal* (December 27, 1984).

21. "Car sales show we're thinking bigger," *USA Today* (January 7, 1985). See also: *Wall Street Journal* (May 3, 1984), p. 14.

22. "Played out: the going gets tough and Madison Avenue dumps the yuppies," *Wall Street Journal* (December 9, 1987), pp. 1, 24.

23. "Establishing travel-volume criteria for fixed guideways," *Railway Age* (June 14, 1982), p. 33 (adapted from *Urban Rail in America*). Based on a 12 m.p.g. average for American automobiles.

24. "MTC historical ridership survey," Metropolitan Transit Commission, memo dated December 20, 1983.

25. "Surviving Minnesota breweries produce a variety of old brands," Minneapolis *Star and Tribune* (August 6, 1986).

26. "Push to treat drug abuse leads firms to bypass doctors and market to patients," *Wall Street Journal* (July 29, 1986).

27. "A Time for Choosing," *Wall Street Journal* (November 23, 1984). Excerpts from a speech delivered by Ronald Reagan in support of Barry Goldwater's presidential campaign on October 27, 1964.

28. St. Paul *Pioneer Press* (December 27, 1974), p. 23. Sign in office of Rep. H.R. Gross.

29. *Wall Street Journal* (June 22, 1978).

30. Minneapolis *Star and Tribune* (February 4, 1985), p. 1M, Dick Youngblood column. Study for the Joint Committee on Taxation of Congress.

31. Minneapolis *Star and Tribune* (December 26, 1983), p. 5B.

32. "The doctor-lawyer war," Minnesota *Daily* (July 8, 1985). Reprinted from the *New Republic,* TRB column, 1985. See also: "Courting disaster: the cost of lawsuits, growing ever larger, disrupts the economy," *Wall Street Journal* (May 16, 1986), p. 11.

33. "Businesses struggling to adapt as insurance crisis spreads," *Wall Street Journal* (January 21, 1986). Also: *Wall Street Journal* (May 16, 1986), p. 1.

34. "Risky business: liability insurance is difficult to find now for directors, officers," *Wall Street Journal* (July 10, 1985), p. 1. Quotes W. Grogan Lord, former director of Verna Corporation.

35. "Spending surge fails to match retailers' hopes," *Wall Street Journal* (December 27, 1984), p. 4.

36. *Wall Street Journal* (May 9, 1986), p. 19; source: Greeting Card Association.

37. "Santa turns grumpy as retailers decide he is unnecessary," *Wall Street Journal* (December 9, 1983), p. 1.

38. Report on Minneapolis-St. Paul radio station (February 18, 1985) disclosed that $515 million was spent that year on Valentine's Day candy. *Wall Street Journal* (May 9, 1986), p. 19; Source: Greeting Card Association. See also "Florists see rosy Valentine's day," *USA Today* (February 7, 1985), p. 3B.

39. St. Paul *Pioneer Press* (October 13, 1975), p. 8.

40. Arthur R. Pinto and Norman Poser, "Brokers who trade too often," *Wall Street Journal* (May 20, 1985).

41. Charles Dickens, *Bleak House,* 1853; quoted in *Forbes* (April 21, 1986), p. 118.

42. "Rising costs force doctors into rationing," Minnesota *Daily* (March 1, 1985); quotes Dr. Ronald Crawford, University of Minnesota neurologist.

43. James Bovard, "Can Sunkist wrap up the lemon industry?" *Wall Street Journal* (January 24, 1985).

44. St. Paul *Pioneer Press* (August 5, 1974), p. 2.

45. B. Charles Ames, "Corporate strategies for a shrinking market," *Wall Street Journal* (January 13, 1986).

46. "Merger advisers say the big fees they're charging are warranted," *Wall Street Journal* (July 17, 1981), p. 21.

47. "Back to School," *Wall Street Journal* (September 6, 1985); source: College Board.

48. "Educator says glut of PhDs driving students away from graduate schools," Minneapolis *Star and Tribune* (March 20, 1985), p. 13A; quotes Michael Sovern, president of Columbia University.

49. *Statistical Abstract, 1985,* Table 213, "Years of school completed, by age and race, 1940 to 1983," p. 134.

50. Peter Drucker, "A growing mismatch of jobs and job seekers," *Wall Street Journal* (March 26, 1985).

51. *Monthly Labor Review* (March 1986), p. 31. Quote from "Investing in America's Future: A Policy Statement by the National Council on Employment Policy" (Washington, D.C.: National Council on Employment Policy, 1984), pp. 24–25.

52. "College SAT's grow in importance despite long history of criticism," *Wall Street Journal* (February 5, 1985).

53. "Ah, Maui: the Mai Tais, the surf and, oh yes, the medical classes," *Wall Street Journal* (April 11, 1985).

54. "Some trade schools make big money by recruiting students who drop out," *Wall Street Journal* (April 5, 1985).

55. "Sartorial edge in job hunting," *Wall Street Journal* (November 9, 1981).

56. Tadashi Hanami, "Worker Motivation in Japan"; in *Highlights of Japanese Industrial Relations* (Tokyo: Japan Institute of Labour, 1983), p. 70.

57. Peter Drucker, "Playing in the information-based orchestra," *Wall Street Journal* (June 4, 1985).

58. *Wall Street Journal* (November 23, 1984), p. 7; review of Lawrence J. Peter's book, *Why Things Go Wrong.*

59. *Wall Street Journal,* January 16, 1986.

60. From a letter of Chief Tecumseh to Indiana territorial governor William Henry Harrison, 1810. Quoted in *I Have Spoken,* compiled by Virginia Irving Armstrong (New York: Sage Books, 1971), p. 44.

61. "Merged patent office yields improved efficiency," *Minnesota Daily* (January 14, 1985), p. 5.

62. "Right-wing thinkers push ideas," *Wall Street Journal* (December 7, 1984); p. 46.

63. *Handbook of Labor Statistics, 1985,* p. 123, Table 54, "Labor force and labor

force participation rates of married women, spouse present by presence and age of children, March 1948 to 1984."

64. "Americans spend less on food, eat out more often," Minneapolis *Star and Tribune* (February 12, 1985), p. 3A.

65. "Homes get dirtier as women seek jobs and men volunteer for the easy chores," *Wall Street Journal* (February 12, 1985).

66. "A nation of advice," *U.S. News & World Report* (March 24, 1986), p. 65.

67. St. Paul *Pioneer Press and Dispatch* (December 18, 1985), p. 6A.

68. "Age of anxiety: stress of American life is increasingly blamed for emotional turmoil," *Wall Street Journal* (April 2, 1979), p. 1.

69. Twin Cities *Reader* (August 27, 1981). Answer to question posed by Arthur Naftalin on public-television program, "Minnesota Issues," December 14, 1980.

70. "Laundry service: how the mob is using financial institutions to disguise its gains," *Wall Street Journal* (March 12, 1985), p. 1.

71. "Not all private eyes go around tracking wayward spouses," *Wall Street Journal* (May 23, 1985), p. 1.

72. "Presidential panel says 4 major unions have connections to organized crime," *Wall Street Journal* (January 15, 1986); "Panel calls on states to fight criminal groups," *Wall Street Journal* (April 2, 1986). Financial analysis prepared by Wharton Econometric Forecasting Associates, Inc.

73. Robert E. Taylor, "Shutting down the LEAA," *Wall Street Journal* (December 2, 1980).

74. "Jail inmates—selected characteristics: 1978," *Statistical Abstract, 1984*, Table 324, p. 194.

75. *Statistical Abstract, 1984*, Table 307, "Criminal justice system—public expenditures and employment, by level of government: 1970 to 1979," p. 185.

76. "Hired guns: One big security risk is the security guards, some companies find," *Wall Street Journal* (August 30, 1983), p. 1.

77. "Domestic arrests up, study says," St. Paul *Pioneer Press and Dispatch* (January 27, 1986), p. 8A.

78. Douglas J. Besharov, "How one group found a path out of the liability jungle," *Wall Street Journal* (April 17, 1986), p. 28.

79. Talk delivered by Minnesota state representative Connie Levi at White Bear Unitarian Church on December 9, 1984.

80. Philip Weiss, "I'm sick, you're sick," *City Pages* (April 11, 1984), p. 7; Nancy Livingston, "Habitually late mate often cause for alarm," St. Paul *Pioneer Press and Dispatch* (May 9, 1986), p. 1D.

81. Personal recollection of a segment on CBS program "60 Minutes" in late January 1985.

82. "Counseling is ace in the hole: compulsives need help to overcome gambling craving," St. Paul *Pioneer Press and Dispatch* (January 17, 1985), p. 1.

83. St. Paul *Pioneer Press* (April 12, 1981).

84. "Congress, cigarettes and tobacco carnage," Minneapolis *Star and Tribune* (June 4, 1985).

85. "Interest groups pay millions in appearance fees to get legislators to listen as well as to speak," *Wall Street Journal* (June 4, 1985).

86. "Beverage makers are thirsting to claim booze is healthy; critics don't

swallow it," *Wall Street Journal* (May 9, 1985). Study by Dr. Arthur Klatsky at Kaiser-Permanente Medical Center in Oakland, California.

87. "Pot group says U.S. crop worth $18.6 billion in '85," St. Paul *Pioneer Press and Dispatch* (January 11, 1986).

88. "Inside jobs: how GM began using private eyes in plants to fight drugs, crime," *Wall Street Journal* (February 27, 1986), pp. 1, 17.

89. Stanley Penn, "The bottom line: despite the dangers, more executives are using cocaine at work and play," *Wall Street Journal* (April 21, 1986), Section 4, "A special report: the business of leisure,", p. 19D.

90. *Runzheimer Report* (September 1985).

91. "For Reginald Giles, potholes aren't so bad; they're a blessing," *Wall Street Journal* (May 13, 1985), p. 1.

92. "Security-consulting firms spread: are they worth it?" *Wall Street Journal* (April 29, 1986).

93. "Subliminal messages take hold as stores struggle to deter shoplifting," *Wall Street Journal* (January 30, 1986).

94. *Statistical Abstract, 1984,* p. 84.

95. "Divorce becomes a big business as cases grow in size and complexity," *Wall Street Journal* (August 28, 1985).

96. Jeffrey A. Trachtenberg, "Shake, rattle, and clonk," *Forbes* (July 14, 1986), pp. 71–74.

CHAPTER 7

1. "Hmong refuse to move into U.S. culture shock," St. Paul *Pioneer Press* (January 13, 1985), pp. 1A, 12A.

2. St. Paul *Pioneer Press* (February 9, 1982).

3. "The Macho of Time," *New Republic* (August 20–27, 1977), TRB column, p. 42.

4. "Child care key to job programs, study reports," St. Paul *Pioneer Press and Dispatch* (January 12, 1986). Cites report by House Government Operations Committee.

5. Joan Beck, "Work structures need to bend, not just family," St. Paul *Pioneer Press and Dispatch* (December 31, 1985), p. 7A.

6. *Skyway News* (September 16, 1981).

7. *Wall Street Journal* (April 29 and June 5, 1981).

8. "Rapid reshaping: Gulf & Western changes image under new chief," *Wall Street Journal* (March 16, 1983), p. 18.

9. "Money was the only way," *Time* (December 1, 1986), p. 51.

10. Jolie Solomon, "Working at relaxation: in spite of unprecedented afflu-ence, Americans labor to find the time for leisure pursuits," *Wall Street Journal* (April 21, 1986), Section 4, "A special report: the business of leisure," p. 2.

11. Steve Lipson, reporter for the Stamford *Advocate*, "Company picnic haz-ardous: behavior can make or break a promising career," St. Paul *Pioneer Press and Dispatch* (August 9, 1985).

12. *Wall Street Journal* (November 30, 1982), p. 1. Probably at IBM.

13. "The workaholic boss: an 18-hour-a-day menace," *Wall Street Journal* (May 10, 1982).

14. *Wall Street Journal* (April 17, 1984).

15. "GE union workers clear contract with 12-hour shifts," *Wall Street Journal* (June 28, 1984).

16. "If you want to make a retailer red hot, talk about blue laws," *Wall Street Journal* (February 4, 1985).

17. "West German law on shopping hours prevails in Stuttgart," *Wall Street Journal* (July 16, 1985).

18. "There's more to life than bocce ball & windmills," *Twin Cities Reader* (June 22, 1983), p. 10.

19. "Hoffman's decade of aid," *Time* magazine (January 17, 1972), p. 31.

20. Paul Craig Roberts, "The Keynesian attack on Mr. Reagan's plan," *Wall Street Journal* (March 19, 1981).

21. "Economics for the birds as scholar pays peanuts," St. Paul *Pioneer Press* (May 27, 1983). Cites work of Prof. Leonard Green of Washington University in St. Louis, Missouri.

22. Henry Ford interview, *Monthly Labor Review* (December 1926), p. 1166.

23. Frederick Engels, "Socialism, Utopian and Scientific," in *Ten Classics of Marxism* (New York: International Publishers, 1946), p. 65.

24. Ibid., pp. 62–63, 71–72.

25. Karl Marx, "Wage-Labour and Capital," *Ten Classics of Marxism*, pp. 45–46.

CHAPTER 8

1. *Wall Street Journal* (June 3, 1981).

2. "Going into hock: soaring levels of debt, national and private, cause rising worries," *Wall Street Journal* (May 9, 1985), p. 1; "Economics plus: consumers continue fast spending pace despite steep debts," *Wall Street Journal* (January 31, 1986), pp. 1, 7.

3. Flora Lewis, "Money soars, but economy drifts perilously," St. Paul *Dispatch and Pioneer Press* (January 2, 1986), p. 11. Estimate of $4.1 trillion actuarial deficit in Social Security trust fund in *Wall Street Journal* (November 26, 1977), p. 18.

4. "Delaying the day: deferred loan losses at thrifts and banks snowball across U.S.," *Wall Street Journal* (January 8, 1986), p. 1. Also "The outlook: financial system is sound, analysts say," *Wall Street Journal* (April 29, 1985), p. 1.

5. Flora Lewis, St. Paul *Dispatch and Pioneer Press* (January 2, 1986), p. 11. Quotes financier Felix Rohatyn. See also: "Delaying the day: deferred loan losses at thrifts and banks snowball across U.S.," pp. 1, 19.

6. *Wall Street Journal* (January 8, 1986), p. 1.

7. Adam Smith, *Wealth of Nations*, p. 882.

8. *Statistical Abstract, 1987*, p. 298; Table 486, "Public debt and interest paid of the federal government: 1940 to 1984," p. 311.

9. *Statistical Abstract 1987*, Table 678, p. 401.

10. Ibid., Table 497, p. 303; *Statistical Abstract 1979*, Table 438, p. 264.

11. James Fallows, "No-Fat City," *Atlantic Monthly* (November 1986), pp. 24–28.

CHAPTER 9

1. Henry Ford interview by Samuel Crowther, *World's Work* (October 1926). Quoted in *Monthly Labor Review* (December 1926); p. 1163.

2. Ralph Waldo Emerson, "Man the Reformer," *The Collected Works of Ralph Waldo Emerson*, Vol. I: Nature, Addresses & Lectures, notes by Robert E. Spiller, text established by Alfred R. Ferguson (Cambridge, MA: Belknap Press of Harvard University, 1971), pp. 150–51.

3. Wassily Leontief, "Employment policies in the age of automation," *ILO Information* 6, No. 1 (1978), pp. 1, 6.

4. *Fair Labor Standards Act of 1938 as Amended* (29 USC 201), U.S. Department of Labor publication 1318, printed October 1975.

5. *Reducing Standard Hours of Work: An Analysis of Australia's Recent Experience*, Research Report #15 (Canberra: Bureau of Industry Economics, 1984), pp. 127, 132, 145, 147. Rostered schedules are explained in the national newsletter of the Amalgamated Metal Workers and Shipwrights' Union, February 1982.

6. Rolande Cuvillier, *The Reduction of Working Time* (Geneva: International Labor Organization, 1984), pp. 105–06. The German estimates were made by the Institute for Labour Market and Occupational Research in Nuremberg. The French estimates were made by the Commission for Employment and Industrial Relations in preparation for eighth plan, May 1980. See also: Lionel Stolera, "Deux atouts contre le chomage," *L'Expansion* (Paris) (October 1979), pp. 136–39.

CHAPTER 10

1. Martin Nemirow, "Work Sharing approaches: past and present," *Monthly Labor Review* (September 1984); p. 38.

2. "Eastern time: Japanese firms move toward a 5-day week, but output isn't hurt," *Wall Street Journal* (January 18, 1973), p. 1.

3. "BIE says shorter week caused little strain to the economy," *Financial Review* (Australia) (July 23, 1984); *Reducing Standard Hours of Work: Analysis of Australia's Recent Experience*, pp. 124, 146.

4. *The International Labour Organization: The First Decade* (London: Allen and Unwin, 1931), p. 30. Quoted in Rolande Cuvillier, *The Reduction of Working Time*, p. 30.

5. Archibald A. Evans, *Hours of Work in Industrialised Countries* (Geneva: International Labor Organization, 1975), pp. 6–7.

6. "Leading the way into the 21st century," *ILO Information* 22, No. 1 (February 1986), pp. 5–6.

7. "Swedes gain leisure, not jobs, by cutting hours," *Wall Street Journal* (January 7, 1985); also, author's personal conversations with two Danish scholars, Karin Borg and Birger Linde.

8. Bernard Mertens, "Employment policy, organization of working time and unemployment in Belgium," in *New Patterns in Employment*, edited by Leonce Bekemans (Maastricht: European Centre for Work and Society, 1982), pp. 45–

62. See *Practical Experiences with the Reduction of Working Time in Europe* (Brussels: European Trade Union Institute, 1984).

9. "As 38.5 hour workweek takes effect in West Germany, the debate continues," *Wall Street Journal* (April 1, 1985); Brian Groom, "Why time may be up for the 40-hour week," *Financial Times* (UK) (July 1984).

10. See *Report on Employment and the Adaptation of Working Time*, rapporteur D. Ceravolo, document 1–425/81 (Strasbourg: European Parliament, Committee on Social Affairs and Employment, 1981), p. 9.

11. Georges Debunne, "Working time and jobs," *ILO Information* 11, No. 5 (December 1983), p. 4.

12. *Memorandum on the Reduction and Reorganisation of Working Time* (Brussels: Commission of the European Communities, COM(82) 809 final, 1982), p. 60.

13. *On the Reduction and Reorganisation of Working Time* (Brussels: Council of the European Communities, draft council recommendation, COM(83) 543 final, 1983), p. 2.

14. *Report on the Memorandum from the Commission of the European Communities on the Reduction and Reorganisation of Working Time*, rapporteur D. Ceravolo, document 1–71/83 (European Parliament, Committee on Social Affairs and Employment, 1983), p. 9.

15. Francis Blanchard, ILO Director-General, "More leisure—more work?" *ILO Information* 7, No. 4 (October 1979); p. 2.

16. Bernard Wysocki Jr., "Lust for labor: Japanese officials mount frenzied effort to persuade the nation's workers to take it easy," *Wall Street Journal* (April 21, 1986), Section 4, "A Special report: the business of leisure," pp. 9D–10D.

17. Masahiko Ishizuka, "Japan needs a 'cultural revolution,'" *The Japan Economic Journal* (May 10, 1986); Flora Lewis, "Nakasone wants Japan to act more like grasshopper than ant," St. Paul *Pioneer Press and Dispatch* (May 9, 1986), p. 13A.

18. Motoyuki Miyano, letters to the author, 1988.

19. "Mixed blessing: do multinationals really create jobs in the third world?" *Wall Street Journal* (September 25, 1979), p. 1; "Third world seen losing war on rural poverty," *ILO Information* 8, No. 1 (February 1980), p. 8; report on book, *Profiles of Rural Poverty* (Geneva: International Labor Office, 1979).

20. "Multinationals' role in third world employment," *ILO Information* 17, No. 4 (October 1981), p. 2; report on book, *Employment Effects of Multinational Enterprises in Developing Countries* (Geneva: International Labor Office, 1981).

21. "Weighing pros and cons of Asian processing 'zones,'" *ILO Information* 11, No. 3 (August 1983), p. 2; based on R. Maex, *Employment and multinationals in Asian export processing zones*, working paper #26 (Geneva: International Labor Office, 1983).

22. Louis Harrell and Dale Fischer, "The 1982 Mexican peso devaluation and border area employment," *Monthly Labor Review* (October 1985), p. 28.

23. "Of recovery and jobs," *ILO Information* 11, No. 3 (August 1983), p. 3.

24. *Preparation for the Special Session of the General Assembly in 1980*, Preliminary report of ILO, Annex, introduction, paragraphs 1–3, 7. See also, Francis Blanchard, "A will to adapt," *ILO Information* 17, No. 4 (October 1981).

25. "Glutted markets: a global overcapacity hurts many industries; no easy cure is seen," *Wall Street Journal* (March 9, 1987), pp. 1, 10.

26. "A need to adjust," *ILO Information* 17, No. 4 (October 1981), p. 1; interview with ILO researcher Geoffrey Renshaw.

CHAPTER 11

1. Jacques Ellul, "From the Bible to a history of nonwork," translated by David Lovekin, *Cross Currents* (Spring 1985), pp. 45–46.
2. Exodus 5:1, 4, 8, *The New English Bible* (Oxford University Press and Cambridge University Press, 1970).
3. Exodus 20: 8–10.
4. Matthew 22:21.
5. Harold L. Wilensky, "The uneven distribution of leisure: the impact of economic growth on 'free time'," *Social Problems* (January 1961), p. 33.
6. Ibid.
7. Wladimir Woytinsky, "Hours of labor," *Encyclopedia of the Social Sciences* VII (New York: Macmillan, 1935), p. 479.
8. Wilensky, "The uneven distribution of leisure," p. 34.
9. Woytinsky, "Hours of labor," p. 479.
10. Ibid., pp. 479–80.
11. Ibid., p. 490. See Robert Owen, *Crisis,* vol. iii, p. 125.
12. John Canning, *One Hundred Great Events that Changed the World,* chapter entitled "The ten-hours' day" (London: Odhams, 1966), p. 446.
13. Karl Marx, "Value, Price and Profit," in *Ten Classics of Marxism,* edited by Eleanor Marx Aveling (New York: International Publishers, 1946), p. 17.
14. O.L. Harvey, "The 10-hour day in the Philadelphia Navy Yard," *Monthly Labor Review* (March 1962), pp. 258–60.
15. Philip S. Foner, *History of the Labor Movement in the United States,* Vol. I (New York: International Publishers, 1947), p. 201.
16. Quoted in Riva Poor, *4 Days, 40 Hours and Other Forms of the Rearranged Workweek* (Cambridge: Bursk & Poor, 1973), p. 142.
17. Woytinsky, "Hours of labor," p. 492. Quoted from *A Documentary History of American Labor,* vol. IX, edited by J.R. Commons & Assoc., (Cleveland, 1910), p. 285.
18. *George Brooks, "Historical background," The Shorter Work Week: Papers Delivered at the Conference on Shorter Hours of Work, Sponsored by the AFL-CIO* (Washington: Public Affairs Press, 1957), pp. 9–10.
19. Foner, *History of the Labor Movement,* Vol. I, p. 381. Quotation appeared in the *New York Times* (June 12, 1872).
20. Foner, *History of the Labor Movement,* Vol. II, p. 98; *Proceedings,* Federation of Organized Trades, 1884, pp. 128–29.
21. Foner, *History of the Labor Movement,* Vol. II, p. 103. Quoted from *John Swinton's Paper,* May 16, 1886.
22. Thomas Greer, *American Social Reform Movements* (New York: Prentice Hall, 1947); p. 28. Quoted from Jacob B. Hardman, *American Labor Dynamics* (New York: Harcourt Brace, 1928): pp. 99–101.
23. *New York Times Magazine,* February 4, 1962, p. 62. Statement made by Samuel Gompers in 1887.

24. Foner, *History of the Labor Movement*, Vol. I, p. 369. Quoted from Karl Marx, *Capital*, Vol. I, p. 309.

25. Foner, *History of the Labor Movement*, Vol. II, p. 180. Quoted from *American Federationist*, Vol. I, May 1894, p. 52.

26. Alexander Trachtenberg, *The History of May Day*, (New York: International Publishers, 1931), p. 16. Quoted from Engels' preface to the fourth German edition of *The Communist Manifesto*, 1890.

27. Archibald Evans, *Hours of Work in Industrialised Countries*, p. 2; Lochner v. New York (198 U.S. 45).

28. *Too Many Hours: Labor's Struggle to Shorten the Work Day* (New York: United Electrical, Radio & Machine Workers of America, 1978), p. 17.

29. William T. Moye, "The end of the 12-hour day in the steel industry," *Monthly Labor Review* (September 1977), p. 23. Quoted in The Commission of Inquiry, the Interchurch World Movement, *Report on the Steel Strike of 1919* (New York: Harcourt Brace, 1920), p. 81.

30. Ibid., p. 23. Quoted from "Industrial relations and labor conditions," *Monthly Labor Review* (May 1923), p. 923.

31. Ibid., pp. 23–24. Quoted from Robert H. Zieger, *Republicans and Labor, 1919–1929* (Lexington: University of Kentucky Press, 1969), p. 99.

32. Evans, *Hours of Work*, p. 8; *Treaty of Versailles*, 1919, Part XIII, article 427.

33. Henry Ford interview with Samuel Crowther, *Monthly Labor Review* (December 1926), p. 1163. Originally in *World's Work* (October 1926).

34. Elbert H. Gary, *Monthly Labor Review* (December 1926), p. 1168. Statement originally in the *New York Times* (October 17, 1926).

35. George Brooks, "Historical background," *The Shorter Work Week*, p. 18.

36. See Benjamin Kline Hunnicutt, "The end of shorter hours," *Labor History* (Summer 1984), pp. 394–400.

37. Gerhard Bosch, "Reduction and flexibilisation of the working week in the FRG," first draft of report to the international symposium on working time, Brussels, April 1987, p. 26. Prepared under the auspices of the Economic and Social Research Institute, West German Trade Union Federation.

CHAPTER 12

1. Jacques Ellul, "From the Bible to a history of nonwork," pp. 43–44.

2. Ibid., p. 46.

3. Ibid., p. 45.

4. Ibid., pp. 46–47.

5. St. Thomas Aquinas, *Summa Theologiae*, 2a2ae.187, 3, in section on "the pastoral and religious lives." See Blackfriars translation by Jordan Anmann, Vol. 47, pp. 157, 159 (New York: McGraw-Hill, 1964).

6. John Paul II, *Laborem Exercens* (On Human Work), Third Encyclical Letter, September 14, 1981 (Washington: U.S. Catholic Conference, 1981); pp. 14–15.

7. Ibid., pp. 15–16.

8. Ibid., pp. 25–26.

9. Ibid., pp. 26–27.

10. Ibid., pp. 27–29.

11. Ibid., p. 30.

12. Max Weber, *The Protestant Ethic and the Spirit of Capitalism,* translated by Talcott Parsons (New York: Charles Scribner's Sons, 1958), pp. 50–51.

13. Ibid., pp. 59–60.

14. Ibid., pp. 60–62.

15. Ibid., pp. 53–54.

16. Ibid., p. 2. Foreword by R. H. Tawney.

17. Plato, *Laws,* Book II, 653(d), in Plato, *Collected Dialogues* (New York: Pantheon, 1961), p. 1250.

18. Josef Pieper, *Leisure the Basis of Culture,* introduction by T.S. Eliot (New York: Pantheon, 1952), pp. 3–5.

19. Ibid., pp. 24–27.

20. Ibid., p. 48.

21. *Matthew,* 6:28–30.

22. National Conference of Catholic Bishops, *Economic Justice for All: Catholic Social Teaching and the U.S. Economy,* Third Draft, June 4, 1986, Washington, p. 92.

SOURCES FOR STATISTICAL TABLES

1.1: Bureau of Labor Statistics, *Workers without Jobs: A Chartbook on Unemployment* (Washington, D.C.: GPO, 1983): Chart 17, "Unemployment rate, 1948–83," pp. 38–39.

1.2: Ibid., Chart 19, "Unemployment measures based on alternative definitions of unemployment and the labor force, 1970–83," pp. 42–43.

1.3: *Economic Report of the President and Annual Report of the Council of Economic Advisors* (Washington: GPO, 1987): Table B–32, "Civilian employment and unemployment by sex and age, 1947–86," p. 282.

1.4: Ewan Clague, Commissioner of the Bureau of Labor Statistics, testimony before House Select Subcommittee on Labor, hearings on H.R. 355, H.R. 3102, and H.R. 3320, Table I, page 76. Included in testimony of George G. Hagedorn before the House Select Subcommittee on Labor, November 21, 1963. Also *Employment and Earnings* (January 1966, 1971, 1976, 1981, 1986, 1988), Table 30, "Persons at work by hours of work and type of industry."

1.5: U.S. Department of Commerce, *Statistical Abstract of the United States,* 1988, 108th Edition, (Washington: U.S. Department of Commerce, Bureau of the Census, 1987), Table 700, "Money Income of Families—Median Family Income in Current and Constant (1986) Dollars by Race and Hispanic origin of Householder: 1960 to 1986, p. 427.

1.6: Paul O. Flaim, "The spendable earnings series: has it outlived its usefulness?" *Monthly Labor Review* (January 1982); p. 3.

2.1: A calculation of index numbers based on 1947 has been made from unpublished data compiled by the Bureau of Labor Statistics and delivered to the author. The computer report, dated December 3, 1987, is entitled, "Basic Industry Data for the Farm Sector, All Persons."

2.2: Kazutoshi Koshiro, "The employment effect of microelectronic technology," in *Highlights in Japanese Industrial Relations,* appendix 2 (Tokyo: The Japan Institute of Labour, 1984), p. 88.

3.1: *Historical Statistics of the United States, 1970,* Series W 1–11, "Indexes of

National Productivity: 1889 to 1970," p. 948. John W. Kendrick's productivity studies were published by the National Bureau of Economic Research in 1961 and 1973. *Handbook of Labor Statistics, 1980,* Table 1, p. 5; Table 103, p. 205; *Monthly Labor Review* (June 1986), Table 1, p. 64; Table 42, p. 93; *Monthly Labor Review* (October 1987), Table 44, p. 94. *Employment and Earnings* (January 1988), Table1, p. 158. *Historical Statistics of the United States, Colonial Times to 1957,* Series D 46–47. Productivity statistics from 1960 pertain to the private business sector.

3.2: *Statistical Abstract 1988,* Table 701, "Money income of families - income and percent of aggregate income at selected positions received by each fifth and top 5 percent of families: 1986," p. 428.

4.1: Household series: "Mean hours worked by all persons at work, 1943–1976, annual averages," unpublished table compiled by Bureau of Labor Statistics. *Employment and Earnings,* January issue, 1977–1988, "Persons at work by hours of work and type of industry"; payroll series: *Handbook of Labor Statistics, 1970* Table 84, "Average weekly hours of production or nonsupervisory workers on private nonagricultural payrolls by industry division, selected years, 1932–69," p. 149; *Monthly Labor Review* (October 1985), Table 12, "Average hours and earnings, by industry 1968–84," p. 75; *Employment and Earnings,* (January 1988): Table 65, p. 228.

4.2: Testimony of Ewan Clague: Select Subcommittee on Labor, Hearings on H.R. 355, H.R. 3102, and H.R. 3320, Table I, page 76. *Employment and Earnings,* January 1971, 1981, 1988, Table 30, "Persons at work by hours of work and type of industry." *Employment and Earnings* (January 1988), Table 1, "Employment status of the civilian noninstitutional population, 1929 to date," p. 158.

4.3: *Handbook of Labor Statistics, 1980,* Table 74, "Production or nonsupervisory workers on private nonagricultural payrolls by industry division, selected years, 1939–79," p. 153; *Employment and Earnings* (January 1988), Table 64, p. 227; Table 65, p. 228.

4.4: *Employment and Earnings* (January 1988): Table 7, "Full- and part-time status of the civilian labor force by sex, age, and race," p. 167; Table 29, "Employed civilians with a job but not at work by reason, sex, and pay status," p. 195; Table 30, "Persons at work by hours of work and type of industry," p. 195; Table 31, "Persons at work 1 to 34 hours by reason for working less than 35 hours, type of industry, and usual status," p. 196.

4.5: *Monthly Labor Review* (March 1962), p. 256; *Monthly Labor Review* (February 1971), p. 6; *Monthly Labor Review* (March 1980), p. 10, footnote 9.

4.6: "Holidays with Pay—Europe," table compiled by International Labor Organization, Geneva, circa 1983. French public holidays taken from 1981 Labor Code, L 222–1.

4.7: *Monthly Labor Review* (March 1973): Table 1, "Distribution of persons not in the labor force, by reason, 1967–72," p. 10; *Handbook of Labor Statistics, 1980,* Table 17, "Job desire of persons 16 years and over not in labor force and reasons for not seeking work by sex and race, 1970–79," p. 37; *Employment and Earnings* (January 1981): Table 39, "Persons not in labor force by reason, sex, and age," p. 194; *Employment and Earnings* (January 1988): Table 35, "Persons in labor force by reason, sex and age," p. 199.

5.1: Calculations of index numbers based on 1947 were made from unpublished data compiled by the Bureau of Labor Statistics and delivered to the author. The computer reports, data December 3, 1987, are entitled "Basic industry data for the business sector, all persons" and "Industry analytical ratios for the business sector, all persons."

5.2: *Statistical Abstract, 1986,* Table 198, "Per capita consumption of major food commodities: 1960 to 1984," p. 121. Source: U.S. Department of Agriculture, Economic Research Service, *Food Consumption, Prices and Expenditures,* November 1984.

6.1: *Statistical Abstract, 1988,* Table 898, "Advertising—estimated expenditures by medium: 1970 to 1986," p. 530. Source: McCann-Erickson Inc., New York. Also, Table 671, p. 410.

6.2: *Statistical Abstract, 1988,* Table 508, "National defense outlays and veterans benefits: 1960 to 1987," p. 314; *Statistical Abstract, 1979,* Table 587, p. 364.

6.3: *Statistical Abstract, 1988,* Table 129, "National health care expenditures: 1970 to 1986," p. 86; Table 738, "Consumer price indexes, by major groups: 1950 to 1986," p. 450.

6.4: *Handbook of Labor Statistics, 1985,* Table 67, "Number and percent of nonproduction workers on manufacturing payrolls by industry, 1939–83," p. 179. *Monthly Labor Review* (June 1986), Table 13, p. 72; *Employment and Earnings* (January 1988); Tables 63 and 64, pp. 226–27.

6.5: *Statistical Abstract, 1988,* Table 305, "Federal and state prisoners: 1950 to 1986," p. 175. Source: U.S. Bureau of Justice Statistics, *Prisoners in State and Federal Institutions on December 31.*

10.1: *Yearbook of International Trade Statistics, 1984* (New York: United Nations, 1986); *Yearbook of Labor Statistics, 1975,* Table 13, "Hours of work in manufacturing" (Geneva: International Labor Organization, 1976), pp. 491–3; *Yearbook of Labor Statistics, 1986,* Table 12, "Hours of work per week in manufacturing" (Geneva: International Labor Organization, 1986), pp. 628–33.

10.2: Edwin Dean, Harry Boissevain, and James Thomas, "Productivity and labor costs trends in manufacturing, 12 countries," *Monthly Labor Review* (March 1986), Table 1, p. 4; Table 2, p. 5; Table 3, p. 6.

10.3: *Yearbook of Labor Statistics, 1965,* Table 13, "Hours of work in manufacturing" (Geneva: International Labor Organization, 1966), pp. 397–88; *Yearbook of Labor Statistics, 1975,* Table 13, "Hours of work in manufacturing," pp. 491–93; *Yearbook of Labor Statistics, 1986,* pp. 628–33, Table 12, "Hours of work per week in manufacturing." See also: Archibald A. Evans, *Hours of Work in Industrialised Countries,* Appendix II, table 1, pp. 141–142.

BIBLIOGRAPHY

Amalgamated Metal Workers and Shipwrights' Union (Australia). National news-
  letter, February 1982.
Amway Corporation. *Amway—the Industry Leader*. 1980 and 1984.
Aquinas, St. Thomas. *Summa Theologiae*. Blackfriars edition. New York: McGraw-
  Hill, 1964.
Beck, Joan. "Work Structures Need to Bend, not Just Family," St. Paul *Pioneer
  Press and Dispatch*, December 31, 1985.
Bednarzik, Robert W. "The Impact of Microelectronics on Employment: Japan's
  Experience," *Monthly Labor Review*, September 1985.
Besharov, Douglas J. "How One Group Found a Path out of the Liability Jungle,"
  Wall Street Journal, April 17, 1986.
Blanchard, Francis. "More Leisure—More Work?" *ILO Information*, October
  1979.
———. "A Will to Adapt," *ILO Information*, October 1981.
Bluestone, Barry, and Bennett Harrison. *The Great American Job Machine: The
  Proliferation of Low Wage Employment in the U.S. Economy*. Washington: Joint
  Economic Committee, 1986.
Bosch, Gerhard. "Reduction and Flexibilisation of the Working Week in the
  FRG"; first draft of a report to the international symposium on working
  time, Brussels, April 1987. West German Trade Union Federation.
Brooks, George. "Historical Background," in *The Shorter Work Week: Papers De-
  livered at the Conference on Shorter Hours of Work, Sponsored by the AFL-CIO*.
  Washington: Public Affairs Press, 1957.
Bureau of Economic Analysis. *Business Conditions Digest*. Washington: U.S. De-
  partment of Commerce, January 1987.
Bureau of Labor Statistics. "Basic Industry Data for the Business Sector, All
  Persons"; "Industry Analytical Ratios for the Business Sector, All Per-
  sons"; "Basic Industry Data for the Farm Sector, All Persons." Computer
  print-out dated December 3, 1987.

Business Week: August 3, 1981; June 16, 1986.

Canning, John. *One Hundred Great Events that Changed the World*. London: Odhams, 1966.

City Pages: April 11, 1984.

Clague, Ewan. *Testimony before House Select Subcommittee on Labor, Hearings on H.R. 355, H.R. 3102, and H.R. 3320,* included in testimony before same committee by George F. Hagedorn on November 21, 1963.

Cuvillier, Rolande. *The Reduction of Working Time*. Geneva: International Labor Organization, 1984.

Dean, Edwin, Harry Boissevain, and James Thomas. "Productivity and Labor Costs Trends in Manufacturing," *Monthly Labor Review,* March 1986.

Debunne, Georges. "Working Time and Jobs," *ILO Information,* December 1983.

Dickens, Charles. *Bleak House,* 1853 (*Forbes,* April 21, 1986).

Diebold, John. Testimony before Subcommittee on Automation and Energy Resources, Joint Economic Committee, 1960.

Disraeli, Benjamin. Speech to the Conservatives of Manchester on April 3, 1872 (*Bartlett's Familiar Quotations,* Boston: Little Brown, 1937).

Douglas, Paul H. *The Theory of Wages*. New York: Macmillan, 1934.

————. *Real Wages in the United States, 1890–1926*. Boston: Houghton Mifflin, 1930.

Drucker, Peter. "A Growing Mismatch of Jobs and Job Seekers," *Wall Street Journal,* March 26, 1985. "Playing in the Information-Based Orchestra," *Wall Street Journal,* June 4, 1985.

Economic Justice for All: Catholic Social Teaching and the U.S. Economy, Third Draft. Washington: National Conference of Catholic Bishops, 1986.

Economic Report of the President and Annual Report of the Council of Economic Advisors. Washington: GPO, 1987.

Elder, Peyton K. "The 1977 Amendments to the Federal Minimum Wage Law," *Monthly Labor Review,* January 1978.

Peyton K. Elder and Heidi D. Miller. "The Fair Labor Standards Act: Changes of Four Decades," *Monthly Labor Review,* July 1979.

Ellul, Jacques. "From the Bible to a History of Non-Work," translated by David Lovekin. *Cross Currents,* Spring 1985.

Emerson, Ralph Waldo. "Man the Reformer," in *The Collected Works of Ralph Waldo Emerson,* Volume I. Cambridge: Belknap Press of Harvard University, 1971.

Engels, Frederick. "Socialism, Utopian and Scientific," in *Ten Classics of Marxism*. New York: International Publishers, 1946.

Evans, Archibald A. *Hours of Work in Industrialised Countries*. Geneva: International Labor Organization, 1975.

Employment and Earnings: January issue, 1971, 1977–88. Washington: Bureau of Labor Statistics.

Fair Labor Standards Act of 1938 as Amended (29 USC 201). U.S. Department of Labor publication 1318, printed October 1975.

Fallows, James. "No-Fat City," *Atlantic Monthly,* November 1986.

Financial Review (Australia): July 23, 1984.

Financial Times (U.K.): July 1984.

Flaim, Paul O. "The Spendable Earnings Series: Has It Outlived its Usefulness?" *Monthly Labor Review,* January 1982.

Focus Japan: October 1982.

Foner, Philip S. *History of the Labor Movement in the United States,* Vol. I and II. New York: International Publishers, 1947 and 1955.

Forbes: July 14, 1986.

Ford, Henry. Interview with Samuel Crowther, *Monthly Labor Review,* December 1926.

Franklin, Benjamin. Letter to Benjamin Vaughan, July 26, 1784, in *A Benjamin Franklin Reader,* edited by Nathan G. Goodman. New York: Thomas Y. Crowell, 1945.

Gary, Elbert H. *Monthly Labor Review,* December 1926.

Gordon, Robert A. *Measuring Employment and Unemployment.* Washington: GPO, 1962.

Greer, Thomas. *American Social Reform Movements.* New York: Prentice Hall, 1947.

Hamilton, David. *The New Mexico Independent.* August 15, 1975.

Hanami, Tadashi. "Worker Motivation in Japan," in *Highlights of Japanese Industrial Relations.* Tokyo: Japan Institute of Labour, 1983.

Handbook of Labor Statistics. Washington: Bureau of Labor Statistics, 1980 and 1985.

Harrell, Louis, and Dale Fischer. "The 1982 Mexico Peso Devaluation and Border Area Employment," *Monthly Labor Review,* October 1985.

Harvey, O.L. "The 10-Hour Day in the Philadelphia Navy Yard," *Monthly Labor Review,* March 1962.

Hedges, Janice Neipert. "Job Commitment in America: Is it Waxing or Waning?" *Monthly Labor Review,* July 1983.

————, with Geoffrey H. Moore. "Trends in Labor and Leisure," *Monthly Labor Review,* February 1971.

————, with Daniel E. Taylor. "Recent Trends in Work Time: Hours Edge Downward," *Monthly Labor Review,* March 1980.

Henle, Peter. "Recent Growth of Paid Leisure for U.S. Workers," *Monthly Labor Review,* March 1962.

————. "Leisure and the Long Workweek," *Monthly Labor Review,* July 1966.

Historical Statistics of the United States, Colonial Times to 1957. Washington: Bureau of the Census.

Historical Statistics of the United States, 1970. Washington: Department of the Census.

Holidays with Pay—Europe. Geneva: International Labor Organization, 1983.

Hunnicut, Benjamin Klein. "The End of Shorter Hours," *Labor History,* Summer of 1984.

ILO Information: October 1979, February 1980, October 1981, August 1983, October 1983, December 1983, February 1986, October 1987.

International Labor Organization. *Convention Concerning Annual Holidays with Pay* (Revised), 1970.

Ishizuka, Masahiko. "Japan Needs a 'Cultural Revolution'," *The Japan Economic Journal,* May 10, 1986.

John Paul II. *Laborem Exercens* (On Human Work). Washington: U.S. Catholic Conference, 1981.

Killingsworth, Charles C. "Structural Unemployment without Quotation Marks," *Monthly Labor Review,* June 1979.

Koshiro, Kazutoshi. "The Employment Effect of Microelectronic Technology," in *Highlights in Japanese Industrial Relations.* Tokyo: Japan Institute of Labour, 1984.

Labour Administration in Japan. Tokyo: Ministry of Labour, 1980.

Leontief, Wassily. "Employment Policies in the Age of Automation," *ILO Information* 6, No. 1, 1978.

Levi, Connie. Speech at White Bear Unitarian Church, December 9, 1984.

Lewis, Flora. "Nakasone Wants Japan to Act More Like Grasshopper than Ant," St. Paul *Pioneer Press and Dispatch,* May 9, 1986.

———. "Money Soars, but Economy Drifts Perilously," St. Paul *Pioneer Press and Dispatch,* January 2, 1986.

Marx, Karl. "Wage-Labour and Capital" and "Value, Price and Profit," in *Ten Classics of Marxism.* New York: International Publishers, 1946.

"Mean Hours Worked by all Persons at Work, 1943–1976, Annual Averages" (unpublished), Washington: Bureau of Labor Statistics, 1977.

Mellor, Earl F. "Investigating the Differences in Weekly Earnings of Women and Men," *Monthly Labor Review,* June 1984.

Memorandum on the Reduction and Reorganisation of Working Time. Brussels: Commission of the European Communities, COM(82) 809 final, 1982.

Mertens, Bernard. "Employment Policy, Organization of Working Time and Unemployment in Belgium," in *New Patterns in Employment,* edited by Leonce Bekemans. Maastricht: European Centre for Work and Society, 1982.

Metropolitan Transit Commission (Minneapolis-St. Paul). "MTC Historical Ridership Survey," 1983.

Minnesota Daily: January 14, 1985; March 1, 1985; July 8, 1985.

Monthly Labor Review: May 1923; December 1926; January, July 1958; March 1962; July 1966; February 1971; September 1977; January 1978; June, July 1979; March, May 1980; May 1982; July 1983; April, July, September 1984; May, August, September, October 1985; March, June 1986; October 1987.

Moore, Geoffrey H., and Janice N. Hedges. "Trends in Labor and Leisure," *Monthly Labor Review,* February 1971.

Moy, Joanna. "Recent Trends in Unemployment and the Labor Force, 10 Countries," *Monthly Labor Review,* August 1985.

Moye, William T. "The End of the 12-Hour Day in the Steel Industry," *Monthly Labor Review,* September 1977.

National Association of Manufacturers. *What Is at Stake in a Shorter Workweek?* New York: NAM, 1964.

Nemirow, Martin. "Work Sharing Approaches: Past and Present," *Monthly Labor Review,* September 1984.

New English Bible. Oxford University Press and Cambridge University Press, 1970.

New Republic: August 20, 1987.

New York Times: June 12, 1872; February 4, 1987.

New York Times Magazine: February 4, 1962.

Pieper, Josef. *Leisure the Basis of Culture*, introduction by T.S. Eliot. New York: Pantheon, 1952.

Plato, *Laws*, Book II. *Collected Dialogues*. New York: Pantheon, 1961.

Poor, Riva. *4 Days, 40 Hours and Other Forms of the Rearranged Workweek*. Cambridge: Bursk & Poor, 1973.

Practical Experiences with the Reduction of Working Time in Europe. Brussels: European Trade Union Institute, 1984.

Preparations for the Special Session of the General Assembly in 1980, preliminary report of the ILO, Annex. Geneva: International Labor Organization.

Railway Age: June 14, 1982.

Readers Digest: January 1984.

Reagan, Ronald. Speech delivered in support of Sen. Barry Goldwater's presidential campaign on October 27, 1964.

Reducing Standard Hours of Work: An Analysis of Australia's Recent Experience, Research Report #15. Canberra: Bureau of Industry Economics, 1984.

Report on Employment and the Adaptation of Working Time, rapporteur D. Ceravolo, document 1–425/81. European Parliament, Committee on Social Affairs and Employment, 1981.

Report on the Memorandum from the Commission of the European Communities on the Reduction and Reorganisation of Working Time, rapporteur D. Ceravolo, document 1–71/83. European Parliament, Committee on Social Affairs and Employment, 1983.

Roberts, Paul Craig. "The Keynesian Attack on Mr. Reagan's Plan," *Wall Street Journal*, March 19, 1981.

Runzheimer Report: September 1985.

Samuelson, Paul A. *Economics*, 5th edition. New York: McGrawHill, 1961.

Sider, Hal, and Cheryl Cole. "The Changing Composition of the Military and the Effect on Labor Force Data," *Monthly Labor Review*, July 1984.

Skyway News (St. Paul): September 16, 1981.

Smith, Adam. *Wealth of Nations*. New York: The Modern Library, 1937.

Star and Tribune (Minneapolis): December 26, 1983; October 10, 1984; February 4, 1985; February 6, 1985; February 12, 1985; March 20, 1985; May 7, 1985; June 4, 1985; June 12, 1985; October 8, 1985; December 23, 1985; January 12, 1986; August 6, 1986.

Statistical Abstract of the United States: 1979, 1984–1987. Washington: U.S. Department of Commerce, Bureau of the Census.

St. Paul Pioneer Press and Dispatch: August 5, 1974; December 27, 1974; October 13, 1975; April 12, 1981; February 9, 1982; May 27, 1983; January 12, 1984; January 27, 1984; August 8, 1984; January 13, 1985; January 17, 1985; August 9, 1985; December 18, 1985; December 31, 1985; January 2, 1986; January 11, 1986; January 27, 1986; May 9, 1986; December 15, 1987.

Tawney, R.H. Foreword to *The Protestant Ethic and the Spirit of Capitalism* by Max Weber. New York: Charles Scribner's Sons, 1958.

Taylor, Daniel E., and Edward S. Sekscenski. "Workers on Long Schedules, Single and Multiple Jobholders," *Monthly Labor Review*, May 1982.

Tecumseh. Letter to Indiana territorial governor William Henry Harrison, 1810. Virginia Irving Armstrong, *I Have Spoken*. New York: Sage Books, 1971.

Time: January 17, 1972; December 1, 1986.

Trachtenberg, Alexander. *The History of May Day*. New York: International Pamphlets, 1931.

Too Many Hours: Labor's Struggle to Shorten the Work Day. New York: United Electrical, Radio & Machine Workers of America, 1978.

Twin Cities Reader: August 27, 1981; June 22, 1983.

United States Trade: Performance in 1984 and Outlook. Washington: U.S. Department of Commerce, 1985.

U.S. News & World Report: March 24, 1986.

Veblen, Thorstein. *The Theory of the Leisure Class*. New York: New American Library, 1953.

Wages and Hours of Work. Tokyo: The Japan Institute of Labour, 1984.

Wall Street Journal: January 18, 1973; November 26, 1977; June 22, 1978; April 2, 1979; September 25, 1979; December 2, 1980; March 19, 1981; April 29, 1981; June 3, 1981; June 5, 1981; July 17, 1981; November 9, 1981; May 10, 1982; November 2, 1982; November 30, 1982; March 16, 1983; April 13, 1983; August 30, 1983; December 9, 1983; April 6, 1984; April 17, 1984; May 3, 1984; June 28, 1984; July 9, 1984; November 23, 1984; December 6, 1984; December 7, 1984; December 27, 1984; January 7, 1985; January 24, 1985; January 31, 1985; February 4, 1985; February 5, 1985; February 12, 1985; March 12, 1985; March 26, 1985; April 1, 1985; April 5, 1985; April 11, 1985; April 29, 1985; May 9, 1985; May 13, 1985; May 20, 1985; May 23, 1985; June 4, 1985; June 10, 1985; July 5, 1985; July 10, 1985; July 16, 1985; August 1, 1985; August 8, 1985; August 13, 1985; August 26, 1985; August 28, 1985; September 6, 1985; September 10, 1985; September 23, 1985; January 8, 1986; January 10, 1986; January 13–16, 1986; January 21, 1986; January 23, 1986; January 29–31, 1986; February 18, 1986; February 27, 1986; April 2, 1986; April 17, 1986; April 21, 1986; April 29, 1986; May 9, 1986; May 13, 1986; May 16, 1986; July 29, 1986; August 7, 1986; March 9, 1987; November 30, 1987; December 9, 1987; December 15, 1987.

Weber, Max. *The Protestant Ethic and the Spirit of Capitalism,* translated by Talcott Parsons. New York: Charles Scribner's Sons, 1958.

Wilensky, Harold. "The Uneven Distribution of Leisure: The Impact of Economic Growth on 'Free Time'," *Social Problems,* January 1961.

Workers Without Jobs: A Chartbook on Unemployment. Washington: Bureau of Labor Statistics, 1983.

Woytinsky, Wladimir. "Hours of Labor," article in *Encyclopedia of the Social Sciences*, Vol. VII. New York: Macmillan, 1935.

Yearbook of International Trade Statistics, 1984. New York: United Nations, 1986.

Yearbook of Labor Statistics, 1965, 1975, 1986. Geneva: International Labor Organization.

Zalusky, John. "Shorter Hours—the Steady Gain." *AFL-CIO American Federationist,* January 1978.

Zeisel, Joseph. "The Workweek in American Industry, 1850–1956," *Monthly Labor Review,* January 1958.

INDEX

197–98; in European labor policy, 148

socialism, 107–9, 169–70, 174, 187, 194–95

Society for Promoting National Regeneration, 163

soft drinks, 61–62

South Africa, Republic of, 140

South Korea, Republic of, 140

Southland Corp., 104

Soviet Union, 173–74, 194–95

standard of living: predicted gains, 10; statistical evidence, 11–12; per-capita output, 52–53; doubts, 53; fewer goods, 91; in developing nations, 150–52; after 1848 law, 164; Ira Steward's theory, 166; improved by leisure, 174

Standard Oil of New Jersey, 175

standard workweek, 131–32

statistics, interpretation of: spurious employment growth, 29; two hours averages, 36; shifts in employment composition, 36–38, 40; three reasons for change in average hours, 44; questions regarding output, 53; difficult to interpret trade balances, 142–43; excluded kinds of work, 181

status-seeking consumption, 56, 73–76

steel industry, 172–73

Steward, Ira, 166–67

Stockman, David, 73

stock market, 80, 117

Strasser, Adolf, 169

strikes for shorter hours, 44–45, 164, 167–74, 178–79

suburbs, 75

suicide, 101

Sunkist Corp., 82

sun-up to sun-down, work day, 161, 164–65

superstores, 69

supply-side economics, 65, 106

Supreme Court, U.S., 167, 171–72, 176–77

Sweden, 147

"Sweetest Day," 79

tariff, proposed, 123, 155–56

Tawney, R. H., 192

taxation, 76–77, 106, 119–20

Taylor, Daniel E., 46

Tecumseh, 88

telemarketing, 68

television, 55, 67, 136

ten-hour day, 164–66

Ten Hours State Convention (Massachusetts), 165

terrorism, international, 97

Texans for Blue Law Reform, 104

Theory of Leisure Class, 56

Theory of Wages, 36

third-party-payment-driven diagnosis, 94

thirty-hour workweek, 175

Thurow, Lester, 153

time-starved consumer, 62–63, 69, 129–31

Tobacco Institute, 96

total work, 195

trade competition: excuse to trim jobs, 25; hours reductions and, 139–44; Japanese policies, 149; labor standards, 154–56

tradeoff: between hours and employment, 16, 128; between leisure and living standards, 10–11, 36, 128, 143

tripartite policy discussions, 145

T. Rowe Price Associates., 115

"two-holidays system," 149

Tylenol, 70

underground economy, 116

unemployment: escalating rate in postwar decades, 4–5; failure of conventional remedies, 5–6; indifference to, 7; not correlated with productivity index, 27; changes in definition, 27–28; Amway's impact, 29; demographic coloration, 31; labor-force category, 48; linked with social problems, 92; shifted to fu-

About the Authors

A native of Watkins, Minnesota, *Eugene McCarthy* taught high school and college until his election to Congress as a Democrat from Saint Paul in 1948. He served for five terms in the House. In 1958, he was elected to the U.S. Senate from Minnesota, and was reelected in 1964. During his first term, he was chairman of the Senate Special Committee on Unemployment, whose recommendations led to the enactment of labor legislation in the early 1960s. In 1968, he was a candidate for the Democratic presidential nomination, and he has subsequently conducted several independent campaigns for the presidency. He has lectured extensively and published a number of books, including *The Hard Years, Other Things and the Aardvark, America Revisited, The Ultimate Tyranny*, and *Up 'Til Now*.

William McGaughey, Jr., is a native of Detroit and a graduate of Yale University. Since 1965, he has lived in the Minneapolis-Saint Paul area, where he has pursued a career in accounting. He has worked primarily in the fields of heavy manufacturing and mass transit. He has also helped to organize a political action group in Minnesota to support federal hours legislation. In 1981, he published a book, *A Shorter Workweek in the 1980s*, and he has also written newspaper articles on this and other topics.